Blood in the Streets

Blood in the Streets

Histories of Violence in Italian Crime Cinema

Austin Fisher

EDINBURGH
University Press

Edinburgh University Press is one of the leading university presses in the UK. We publish academic books and journals in our selected subject areas across the humanities and social sciences, combining cutting-edge scholarship with high editorial and production values to produce academic works of lasting importance. For more information visit our website: edinburghuniversitypress.com

© Austin Fisher, 2019, 2020

Edinburgh University Press Ltd
The Tun – Holyrood Road
12 (2f) Jackson's Entry
Edinburgh EH8 8PJ

First published in hardback by Edinburgh University Press 2019

Typeset in Ehrhardt MT by
Servis Filmsetting Ltd, Stockport, Cheshire

A CIP record for this book is available from the British Library

ISBN 978 1 4744 1172 1 (hardback)
ISBN 978 1 4744 7772 7 (paperback)
ISBN 978 1 4744 1173 8 (webready PDF)
ISBN 978 1 4744 1174 5 (epub)

The right of Austin Fisher to be identified as author of this work has been asserted in accordance with the Copyright, Designs and Patents Act 1988 and the Copyright and Related Rights Regulations 2003 (SI No. 2498).

Every effort has been made to trace copyright holders for permission to reproduce material previously published elsewhere, but if any have been inadvertently overlooked, the publisher will be pleased to make the necessary arrangements at the first opportunity.

Contents

List of Figures	vi
List of Tables	viii
Acknowledgements	ix
Introduction	1
1. Italian Crime Films and the Years of Lead	20
2. Corruption and Conspiracy in the *Poliziotteschi* and the Vigilante *Filone*	42
3. Nostalgic Gangsters and the Mafia *Filone*	77
4. Serial Killing and the *Giallo*	114
5. Enter . . . If You Dare! The Cross-cultural Reception of Crime *Filoni*	148
Conclusion	180
Appendices	193
Bibliography	214
Index	229

Figures

I.1	The police watch undercover footage of a riot in *La polizia chiede aiuto*	2
1.1, 1.2	Carlo's vandalised manifesto points to underlying historical motivations in *Il cittadino si ribella*	21
2.1	Ricciuti and Bertone debate the politics of violence in *La polizia ringrazia*	43
2.2–2.7	Each assassination is accompanied by an inadequately informed media report at the start of *La polizia accusa: il servizio segreto uccide*	55
2.8	Vito Cipriani capitulates to the corrupt system in *Revolver*	66
3.1, 3.2	Don Vincenzo in *Milano calibro 9* and Don Corrasco in *Il boss* lament the debasement of modern criminality	81
3.3, 3.4	Tony is framed in stark contrast to the overtly Sicilian *mise en scène* in *Quelli che contano*	105
3.5	A mafia hit is framed by a quintessentially Sicilian setting in *La violenza: quinto potere*	106
3.6, 3.7	The natural beauty and antiquity of Sicily are conflated with mafia violence by the editing in *Afyon oppio*	107
4.1	Victims of the Holocaust are marched to their deaths in *Nelle pieghe della carne*	120
4.2	Manfredi is tortured by the Nazis in *Roma città aperta*	120
4.3, 4.4	The opening pan shot of *Non si sevizia un paperino* juxtaposes the modern *autostrada* with its primordial surroundings	141
5.1	Banner ad for *Reazione a catena* in *The Morning News* (Wilmington, Delaware), 24 July 1972	149
5.2, 5.3	Banner ads for *Quelli che contano* in *Corriere della Sera*, 5 June 1974, and the *Clarion-Ledger* (Jackson, Mississippi), 19 August 1977	160
5.4	Banner ad for *La polizia ha le mani legate* in *La Stampa*, 4 April 1975	162
5.5	Italian publicity poster for *La polizia ringrazia*	162

5.6	Banner ad for *Il consigliori* in the *Santa Cruz Sentinel*, 10 September 1975	164
5.7	Banner ad for *Città violenta* in the *Star Tribune* (Minneapolis), 13 April 1973	164
5.8–5.10	Banner ads for *I corpi presentano tracce di violenza carnale* in *The Indianapolis Star*, 6 February 1975, the *Asheville Citizen-Times* (North Carolina), 8 November 1975, and the *San Antonio Express*, 2 December 1977	167
5.11	Banner ad for *L'uccello dalle piume di cristallo* in *The Philadelphia Enquirer*, 16 September 1970	169
5.12	Banner ads for *Reazione a catena* and *Dumbo* in *The Palm Beach Post*, 9 December 1972	171
5.13	Banner ads for *I corpi presentano tracce di violenza carnale*, *Winnie the Pooh and Tigger Too* and *The Island at the Top of the World* in *The Republic* (Columbus, Indiana), 7 February 1975	171

Tables

3.1 Italian mafia *filone* films, August 1972–March 1974 — 100
C.1 The mafia *filone* mapped onto Richard Nowell's 'film cycle' model — 185
C.2 The vigilante *filone* mapped onto Richard Nowell's 'film cycle' model — 186
C.3 The 'conspiracy' *poliziottesco* mapped onto Richard Nowell's 'film cycle' model — 187

Acknowledgements

No book is the result of one person's solo effort, and 'Acknowledgements' sections are always revealing for how they register an author's understanding of this fact. This volume would certainly not have seen the light of day had it not been for many people's input, support, feedback and assistance over the course of several years. I am sure that I have accidentally missed some of these people out here, and for that I apologise in advance.

I am eternally indebted to Gillian Leslie and all at Edinburgh University Press for their endless patience, good humour and support while I crawled to the finish line. Equally, the long process of researching and writing this book has only been possible due to the intervention of many friends and scholars at various points along the way. Alan O'Leary has invited me to several workshops and symposia at which I have been able to air my ideas in a welcoming and supportive environment. These ideas have also developed through the presentation of many conference papers, and the resultant kind words, effusive encouragement and valuable feedback from Robert Burgoyne, Peter Alilunas, Karen Randell, Mark Kermode, Emma Pett, Kate Egan, Peter Stanfield and Áine O'Healy have stuck in my memory as invaluable reassurances that I would be able to complete this project. Giulio Olesen will be very relieved that I have indeed finished this book, since I will now stop hassling him for linguistic advice, archival assistance and feedback on draft chapters. Phyll Smith, Johnny Walker and Neil Jackson also stepped in at crucial points in the research process to point me in the right direction.

I am also very grateful to Stefano Baschiera, Russ Hunter, Flavia Laviosa and Frank Burke for inviting me to write articles and chapters that sparked the whole idea for this volume many moons ago. Accordingly, parts of Chapters 2 and 4 have previously appeared in different forms in the *Journal of Italian Cinema and Media Studies* (2:2, 2014), *Italian Horror Cinema* (Edinburgh University Press 2016) and *A Companion to Italian Cinema* (Blackwell 2017).

Finally, this short space is a wholly inadequate one properly to thank my partner Kirsty, and my parents Joyce and John, for their remarkable forbearance as I have self-indulgently allowed this volume to consume my time and attention. Their good humour and endless support have constantly reminded me that there is a life outside academia.

Introduction

La polizia chiede aiuto / What Have They Done to Your Daughters? (Massimo Dallamano, 1974) opens with what appears to be a clear statement of intent, in a caption reading:

> Ogni giorno accadono fatti crudeli e apparentemente inspiegabili. Solo la ricostruzione fedele di questi fatti può farne comprendere il drammatico e inquietante significato.
>
> Every day cruel and apparently inexplicable events happen. Only the faithful reconstruction of these events can make the dramatic and disturbing meaning behind them understandable.

Before a word has been spoken, the film has implicitly promised both an accurate rendition of contemporary society's ills, and an explanation for them. Of course, neither of these is possible, and neither is attempted with any real conviction. What instead makes Dallamano's film interesting is the shorthand rendering of a broad and generalised 'contemporary' milieu that then ensues. Within the opening few minutes, the naked corpse of a fourteen-year-old girl is found hanging in a garret. The police then deduce that this was a murder rather than a suicide purely by chance, when they are watching undercover footage of a recent city-centre riot instigated by students and political extremists (Figure I.1). After Inspector Silvestri later proceeds to uncover a related child prostitution ring, the District Attorney makes it clear to him that the investigation will go no further, as the people he has implicated are untouchable, clearly pointing to a government-level cover-up.

Though the above synopsis might suggest otherwise, *La polizia chiede aiuto* is no investigation into high-level corruption or politically motivated violence. Instead, political extremism, militant youth countercultures and official cover-ups appear fleetingly, as component parts of a common sense backdrop that signifies the 'here and now'. They provide scene-setting

Figure I.1 The police watch undercover footage of a riot in *La polizia chiede aiuto* (Massimo Dallamano, 1974).

details and plot devices to aid the film's murder mystery, betraying a perfectly reasonable assumption on the part of the filmmakers that an Italian audience in August 1974 will immediately recognise these as integral and inevitable parts of the tapestry of contemporary society.

Above all, *La polizia chiede aiuto*'s immersion in its immediate contexts is manifested in its opportunistic use of cinematic conventions. It was a product of a highly prolific industrial system that flourished in 1960s and 1970s Italy by seeking to capitalise on popular tastes with concentrated bursts of activity around particular categories of film, known locally as *filoni* (literally 'traditions' or 'veins', but also hinting at *filo*, meaning 'thread').[1] Dallamano's film is a purposeful and unashamed exploitation of two of the most dominant *filone* categories by 1974, which have become known as the *poliziottesco* (police procedural) and the *giallo* (murder mystery). Its plot, themes and *mise en scène* are meticulously culled from each. The masked, leather-clad, knife-wielding psychopath committing gruesome murders, along with the clear indication of contemporary society's moral depravity, are lifted straight from the *giallo*. The setting in a *questura* (police station), the trench-coated police inspector protagonist, the car chases, the recurrent use of newspaper headlines to aid plot development, and the unambiguous indications of political corruption explicitly evoke the *poliziottesco*. Put simply, this film can only really be understood through its relationship to other films.

This book will analyse these cultural, political and industrial contexts, to understand how and why such representations of corruption, depravity and political violence became staples of *filone* cinema in 1970s Italy. It is not my purpose here to provide an all-encompassing survey of either the *poliziottesco* or the *giallo*, and I have therefore missed out many films whose inclusion might have added to the discussion. Instead, I have identified a collection of smaller *filone* strands that fragment these convenient categorisations, and that possess a particular unifying thematic focus of their own. Italy's 1970s were notable for an unprecedented increase in politically motivated violence and high-level cover-ups around its culpabilities, but also for underlying disputes concerning the nation's recent past. My aim in these pages is to understand how these competing narratives were negotiated through a variety of *filoni* that depicted violent crime in contemporary Italy[2] between the years 1968 and 1980. These include conspiracy thrillers, serial killer films, murder mysteries set in rural Italy, and films that passed comment on the nation's crises through vigilante, mafia and gangster narratives. Taken together, these films engaged with both contemporary events and the traumatic schisms of the past, thereby offering insights into wider anxieties of the 1970s around the Second World War and its ongoing political aftermath.

The ferments that followed the December 1969 bombing of Milan's Piazza Fontana, intensified with the official cover-up that surrounded the atrocity's neofascist culpability, and then continued throughout the next decade and beyond, are well documented. The Italian Ministry of the Interior's bare statistics record 14,591 'politically motivated' acts of violence on people or property between 1969 and 1987, resulting in 491 deaths and 1,181 injuries (Bull and Cooke 2013: 13). Equally well studied is the fact that, behind these figures, the acts of violence were diverse in their nature, in their motivations and in the ways they have been represented through cinema (see, for example, O'Leary 2011: 79–83). Clandestine militant groups on the political left – most famously the Red Brigades, or *Brigate Rosse* – broadly emerged from extremist wings of the era of mass protest at the end of the 1960s in defence against rising neofascism. Such groups graduated through sabotage and kidnappings to targeted political killings (most notoriously of former Prime Minister Aldo Moro in May 1978). Clandestine groups on the political right, such as *Ordine Nuovo* and *Avanguardia Nazionale*, instigated the indiscriminate bombing campaign known as *stragismo* ('massacre-ism'), and operated on a considerably more covert level.

The traumatic period of Italian history summarised above has since become known as the *anni di piombo* ('Years of Lead'). Since the films selected for consideration in this volume were made during this period, and since they depict amplified levels of violence in contemporary Italian locales, it may seem logical to read them as direct commentaries on these events. In some cases this is an appropriate, if obvious, reading (particularly in those *poliziotteschi* that depict *coup d'état* conspiracies, which are analysed in Chapter 2). It is, however, a central line of argument in these pages that this period of Italian history also left its mark on these films through more indirect preoccupations with the nation's past, which lay behind the intensification of violent acts. The period between the bombing of Piazza Fontana and the murder of Aldo Moro provides a key case study for John Foot's analysis of Italy's 'divided memory', as an era during which the past and its competing forms of memorialisation were increasingly politicised subjects of dispute (Foot 2009: 183–203). Foot presents a continuum in post-war Italy, whereby the schisms of living memory persist through continual conflict over the details and significance of historical 'truths'. In the 1970s, this intensified battleground over both the facts of the past and their resonance in the present centred on memories of events both decades old (the War, the Resistance and unresolved grievances between communism and fascism) and recent (the bombings and their disputed culpabilities, the 'accidental' death of the anarchist Giuseppe Pinelli in police custody). The picture of Italy's 1970s painted by Foot's study is therefore one of a forum in which open wounds of the local past were being perpetually exposed anew in an ongoing 'memory war' (Foot 2009: 150).

By no means was this exclusively an Italian phenomenon, since similar processes of divisive preoccupation with the living past (and over how that past should continue to be interpreted) were evident across Western Europe in the 1970s. It is a well-studied[3] phenomenon that, as the unprecedented prosperity of the post-war boom began to wane, tensions that had festered since the War began once more to rise to the surface, and this was particularly acute in those former Axis countries where the extent of denazification remained a hot topic of debate. Mark Mazower writes that the terrorism and retaliatory police repression of 1970s West Germany 'raised the spectre of that inter-war political extremism and ideological polarization which most of western Europe hoped had been left behind for good' (Mazower 1999: 324). In a broader sense, therefore, this can be seen as a period of reflection on the rapid changes of the previous three decades, as well as one of renewed crisis as untreated wounds of living memory were being opened up to haunt the present. The supranational nature of this phenomenon allows us to observe a process of crisis that fluctuated and responded according to the demands of particular cultural–political (rather than strictly 'national') contexts.

When we consider these contexts of negotiable and disputed outlooks on the past, the films analysed in these pages become intriguing documents of Italy's cultural and political histories. The plural word 'histories' is crucial for a number of reasons. It firstly emphasises the milieu of competing historical narratives summarised above. It also points to the varying modes of historical engagement to be found in this book's key films. These will be analysed variously as films that demonstrate a preoccupation with the past, films that are directly about the historical past, films that act as documents of their surrounding historical–political conditions, and films that register conditions of cinematic reception, distribution and consumption that characterised their own historical moment.

Since hardly any of the case studies I am analysing here were set in the past, I will stop short of claiming that they are 'historical films'. This category is not, however, as obvious or as self-evident as it may seem, since it has long been a bone of scholarly contention. Though these films are physically set in their present moment, they still raise questions about what it means when we categorise a film as 'historical'. This is because they are not only 'documents' of what is now the past (the 1970s), but also films that explore conceptions of the recent past from their own subjective present, as often inexplicit manifestations of broader silences, traces and residues within post-war Western Europe. They are resolutely contemporary, yet this very contemporaneity demands that they demonstrate that moment's place in its broader historical continuum. It is therefore worth considering how scholarly debates around the 'historical film' can frame the arguments to come.

Robert Burgoyne has compellingly written that historical films should give us access to the 'emotional archaeology' of the past. For Burgoyne, rather than seeking faithfully to 'relive' past events, the historical film should render what Paul Ricoeur calls the 'inside' of those events: an imaginative process of critically rethinking the past and its relationship to the present (Burgoyne 2013: 353). Such an approach frees the category up to include various modes of critical engagement with the past, including films that are set in their contemporary moment, but which invite contemplation of the weight of history on that moment. It is therefore precisely because the films in question are set in the present that I have chosen them for this analysis. All of them can be seen to pass comment on the immediate events of 1970s Italy, but they also illuminate the 'historicity' of their present subjectivity. Philip Rosen builds on the theories of André Bazin to argue that the 'historicity' of cinema rests upon its innate investment in temporality. For Rosen, cinema's need to represent the 'reality' of particular points in time is manifested in a combination of or tension between two moments: 'One is *historiography*, the writing of history . . . The other is *history*, the actual past the writing claims to convey' (Rosen 2001: 6; emphasis in original). The films under scrutiny in this volume demonstrate and embody such tensions between 'then' and 'now', by revealing their contemporary moment to be one particularly charged with such historicity and shot through with traces of the past.[4] Perhaps we might therefore think of these as belonging to a 'presentist' subset of the category 'historical film'.

If such a categorisation is to avoid seeming tokenistic, it requires clarification in relation to established scholarly approaches to historical films, which tend to assume their subject matter to be purposeful and direct representations of the past. As Burgoyne has elsewhere put it, historical films 'are centred on documentable historical events, directly referring to historical occurrences through their main plotlines' (Burgoyne 2007: 4). It is, however, notable that, when definitions for historical films are offered, they often do not delineate the setting so strictly as being 'in the past'. I have already argued that Burgoyne's more recent work allows consideration of contemporary-set narratives, while Robert A. Rosenstone (preferring the term 'history film') defines the category as one that 'evokes and makes meaningful the world of the past' (Rosenstone 2012: xi). Marnie Hughes-Warrington goes further:

> What makes a film 'historical' ... is its location in a timebound network of discussions – more or less explicit – on what history is and what it is for. On this definition, any film may be historical because it is viewed as offering indexical markers – on-screen phenomena seen as capturing or connected with past phenomena – or because it suggests something about how and why histories are made. (Hughes-Warrington 2007: 191)

By these definitions, the category 'historical film' comprises films which invite the viewer to contemplate historical narratives and their relationship to the present, be they set in the past or not.

Such tensions between past and present have long been at the centre of historical enquiry. E. H. Carr, in his seminal work *What is History?*, described the discipline as 'a dialogue between the historian in the present and the facts of the past' (Carr 2001: 29). In other words, 'history' is not merely an accumulation of facts, but is rather the process by which perceived facts are selected and utilised to address present concerns. Unsurprisingly, this tension has also long been characteristic of scholarship on the historical film. The works of Marc Ferro (1988) and Pierre Sorlin (1980), for example, influentially investigated how cinematic representations of the past illuminate films' contemporary conditions. Rosenstone (1995) has conversely sought to uncover what history films tell us about the periods being represented on screen, considering the particular registers through which cinema (as opposed to written history) allows us to teach, research and think 'historically'. In dialogue with Rosenstone's ideas, Hayden White coined the word 'historiophoty' to distinguish 'the representation of history and our thought about it in visual images and filmic discourse' from 'historiography' ('the representation of history in verbal images and written discourse') (White 1988: 1193). The debate continues, with Rosenstone more recently describing Burgoyne as writing 'as if history films are not really about the past, but about the present' (Rosenstone 2012: xv).

The phenomenon of 'presentism', meanwhile, has often been seen to be a problematic barrier to historical understanding: a process of interpreting all past events through a subjective contemporary prism and thus encouraging, in the words of one president of the American Historical Association, 'a kind of moral complacency and self-congratulation. Interpreting the past in terms of present concerns usually leads us to find ourselves morally superior' (Hunt 2002). The identification and analysis of such 'presentist' tendencies can therefore reveal much about how particular historical periods continued to influence socio-political discourse long after the event. In his study of cinematic representations of Fascism since the Second World War, Giacomo Lichtner diagnoses the 'presentist concerns of so many filmmakers of the 1970s' (Lichtner 2013: 136). For Lichtner, Italian films set in the Fascist period that were made after the events of 1968 addressed the rise of totalitarianism with a marked emphasis on their present concerns, 'thus establishing a chilling link between Fascist violence and the Strategy of Tension'[5] (2013: 137). Rather than seeing this tendency as a barrier to historical understanding, this volume will diagnose it as a repeated attitude towards the recent past within *filone* cinema of the 1970s.

Such an undertaking immediately poses methodological questions: what are we looking for when we seek to identify historical significance in such a 'popular' kind of cinema; by what models can we best pursue a 'historical' approach to an amorphous, frequently unruly cinematic format like the Italian *filone*? Certainly, such films can offer insights into how discourses about the past have been represented and consumed within particular registers of historical address. Foot concludes his study of Italy's 'divided memory' by stating that, for the historian:

> [Italy] provides a rich and complicated kaleidoscope of debates over the past. Our task is not to look for overarching theories or outcomes that suppress these competing visions and narratives, but to understand, explain, and study how the past has been experienced and narrated over time. (Foot 2009: 206)

Foot's central thesis places the nation's history in an osmotic relationship with a contested 'public memory': a relationship that ensures that the past is continually constructed and narrated anew in the negotiated, organic shaping of the present. By thus repudiating perceived boundaries between notions of (empirical) 'history' and (subjective) 'memory', Foot seeks to examine heterogeneous 'lived experiences' of a people's relationship with their national past: as set out by E. H. Carr, analysing not mere 'facts', but the differing ways in which perceived facts have been understood and utilised (Foot 2009: 5–6).

In essence, this approach seeks to appraise history on its audiences' terms, to take account of the diversity of cultural options open to them for its interpretation and negotiation in a given moment. It also draws from a rich heritage in twentieth-century historiographical debate. Isaiah Berlin, responding to Carr's argument that impersonal, ideological 'forces' determine human behaviour, insisted that, though such forces might indeed constrain human room for manoeuvre, the historian's job is to identify what that room for manoeuvre was in a particular historical or political moment (Ignatieff 2000: 206). Italy's 1970s were represented through the distribution and consumption of a variety of popular registers. An apperception of this moment's 'room for manoeuvre' should therefore take this variety into account, if we are to appraise the cultural options open to Italian audiences at the time to 'think historically' by considering their contemporary condition in its broader continuum.

It is of course beyond the scope of this (or any other) book to assess the full range of these options, and it is not my intention to try. If my research has taught me anything, it is that periods of cultural history are not mines of information that can be excavated until they are exhausted of their raw materials, but are more akin to a never-ending, organic cave network whose countless passages and galleries reveal yet more avenues of investigation. My intention is therefore to illuminate one particular register of historical address from 1970s Italian cinema. As has already been discussed, the films that provide this volume with its core focus are commonly categorised under the headings *poliziottesco* and *giallo*, each of which can be said to number hundreds of films by the end of the 1970s. I will question the usefulness of such broad critical constructs for assessing the industrial context of *filone* filmmaking: one in which numerous smaller strands (or, perhaps, '*sub-filoni*') would ebb and flow in response to the whims of the market, often proliferating in a process of concentrated and rapid repetition for a short period of time before ceasing to be profitable. Ultimately, this industrial context will emerge as the central concern for my analysis of how these films addressed their intended audiences: often through hastily constructed, shorthand versions of a recognisably 'contemporary' milieu, which in turn demonstrated the weight of the past on that present moment.

Filoni centring on acts of violence in contemporary Italian locales started to proliferate at the beginning of the 1970s, and flourished during postwar Italy's most traumatic decade. Some of these films sought directly to portray the high-profile terrorism and official cover-ups of the era. A number of *poliziotteschi* in particular depict the unmasking of official culpability behind acts of terror, and much existing scholarship on popular cinematic representation of the era therefore concerns these films. This book will begin by reappraising such direct representations, but will progress to consider how certain films that have often been relegated within critical literature to subsidiary strands of the *poliziottesco* or the *giallo* were situated within Italy's larger political battleground over the facts of the past and their resonance in the present.

Chapter 1 sets the cultural, historical and political scene for the investigation of cinematic strands that follows. Firstly, Italy's 1970s are placed within a broader continuum in post-war Western Europe, in which wartime schisms were silenced and shelved, only to reappear decades later into a transformed cultural landscape. The armed conflicts of the Years of Lead are thus framed as an opening up of old wounds, as the unfinished business of the historical battle between left and right burst once more to the surface of Italian life. In a broader sense, the early 1970s are examined as the period in which the post-war economic boom and socio-political upheavals had at last slowed down, with Italy entering a period of reflection on the changes wrought since 1945. A consequent sense of 'taking stock' manifested itself in an acute awareness of the weight of the past, and of the present moment's significance as a turning point in Italian history. The chapter analyses this point in more detail by looking at the influence of the USA in the post-war years, with a particular focus on Italy's film industry. As a barometer for the intimate economic and cultural relationship between the two nations, Italian cinema embodied wider tensions between the local and the global, and the 'crime film' is taken as a case in point.

The proliferation of Italian crime films in the 1970s is attributed to a confluence of political and cinematic factors at the end of the 1960s. Firstly, these years saw mass protest movements begin to give way to more militant forms of activism, foreshadowing the violent confrontations that were to come in the 1970s. Secondly, this was the peak period for US investment in the Italian film industry: a crucial contextual factor, which points to the decisive influence of Hollywood's output on local production into the 1970s. The films under consideration in this volume, by responding to such box-office successes as *Dirty Harry* (Don Siegel, 1971), *The French Connection* (William Friedkin, 1971), *The Godfather* (Francis Ford Coppola, 1972) and *Death Wish* (Michael Winner, 1974) while simultaneously turning their attention towards local Italian settings and events, embody the above tensions between the local and the global. *Banditi a Milano / The Violent Four* (Carlo Lizzani, 1968) is assessed as a particularly revealing precursor to the period of proliferation, for its careful interweaving of Hollywood genre tropes with preoccupations around recent changes in Italian society. The chapter therefore arrives at the cultural 'moment' of the early 1970s having examined these contextual factors, and considers the tensions that arise between the cultural specificity of the key films and their transnational aspects. As documents for Italy's globally oriented outlook that simultaneously address local concerns, they raise questions relating to national belonging, and offer insights into the complexities at work within the specific national, local and subcultural contexts that surrounded them.

Returning to the central argument that this book's key films demonstrate residues of the national past persisting beneath the surface of the present, the chapter then concludes by considering the concept of 'collective' or 'cultural' trauma. The Years of Lead are thus placed in a cycle of silence and re-emergence of trauma going back to the Second World War, and incorporating not only the violence of the past and the present, but also the rapid socio-cultural changes of the intervening years. These changes were therefore omnipresent, even if frequently 'silent', in attempts to make sense of the 1970s present, whose political events were from the moment of their occurrence sites of contested political memory across diverse strata of cultural and political discourse. Finally, the industrial nature of the *filone* production model is framed as a key contextual factor, with its fast turnaround and its repetitive 'serial' nature proving central to its responsiveness to contemporary concerns. Throughout the remainder of the book, I therefore approach these films as constituent parts of rapidly reproduced formulae, rather than as self-contained units.

The cultural and political coordinates surrounding the emergence of the book's key films thus detailed, Chapter 2 begins by focusing on the trend of 1970s *filone* cinema that most directly commented on the historical and political schisms of its era: the *poliziottesco* or 'police procedural' format. Specifically, the first half of the chapter takes as its subject matter the strand of this *filone* whose plots invest in notions of high-level *coup d'état* conspiracy. The key case studies here are *La polizia ringrazia / Execution Squad* (Stefano Vanzina, 1972), *Milano trema – la polizia vuole giustizia / The Violent Professionals* (Sergio Martino, 1973), *La polizia sta a guardare* / *The Great Kidnapping* (Roberto Infascelli, 1973), *La polizia accusa: il servizio segreto uccide* / *Silent Action* (Sergio Martino, 1975), *La polizia ha le mani legate* / *Killer Cop* (Luciano Ercoli, 1975), *Poliziotti violenti* / *Crimebusters* (Michele Massimo Tarantini, 1976) and *Il grande racket* / *The Big Racket* (Enzo G. Castellari, 1976).

Each of these films enacts a revelatory unmasking of officially sanctioned corruption or authoritarian conspiracy, on the surface trying to find explanations for the nation's contemporary traumas. This chapter, however, argues that such films seek, not to explain or to 'make sense' of the events, but instead to enact a ritual recognition of only partially understood, but pervasive and therefore assumed, corruption. It is ultimately the 'serial' nature of *filone* cinema that is identified as the key to understanding this process as ritual: a performance of formulaic repetition, which assumes a degree of prior knowledge on the part of its audiences, akin to the ancient Greek concept of *anagnorisis* ('recognition'). Embedded within its immediate moment, this 'conspiracy' strand of the *poliziottesco* thus embodies the incomplete understanding of elusive culpabilities that characterised the period in Italian political discourse. The films are appraised for their immediacy rather than their coherence, as documents of confusion rather than of investigative rigour.

The ritual performances of conspiracy and the *filone* production values evident throughout these films are ultimately seen to serve the primary task of constructing believable backdrops for the cathartic ritual of unmasking. Analysing the unspoken assumptions that make up those backdrops therefore provides a valuable insight into the historical silences that exist in Italian crime films. To explore this point in more detail, the chapter moves on from this *filone* about policemen battling institutional corruption from within, to examine films whose protagonists are private citizens driven to fight against criminal syndicates, and who in the process become caught up in labyrinthine webs of intrigue. The key films analysed in this section are *Città violenta* / *The Family* (Sergio Sollima, 1970), *Ricatto alla mala* / *Summertime Killer* (Antonio Isasi, 1972), *Revolver* / *Blood in the Streets* (Sergio Sollima, 1973), *Il cittadino si ribella* / *Street Law* (Enzo G. Castellari, 1974), *La città sconvolta: caccia spietata ai rapitori* / *Kidnap Syndicate* (Fernando Di Leo, 1975), *Roma violenta* / *Violent City* (Marino Girolami, 1975), *Il giustiziere sfida la città* / *Syndicate Sadists* (Umberto Lenzi, 1975), *L'uomo della strada fa giustizia* / *Manhunt in the City* (Umberto Lenzi, 1975), *Vai gorilla* / *The Hired Gun* (Tonino Valerii, 1975), *Roma, l'altra faccia della violenza* / *Rome: The Other Side of Violence* (Marino Girolami, 1976) and *Torino violenta* / *Double Game* (Carlo Ausino, 1977).

This *filone* strand is considered within a broader international continuum of urban vigilante films that have been seen as nostalgic rejections of globalisation and traumatic processes of rapid socio-cultural change across diverse national contexts. By its very nature, the vigilante film and its 'citizen taking control' trope hankers after an imagined past time of moral certainty, as opposed to a debased present of national crisis. Yet the Italian version is different in one important sense. Building further on the arguments around the pervasiveness of high-level criminality (and the textual assumptions that arise from such an outlook), I assess how these representations of alienated or on-the-run individuals amount to nihilistic assertions of the futility of fighting against a corrupt, faceless system.

Rather than making specific reference to historic failed coup plots that are 'unmasked' for the protagonist, as identified earlier in the chapter, these films tend to be decoupled from specific historical reference points. They instead construct a more diffuse sense of the powerlessness of the individual in the face of an omnipotent machine. This assumed, taken-as-read ubiquity of corruption is shown to manifest itself through seemingly minor scene-setting details and off-guard moments of background exposition, which expose preoccupations with the nation's traumatic past and the historical continuity of systematic institutional brutality. Once again, it is only through analysing the repetitious nature of the *filone* production model that this significance becomes apparent, as these details are not noticeable as standalone commentaries, but instead obtain meaning through serial accumulation. These repeated assumptions informing the construction of believable story worlds include indirect but clear references to continuing neofascist violence and thus pertain to the historical 'silences' analysed in Chapter 1. The films analysed in this second chapter are all explicitly embedded in their contemporary political moment, but it is through that very immediacy that their preoccupation with the past is manifest.

In Chapter 3, I turn my attention to another context of resurgent violence and political corruption plaguing 1970s Italy: that of the mafia. The proliferation of a mafia *filone* between 1972 and 1974 is the core subject matter of this chapter, but I begin by taking the internationally influential gangster films of Fernando Di Leo as case studies: *Milano calibro 9 / Caliber 9* (Fernando Di Leo, 1972), *La mala ordina / The Italian Connection* (Fernando Di Leo, 1972), *Il boss / The Boss* (Fernando Di Leo, 1973) and *I padroni della città / Rulers of the City* (Fernando Di Leo, 1976). Continuing the pattern from Chapter 2, these films' depictions of insidious, far-reaching mafia infiltration into the institutions of state come across as an assumed, self-evident ritual, rather than a revelatory claim requiring in-depth analysis. Of more interest are the ways in which the films repeatedly demonstrate an overt preoccupation with the past, by deploying old-timer *mafioso* protagonists to provide both an elegiac reflection on the passing of a bygone era and a lament at the changes that have visited Italy since the economic boom of the 1950s. Each film thus revealingly positions its branch of the mafia as a mouthpiece for a larger Italian polity, and a conduit for national neuroses.

The chapter then demonstrates how Di Leo's films inherit, recycle and perpetuate a number of pre-existing popular myths about the mafia as a repository for elegiac nostalgia. The most obvious point of reference here is *The Godfather* (Francis Ford Coppola, 1972), but Coppola's film itself emerged from pre-existing traditions of representation and stereotyping, which are inherited and reworked by the mafia *filone* that followed in its wake. The Hollywood 'mafia film' is thus analysed as a chronicle of cultural displacement and a descendent of the early twentieth-century 'immigrant film', which explored the Italian-American experience as a repository for tensions around acculturation and assimilation in US national discourse. The competing pulls of the Old World and the New that ran throughout these 'immigrant films' would eventually feed into the Hollywood mafia genre, and would in turn be appropriated by the Italian mafia *filone*. The chapter also demonstrates, however, that this was not a simple process of transatlantic imitation, since this *filone* is equally indebted to native models of mafia representation.

The Italian mafia film is also seen to invest heavily in discourses around the past. Since the *Risorgimento* (the nineteenth-century unification of the Italian nation), the mafia has been a component part of a broader tendency to stereotype the 'backward' southern regions of Italy as a window into the nation's history and a forum for taking stock of the contemporary moment in relation to a benighted past. Though the mafia *filone* noticeably proliferated in the wake of *The Godfather*, this chapter argues that it inherited, recycled and repurposed all manner of mafia myths – from both sides of the Atlantic – each of which possessed a pre-existing function as a register of national or ethnic identity, a gauge for the historical position of contemporary society in relation to prevailing conceptions of modernity or a locus for tensions between the past and the present. The key films are too numerous to list here in their entirety, but they include *Afyon oppio / The Sicilian Connection* (Ferdinando Baldi, 1972), *L'amico del padrino / The Godfather's Friend* (Frank Agrama, 1972), *Milano rovente / Gang War in Milan* (Umberto Lenzi, 1973), *Baciamo le mani / Family Killer* (Vittorio Schiraldi, 1973), *L'onorata famiglia – Uccidere è cosa nostra / The Big Family* (Tonino Ricci, 1973), *Il consigliori / Counselor at Crime* (Alberto

De Martino, 1973), *Tony Arzenta / No Way Out* (Duccio Tessari, 1973), *Anna, quel particolare piacere / Secrets of a Call Girl* (Giuliano Carnimeo, 1973) and *Quelli che contano / Cry of a Prostitute* (Andrea Bianchi, 1974).

Again, it is through analysing the repetitive, 'serial' nature of this mafia *filone* that these discourses become apparent. These films replicate certain themes time and again in a maze of intertextual references, operating in constant dialogue with both a diverse set of external influences and with one another, rather than as self-contained narrative units. It is through appraising these industrial conditions that the films of Fernando Di Leo are properly contextualised, since his repeated tropes are shown to be embedded within this larger process of rapidly produced variations on a theme. The elegiac laments of elderly *mafiosi*, the focus on transatlantic mafia activity, the fixation on the migration of southern Italians to the north of the country and an investment in stereotyped depictions of Sicily all recur so often in such a short period of time that they provide their viewers with a peculiar sense of déjà vu, as a catalogue of echoes and half-remembered recollections from an amalgam of other mafia films.

What is therefore most interesting about these films is how diverse mafia myths become blended together in this serial use of patterns and trends, across a large number of films released within a short period of time. These films' mode of delivery is a more significant factor than the narrative contents of any one of this *filone*'s source materials, creating an intertextual tension between the past and the present, and between competing cinematic 'Sicilies'. It is precisely in the repetitiveness of these films that their various genre echoes obtain significance through a process of accumulation. This *filone* therefore provides an illuminating document of production decisions, marketing ploys and ruminations on the state of contemporary Italy.

In Chapter 4, I turn my attention to films loosely connected through their depiction of serial killing in contemporary Italy. Specifically, I identify and analyse a number of strands that are usually subsumed within the *giallo* category. These demonstrate a variety of ways in which *filone* cinema was characterised by tensions between cosmopolitanism and parochialism, in turn providing further insights into how particular *filoni* sought to capitalise on a preoccupation with the recent past. While the *poliziottesco* overtly comments on the politically motivated violence of its time and place, the *giallo* is instead analysed as a category that is fixated on the changes wrought on Italian society in the preceding decades.

Firstly, the chapter examines a small set of films that make explicit reference to memories of the Second World War weighing heavily upon the present. Historical memory of this conflict becomes fragmented and positioned as an originary trauma for contemporary violence in *Nelle pieghe della carne / In the Folds of the Flesh* (Sergio Bergonzelli, 1970), *Ragazza tutta nuda assassinata nel parco / Naked Girl Killed in the Park* (Alfonso Brescia, 1972) and *Il gatto dagli occhi di giada / Watch Me When I Kill* (Antonio Bido, 1977). In particular, the oft-silenced history of retributory violence against Nazi collaborators in the immediate post-war era (the *resa dei conti*, or 'settling of accounts') is summoned up, and is most directly represented in *Pensione paura / Hotel Fear* (Francesco Barilli, 1978). These films are analysed as productions that seek to evoke audiences' lived experiences of the War, while simultaneously obfuscating such precise (and traumatic) historical reference points. The *resa dei conti* in particular remains a palpable yet unspeakable presence.

Such themes fit into the *giallo*'s broader obsession with past traumas, fragmented memories and the unravelling of supposed facts. Returning to the concept of collective or cultural trauma explored in Chapter 1, the argument turns to dominant scholarly approaches that identify *gialli* as commentaries on the increasingly globalised lifestyles of affluent post-war modernity. The perceived impact of tourism, bourgeois decadence, consumerist modernity and sexual licentiousness manifests itself in the contemporary urban spaces of Western Europe being rendered culturally alienating and threatening in a significant number of films. These include *Sei donne per l'assassino / Blood and Black Lace* (Mario Bava, 1964), *Il rosso segno della follia / A Hatchet for the Honeymoon* (Mario Bava, 1970), *Paranoia / A Quiet Place to Kill* (Umberto Lenzi, 1970), *Un posto ideale per uccidere / A Quiet Place to Kill* (Lenzi, 1971), *Lo strano vizio della signora Wardh / Blade of the Ripper* (Sergio Martino, 1971), *Cosa avete fatto a Solange? / What Have You Done to Solange?* (Massimo Dallamano, 1972), *Perché quelle strane gocce di sangue sul corpo di Jennifer? / The Case of the Bloody Iris* (Giuliano Carnimeo, 1972) and *Nude per l'assassino / Strip Nude for Your Killer* (Andrea Bianchi, 1975). Again, I argue that the *filone* production model invites a scenario in which the world of the *giallo* accumulates through rapid repetition, as common sense, assumed or taken-as-read 'modern' settings are hastily constructed in an incoherent cacophony of licentious modernity.

The chapter then turns to representations of a parochial Italian underbelly, which I dub the 'rural *giallo*'. To an even greater extent than the mafia films analysed in Chapter 3, these films gaze inwardly to invest in a set of discourses surrounding the nation's past and the onset of modernity. *Reazione a catena / A Bay of Blood* (Mario Bava, 1971) is taken as this strand's trailblazer, followed by *Non si sevizia un paperino / Don't Torture a Duckling* (Lucio Fulci, 1972), *I corpi presentano tracce di violenza carnale / Torso* (Sergio Martino, 1973), *La casa dalle finestre che ridono / The House of the Laughing Windows* (Pupi Avati, 1976) and *Solamente nero / Bloodstained Shadow* (Antonio Bido, 1978). These films deviate from the *giallo*'s more famed 'urban' films through their primitive backwater settings and overt focus on rustic superstition. In so doing, they enact a peculiar form of time travel, in which a representative of modernity investigates the local past, which inescapably haunts the 1970s present. *Non si sevizia un paperino* provides a particularly vivid illustration of this argument, since this film invests in long-standing discourses surrounding the Italian south as both a window into the nation's primitive past and a mirror onto its troubled present.

The chapter concludes with a detailed consideration of *I corpi presentano tracce di violenza carnale*, since this film brings together the various strands so far discussed. Its focus on the clash between cosmopolitan modernity and provincial parochialism goes hand-in-hand with a dual setting pertaining to Italy's heritage industry and its benighted underbelly. It also points towards an important factor when considering *filone* cinema, since it enjoyed more success in anglophone export markets than it did at home. With this in mind, the following chapter shifts the book's focus to a comparison of reception patterns at home and abroad that greeted these various *filone* strands.

With the book having so far examined a collection of *filoni* in their immediate cultural–political contexts, Chapter 5 considers how discourses around these films' releases developed in two specific markets: those of Italy and the USA. In so doing, this chapter tests the claims made in Chapters 2, 3 and 4 that the historical significance of these films lies in their status as overlapping sets of rapidly produced 'serial' repetitions, rather than as self-contained units. This is here more fully interrogated by considering how the films' differing distribution patterns across these markets resulted in contrasting promotional strategies and critical discourses. This introduction's promise to 'appraise the cultural options open to Italian audiences at the time' is therefore extended to assess a dialogue across reception contexts and cultural mores.

Through a wide-ranging survey of newspaper film reviews, the chapter firstly illustrates that the Italian reception of *poliziotteschi* and vigilante films in particular was characterised by accusations of reactionary politics or of oversimplified and irresponsible treatments of the issues surrounding contemporary violence. This betrays an assumption on the part of some critics that such films are aiming for a benchmark of 'serious' political cinema, overlooking the fact that *filoni* were operating according to a different set of rules predicated upon ritual performances in cycles of repetition and renewal. The chapter's most significant insight, however, comes when boundary lines between *filone* categories are disregarded and the sample of reviews is assessed as one entity. By doing this, the analysis discovers that discussions of *filone* cinema's repetitive nature are a constant across the entire eight-year sample. Indeed, many critics used the various *filone* labels more or less interchangeably, viewing them all as a steady stream of repetitive ephemera. Their concentrated patterns of production, distribution and consumption were more often the subject of critical discourse than were the narrative contents of particular cycles.

The chapter then compares the publicity campaigns of Italian crime films in the Italian and US markets, analysing a shift in distribution and exhibition contexts that would have a tangible impact on reception patterns. While Italian adverts tended to emphasise the allure of repetition, the American publicity for the same films contained more lurid and sensationalised promises of aberrant titillation. My analysis suggests that this was in part due to their more sporadic release patterns in the drive-in and grindhouse sectors of the US market. The US critical reception broadly refused to buy into such hype, instead framing these films as unremarkable or incompetent trash. Italian crime films were thus seen as foreign oddities, whose intermittent release patterns in the US market led to amusement, disdain and bewilderment. This marked contrast between the two reception contexts is finally used to illustrate the centrality of 'serial' repetition to an understanding of these films' significance in their place of origin. When the films were removed from the concentrated production and release patterns of the *filone* system, their status as innately serial artefacts failed to register, rendering them laughable peculiarities rather than culturally familiar rituals.

This book concludes by considering issues of categorisation, and discussing the meaning, significance and usefulness of the word '*filone*' for the study of this kind of cinematic output. The previous chapters' consistent recourse to notions of 'seriality' is here discussed as a unifying thread for the book as a whole, by considering *filoni* in relation to prevailing definitions of the 'film cycle'. The cinematic strands discussed throughout the book are found to vary widely in their relationship to such definitions, illuminating the industrial nature of this sector of the Italian film industry. A *filone* is ultimately identified as a product emanating from a marketplace that had a dual *raison d'être*: firstly, to create speculations in an attempt to predict where the next cycle might lie, informed by previous patterns; and secondly, to exploit the short-lived favourable market conditions of profitable cycles. The perpetual attempt to capitalise on topicality that resulted from this business model is ultimately seen to be the key to understanding these films' oscillation between repetition and difference. Their resultant traces of preoccupations with the recent past are key components of a contemporaneity that was assumed to be instantly recognisable to Italian audiences of the 1970s.

Throughout this book, I shall translate films' Italian dialogue into English as faithfully as possible, but I will also mention the Italian in instances where semantic ambiguities arise or where I feel this will aid clarification of meaning. When I make use of written sources in the Italian language, I shall provide the original text alongside my own translation. Finally, I shall use the Italian release titles of films after their initial mentions in any given chapter. This is for the sake of clarity, since many *filone* films have been released in English-speaking markets under numerous different titles over the years.

Notes

1. The word *filone* is generally preferred to 'genre' in scholarship around popular Italian cinema of the 1960s and 1970s, as a way of distinguishing this industrial context from that of Hollywood. This runs the risk of making broad generalisations about both the popular cinema of the USA and the scholarly field of 'genre studies', both of which are vast and heterogeneous: a trap into which I have fallen in the past (Fisher 2011: 36). This caveat notwithstanding, *filone* remains a useful descriptor for a set of culturally and temporally specific production and distribution practices.
2. There are some exceptions where I have chosen to incorporate films that were set in past times, but which nevertheless inform an analysis of the cinematic strands I am considering. For example, Chapter 3 includes analyses of historical mafia dramas *I guappi / Blood Brothers* (Pasquale Squitieri, 1974) and *La mano nera / The Black Hand* (Antonio Racioppi, 1973), while Chapter 4 incorporates *Pensione paura / Hotel Fear* (Francesco Barilli, 1978), which is set during the Second World War. Likewise, a handful of the selected films are in fact set outside Italy, but are similarly useful for contextual analysis of broader trends.
3. For a particularly detailed analysis of the sense of sudden socio-economic and political stagnation that arose in 1970s Western Europe, see Judt (2010: 453–83).
4. My vocabulary here is deliberately alluding to that of Walter Benjamin's 'Theses on the Philosophy of History', in which a historian is described as someone who 'establishes a concept of the present as the "time of the now" which is shot through with chips of Messianic time' (Benjamin 1999: 255). Benjamin's notion of *Jetztzeit*, or 'now time' refers to points in time that are particularly replete with political significance, and remain so as they are remembered and represented throughout subsequent eras, defined as 'a past

charged with the time of the now which [is] blasted out of the continuum of history' (1999: 253). The Second World War can be seen as one such point in time, and its long shadow on 1970s Italy will be a key factor in my analysis.

5. 'Strategy of tension' (*strategia della tensione*) describes a plan enacted by the secret services and other state institutions covertly to support terrorist attacks in an effort to spread fear and promote an authoritarian *coup d'état*. This will be investigated in more detail in Chapters 1 and 2.

CHAPTER 1

Italian Crime Films and the Years of Lead

The opening four minutes of *Il cittadino si ribella* / *Street Law* (Enzo G. Castellari, 1974) present the viewer with a rapid montage of housebreaking, robbery, looting, muggings and assassinations on the streets of Genoa. The protagonist Carlo (played by Franco Nero) then enters the film by walking into a bank, which is immediately held up by more criminals, who take him hostage. On an explicit and obvious level, this catalogue of violence registers a sense of insecurity in 1970s Italian society, as stories of such criminality dominated the headlines.

Yet in the midst of this scene-setting preamble lies an important detail, which points to less explicit, underlying historical factors. As three men break into and vandalise Carlo's flat, one of them finds a framed document on the wall carrying the headline 'Italiani ribellatevi!' ('Italians rebel'), and smashes it. As the flat is set alight and the men retreat, the camera zooms in on this document, now lying on the floor (see Figures 1.1 and 1.2). Its significance is returned to only briefly later in the film, when Carlo explains that it was a manifesto written by his father during the Second World War to urge resistance to the German army. He mentions it because he sees its enduring relevance in the present, as an exhortation to Italians to resist continuing injustice.

This opening sequence literally depicts a breaking open of past conflict to frame the film's narrative. The document and its historical significance are rarely dwelt upon in the film's diegesis, and it only reappears as a framing device in establishing shots to physically place us back in Carlo's flat, but this is emblematic of many of the films analysed in this book: a narrative set in contemporary 1970s Italy, which is on the surface about violence on contemporary streets, but whose preoccupation with the War, the Resistance and their traumatic legacies weighs heavily (even if silently) throughout. This historical backdrop only bursts through to the surface briefly in Castellari's film, and is not therefore the explicit theme, but it is

Figures 1.1 and 1.2 Carlo's vandalised manifesto points to underlying historical motivations in *Il cittadino si ribella* (Enzo G. Castellari, 1974).

the driving force behind all of the protagonist's actions and the reference point of the film's Italian title: 'the citizen rebels'.

This chapter will examine the cultural, historical and political contexts that facilitated such a mode of representation as is outlined above. The notorious events of Italy's 1970s had their roots in the unfinished business of the War, the Resistance and the historical conflict between left and right. The weight of the past lay even more heavily for the fact that the internecine schisms of the War had never been healed, but instead papered over as Italy underwent two decades of unprecedented socioeconomic growth in the post-war period. The late 1960s and the 1970s would see these festering tensions burst into the open once more, but in a fundamentally changed cultural backdrop. The influence of the USA on Italy's post-war outlook had been profound, and nowhere was this more apparent than in the country's film industry. The *filone* production format was testament to a rapid responsiveness to popular tastes and trends, often in reaction to successful Hollywood imports but at the same time addressing the concerns of their immediate time and place. The films under consideration in this volume therefore emerged in a cultural moment at which tensions between the local and the global, and the past and the present, were converging.

'An Unspeakable Past'

The pre-eminent historian of post-war Europe, Tony Judt, examined how Western Europe remade itself after the Second World War through processes of wilful amnesia and silences around the horrors of the recent past. The rebuilt continent was, in Judt's words, 'an imposing edifice resting atop an unspeakable past' (Judt 2010: 3) and 'a prophylactic, to keep the past at bay' (Judt 2010: 6): 'The long shadow of World War Two lay heavy across post-war Europe. It could not, however, be acknowledged in full. Silence over Europe's recent past was the necessary condition for the construction of a European future' (Judt 2010: 10). The picture of this period Judt's compelling account paints is one of swift, arbitrary and cathartic retribution against collaborators with the Nazis, followed by a protracted process of lingering bitterness being silenced, and shelved for later generations to dust off.

Italy, as one of the defeated Axis nations, provided a particularly notable manifestation of this process. Just five days after what would become sanctified as the National Liberation Day of 25 April 1945 (a day whose very purpose is one of remembrance of the War), the Christian Democrat newspaper *Il Popolo* responded to the execution of Benito Mussolini by declaring:

> Nessuno può desiderare che il bagno di sangue si prolunghi oltre i limiti della stessa guerra civile, nessuno può desiderare che lo spettacolo ammonitore di chi ha finalmente pagato per i propri delitti si trasformi in una ripugnante esibizione. Ed ora, abbiamo la forza di dimenticare! Dimenticare al più presto.
>
> Nobody can want the bloodbath to prolong itself beyond this civil war. Nobody can want the admonitory spectacle of those who have finally paid for their crimes to become a disgusting performance. And now, we have the strength to forget! Forget as soon as possible. (Gonella 1945)

Palpable in these words is a need to move on, to not dwell on the traumas and to rebuild a new nation from the rubble of war: a need made more explicit still by the Action Party's newspaper *L'Italia Libera* a day later: 'Now we must look to reconstruct . . . The past must never resurface in any form' (Domenico 1991: 156).

In truth, the bitter schisms within Italian society that had opened up during the War would not be consigned to the past so easily. The political and social divisions arising from the civil war that engulfed the Italian peninsula between 1943 and 1945 would resurface years later, but the immediate desire to move on outlined above nevertheless proved potent. Italy's national mythology around the wartime Resistance movement grew rapidly in the post-war era, with public remembrance of the sacrifices made in the struggle against Nazism becoming a locus for national pride and official ceremony. Yet, as has been analysed by John Foot, the Resistance myth was also a forum for forgetting, since certain elements of that history were silenced or hidden: most notably, the period known as the *resa dei conti* ('settling of accounts') (Foot 2009: 156–82). This period of retributory violence immediately followed the Liberation, and saw an estimated 12,000–15,000 people being killed across Italy as old scores were settled and former Fascists were hunted down (Ginsborg 1990: 68). So strong was the desire to bury such unsavoury elements of the past, the *resa dei conti* was largely overlooked in histories and public memories of the Resistance in what Foot describes as a 'shared silence' (Foot 2009: 168).

Mark Mazower describes equivalent processes of selective memorialisation throughout Western Europe (such as France canonising the memory of a united opposition to the Vichy regime, or Austria positioning itself as 'Hitler's first victim') as 'the foundation myths of a Europe liberated from history; they expunged awkward memories and asserted the inevitability of freedom's triumph' (Mazower 1999: xiii–xiv). It was through precisely such collective amnesia, along with a purposefully light-touch purging of fascism within the institutions of state, that Italy in particular underwent a 'suspiciously painless transition' to becoming a democratic ally of the West in the Cold War years (Judt 2010: 48).

When we fast-forward to the start of the 1970s, after the country had undergone two decades of rapid socio-political change and militant movements on both the extreme left and the extreme right were reappearing, the resurfacing of such memories around the War was ever more pertinent. Antonello and O'Leary have described the Years of Lead as 'the return of the repressed', as part of an ongoing cycle of national trauma (Antonello and O'Leary 2009: 6–7). Putting to one side the psychoanalytical connotations of this phrase, such a perspective serves usefully to illuminate this specific cultural–political moment when memories of the past were being returned to and old scores were being resurrected. Indeed, the actions of both the far left and the far right in these years were driven in large part by the unfinished business of the civil war of 1943–5. While the left drew inspiration from the prominent role played in the Resistance by leftist organisations, neofascists defined themselves as a continuation of Mussolini's conflict with communism. In the words of Leonard Weinberg: 'Each side has been armed with a historical example of its victory through violence over the other' (Weinberg 1986: 149).

It is of course not the case that such schisms between left and right were entirely hidden in 1945, until suddenly reappearing from nowhere in the 1970s. Fear of Italy's strong communist subculture, which had been emboldened by its central role in the victorious Resistance, was a crucial motivating factor for much of the country's ensuing political division. The elections of 1948, for example, saw the centre-right Christian Democrats (DC) defeat the resurgent Italian Communist Party (PCI), and enter government on an avowedly anti-communist mandate. In the early 1960s, the entry of the centre-left Italian Socialist Party (PSI) into coalition government (known as the 'opening to the left') led sections of the military to fear a renewed climate of tolerance towards communism and to forge closer links with the extreme right, who had not conveniently disappeared after defeat in 1945. Neofascist ideologies – broadly characterised by extreme anti-communism and nostalgia for Mussolini's Republic of Salò (1943–5) – remained significant in postwar Italian political life, with a parliamentary presence in the form of the Italian Social Movement (MSI), organised street gangs of *picchiatori* ('dive bombers') assaulting PCI offices (Weinberg 1986: 149), and an active clandestine underbelly in such paramilitary organisations as *Ordine Nuovo* and *Avanguardia Nazionale*.

Bull and Newell identify the 'opening to the left' as the catalyst for the *strategia della tensione*, or 'strategy of tension': a coordinated effort by secret services and other state institutions to spread fear and foment instability through terrorist attacks, thus providing a perceived necessity for an authoritarian takeover (Bull and Newell 2005: 101). Indeed, as Jonathan Dunnage points out, while the Piazza Fontana bombing of December 1969 is commonly seen to be the starting point of the strategy of tension, its roots lay in the anti-communist plots that began in 1964 with the abortive *coup d'état* led by General Giovanni De Lorenzo (Dunnage 2002: 186). The links between the military, the secret services and the far right are neatly illustrated by the personal trajectory of De Lorenzo himself: a former head of the military secret service (SIFAR), the acting head of the *carabinieri*, and subsequently a Member of Parliament and representative of the MSI. While the precise details remain murky, the planned coup was seemingly devised in collusion with the President of the Republic, Antonio Segni (see Ginsborg 1990: 276–8), and had the specific intention of neutralising left-wing influence in Aldo Moro's coalition government with the PSI.

Such a continuous presence of neofascist activity (and collaboration with the state) notwithstanding, the period after 1969 was especially notable because this was when such historical tensions spilled over into armed conflict in a systematic and widespread manner. The bomb that exploded in Milan's Piazza Fontana on 12 December 1969 killed sixteen people and wounded eighty-eight (Ginsborg 1990: 333), but also ushered in a new era which opened up the wounds of the past. The authorities immediately laid the blame on left-wing activists and rounded up anarchist suspects, only for investigative journalists to reveal that the culpability lay with the far-right group *Ordine Nuovo*, with the covert support of the secret services. The clandestine links between institutions of state and the far right had become more virulent, and the ensuing years saw further coup plots (most notably by former Republic of Salò commander Prince Valerio Borghese in December 1970) and the bombing campaign known as *stragismo*[1] (most famously at Peteano in 1972, Brescia and San Benedetto

Val di Sambro in 1974, and Bologna in 1980), amidst cover-ups pointing to further collusion between far right militants and the secret services.

On the political left, responses to the fascist resurgence explicitly drew on reference points from the War. A key dispute by the late 1960s surrounded the means by which the contested memory and legacy of the Resistance would be negotiated and appropriated. This became a pole of identity and pride to a variety of left-wing subcultures, not least those within the protest movements who venerated the partisan struggle as an exemplar of armed resistance to a repressive state. This paradoxically manifested itself in a rejection within the far left of the wartime generation, who were seen to have betrayed the values of the Resistance in the post-war era. The pragmatism and compromise of the PCI's leader Palmiro Togliatti in the years following the Liberation successfully turned his party into a mass movement. Yet the simultaneous failure of the communists to outmanoeuvre the nascent Christian Democrats, to force through much-needed reform of the institutions of state, or to forge a clean break with the Fascist past sewed the seeds for generational conflict in the late 1960s. Antonio Tricomi describes the new generation of young communists as:

> A generation born after the Second World War, brought up in Boom-era Italy and therefore ignorant of the true dynamics of the partisan struggle. This generation would nonetheless include the protagonists of 1968, or of a *lotta armata* [armed struggle] posited on the myth that the PCI had prevented a revolution that was possible in 1948; a revolution that should now, twenty and more years later, be set in motion at last. (Tricomi 2009: 18)

The disputed legacy of the Resistance – claimed at once by the PCI, the PSI and the extra-parliamentary protest movements that proliferated around 1968 – thus served as a locus for anti-fascism within the Italian left. Among the many militant leftist groups that formed in the late 1960s and early 1970s was Giangiacomo Feltrinelli's *Gruppi d'Azione Partigiana* ('Partisan Action Groups'), and their underground publication was entitled *Nuova Resistenza*. The nomenclature of this 'New Resistance' attested to the pertinence of the past for the present: a contested historical memory shaping the rebellion's representation, appropriation and preservation.

Crucially, this preoccupation with the past was a driving factor behind the eventual turn to armed conflict by left-wing extra-parliamentary groups in the early 1970s. The perceived necessity for a new partisan struggle had its roots in the era of mass protest towards the end of the 1960s which, though largely peaceful, had included factions for whom terrorism would subsequently become a justifiable option. These factions had often been inducted into political confrontation through running battles with neofascists, and militant leftist groups formed armed wings (*servizi d'ordine*) in response (Tarrow 1991: 52–8). The post-Piazza Fontana period was accordingly marked by a conviction on the far left that Italy was, in Tricomi's words 'in the same situation it had been in half a century previously, on the brink of fascist dictatorship' (Tricomi 2009: 19). When the *Brigate Rosse* (BR) were founded in 1970, their formation was therefore undertaken with specific reference to the Resistance. Co-founder Renato Curcio drew inspiration from his uncle, who died fighting for the partisans: 'I have picked up the rifle that only death, arriving through the murderous hand of nazi-fascists, had wrested from him' (Weinberg 1986: 148). The BR thus appropriated the symbols and rhetoric of the Resistance as what Raimondo Catanzaro describes as 'a ready-made ideology that was treated as an immediately usable resource for historical legitimation' (Catanzaro 1991: 180).

At this juncture, it is important to stress that preoccupation with the past – and the 1940s in particular – was a phenomenon that reached well beyond such overtly politicised evocations of the War. In a much broader sense, the early 1970s saw the end of an unprecedented period of economic boom and attendant socio-political upheaval. Richard Nixon's abandonment of fixed exchange rates in 1971, the Organization of the Petroleum Exporting Countries (OPEC) oil crisis of 1973 and the ensuing financial downturn across the Western world saw Italy's 'Economic Miracle' come to a halt, as if the years since 1945 had been a heady dream of inexorable growth, from which the nation was being rudely awakened. For Judt, the early 1970s were characterised by a sense that 'Europe's "good times" had gone . . . It was an age depressingly aware of having come *after* the big hopes and ambitious ideas of the recent past' (Judt 2010: 477–8).

A consequent sense of taking stock – of contemplating how far the continent had come in the past thirty years – could be detected in cultural–political discourse across Western Europe. In Italy, an acute awareness of the weight of the past, along with recognition that the present moment constituted a decisive historical crossroads, was a key motivator within mainstream parliamentary politics. From 1973, PCI leader Enrico Berlinguer's 'historic compromise' policy was devised in the belief that the dangers of the Fascist period were once again raising their heads. For Berlinguer, the 1970s presented a moment of danger, with the strategy of tension, the mobilisation of the far right and a deteriorating economic climate providing fertile ground for a return to authoritarianism. His policy proposed a grand alliance in defence of democracy, akin to that which had fought Fascism in the 1940s, uniting the DC, the PSI and the PCI. Crucially, however, Ginsborg explains that the 'historic compromise' was not only drawing inspiration from the 1940s; it arose from an outlook living in the past, 'profoundly out of tune with the radical transformations that had taken place in Italian society since 1945' (Ginsborg 1990: 357). Though the War years continued to shape attitudes and policies alike, mass migration, economic upheaval and the cultural influence of the USA in the intervening decades had ensured that politically, socially and culturally, Italy was a different place.

American Influences, Italian Crime Films

To look back to 1945, and to take stock of how far Italy had come since, was to behold a steady process of alignment with the American sphere of influence. From Allied occupation and political intervention, through economic recovery and the importation of US popular culture, Italy had been fast-tracked to become an advanced capitalist nation. The preceding couple of paragraphs have underlined the extent to which international factors were playing a decisive role in the country's fate by the 1970s, but American influence in Italy should not be seen as an entirely external imposition. Rather, the extent to which American lifestyles, outlooks and cultural artefacts were embraced and appropriated by Italians provides a barometer for transformations in post-war Italian identities, which through their very fluidity cast doubt upon notions of cultural belonging drawn along rigidly national lines.

Nowhere was this more apparent than in the Italian film industry, where tension between the nurturing of a local, national product and the need to negotiate the popular appeal of the USA had long been a defining factor. The years either side of the Second World War provided an extreme illustration of this point. In 1938, the Fascist regime banned Hollywood imports as part of Mussolini's drive to foment a strong local film industry, which included the foundation of Rome's Cinecittà Studios. After the Liberation in 1945, the Allied Military Government steered the nation's cinemas in the opposite direction, facilitating the Motion Picture Export Association of America's 'dumping' policy (whereby the backlog of US films were released in one go, dominating the Italian market).[2] Stephen Gundle has written extensively about the challenges posed by the subsequent Americanisation of everyday life, explaining the ideological purpose of spreading upbeat affirmations of Western democracy as the Cold War loomed large:

> Hollywood did not only educate and amuse. Through its transmission of ideas, fashions, and more modern, less cumbersome modes of interpersonal interaction, it paved the way for the future incorporation of ever wider strata into a pattern of consensus in which entertainment and material life were closely related aspects of a new model of society that had the consumption of goods as its primary rule of social contact. (Gundle 2000: 33)

Indeed, the influence of Hollywood on the Italian film industry acted as a gauge for the USA's wider socio-cultural influence in the post-war years, but this would certainly not be a one-way process of domination. Gundle also explains, for example, that despite the considerable allure of American film stars in post-war Italy, domestic stars such as Anna Magnani and Totò continued to appeal to provincial audiences in the 1950s because they 'provided symbols of continuity with the past combined with varying elements of change during a period of immense, disorienting social and economic development' (Gundle 1996: 316–17). Italians' intimate encounter with US popular culture was therefore one of selectivity rather than wholesale superimposition, and the rate of change was not universally embraced.

In an economic as well as a cultural sense, the cinematic relationship between Italy and the USA was not as unbalanced as it may at first appear. Declining attendances and profits in the USA, coupled with European protectionist measures in the late 1940s, meant that international co-production became a preferred business model for American studios, allowing for the exploitation of multiple markets simultaneously by circumventing national quota systems. From 1950 onwards, US films acquired 50 per cent of their earnings abroad, while their shrinking home market could no longer cover the costs of production (Wagstaff 1995: 106). Italy, as Europe's largest cinema-going market by 1960,[3] was a crucial source of income and a fertile ground for investment. Between 1957 and 1967, US investment in Italian films totalled $350 million, or 21 billion lire: enough to fund over 100 average cost films (Wagstaff 2013: 32–3).

By the end of the 1960s, the entwinement of Italy's film industry with that of the USA was to be expected, given the nation's wider post-war economic development along the lines of US-led modernity and its geopolitical commitments (Italy had joined the North Atlantic Treaty Organization (NATO) in 1949, and in its role as a bulwark against communism became known as 'America's most faithful ally' (Ginsborg 1990: 158)). Though starting out as one of subjugation, the cinematic relationship between the two nations had become one of synergy. Likewise, the cultural, political and economic influence of the USA was characterised as much by ambivalence and uneven development as it was by inexorable progress. While the DC administrations of the 1950s had embraced the bounties of the transatlantic relationship, for example, Dunnage describes 'a ruling class and ecclesiastical hierarchy that, while supportive of economic progress, was fearful of the emancipating effects of social and cultural transformation accompanying the boom' (Dunnage 2002: 166). The fate of Italy's southern regions, meanwhile, remained perilous, with mass migration to the more prosperous north continuing unabated during the 1960s and leaving many rural villages on the brink of extinction (Ginsborg 1990: 232). No matter which way one looked back from the start of the 1970s, Italy had undergone a profound change from twenty-five years previously, and the USA had been an ever-present protagonist in the national narrative.

The Italian crime film is a case in point of the cinematic relationship outlined above, and is the primary subject matter of this book. The label 'crime film' is fluid and potentially amorphous (as are all such categories), but for my purposes it denotes films produced or co-produced in Italy, which explore – directly or indirectly – contemporaneous tensions surrounding the social contract of institutional law or the individual's relationship to judicial power structures. At once local and global, Italian crime films of this era selectively responded to, blended and appropriated American influences to address events and preoccupations at the forefront of the concurrent Italian zeitgeist.

Though this book largely focuses on the spate of crime films that were produced in the 1960s and 1970s, a number of earlier films also fit into the above categorisation. Pasquale Iannone has analysed the ways in which the director Pietro Germi 'sought to address social issues through the prism of uniquely American genre(s)' in such post-war contemporary crime thrillers as *Gioventù perduta* / *Lost Youth* (Germi, 1948) and *In nome della legge* / *In the Name of the Law* (Germi, 1949). Iannone uses Germi's exploration of Italian criminal phenomena such as the Sicilian mafia, via the generic conventions of the Hollywood gangster film and the Western, to chart a lineage of tales of banditry that blended the international and the local (Iannone 2016: 49, 56). Mary Wood (2005: 103–6) emphasises the extent to which Hollywood influences were worked into other films that are commonly categorised under the 'neorealist' label in the immediate post-war period, many of which explore themes of criminality in relation to Italy's economic crisis of the late 1940s. These include the stylistic and thematic debts to 1930s gangster films and *films noir* to be found in *Il bandito* / *The Bandit* (Alberto Lattuada, 1945) and *Senza pietà* / *Without Pity* (Alberto Lattuada, 1948), and the use of melodrama in *Riso amaro* / *Bitter Rice* (Giuseppe De Santis, 1949). The purposefully transatlantic inclination of this latter film is palpable in De Santis' description of the film's star, Silvana Mangano, as a 'Rita Hayworth of the Italian periphery' (Faldini and Fofi 1979: 154).

The Italian crime film was not therefore an entirely new concept by the late 1960s and early 1970s. What sets these years apart is the sheer scale of production, as hundreds of such films were produced or co-produced by Italian studios between 1966 and 1980. This proliferation can be attributed to the confluence of political and cinematic factors already outlined. Firstly, the year 1968 marked a turning point at which sections of the mass protest movements in universities and factories across Italy began to give way to more militant forms of activism, in part sowing the seeds for the violent confrontations of the 1970s. Secondly, the mid-to-late 1960s marked the peak period for American investment in the Italian film industry. As we have seen, Italian crime films had not previously been mere imitations of US formats, but instead selectively responded to and adapted certain cinematic conventions for the negotiation of their local contemporary condition. Accordingly, though the output of Hollywood continued to be a decisive influence on local production into the 1970s – most notably for the chapters that follow, with the Italian releases of *Bullitt* (Peter Yates, 1968), *Dirty Harry* (Don Siegel, 1971), *The French Connection* (William Friedkin, 1971), *The Godfather* (Francis Ford Coppola, 1972) and *Death Wish* (Michael Winner, 1974) – the filmmakers under consideration in this volume were simultaneously turning away from such internationally oriented formats as the Spaghetti Western, adapting the *filone* production model to focus on local Italian settings, issues and events.

Banditi a Milano / *The Violent Four* (Carlo Lizzani, 1968) is a particularly significant moment in the development of the Italian crime film, since it anticipated the impending proliferation in a number of ways. Based on an infamous September 1967 bank robbery in Milan, the film was released just six months later in March 1968. It thus provided a model for how such films could respond rapidly to events, to represent anxieties around violence in contemporary Italian society. On a superficial level, *Banditi a Milano* also exploits a number of conventions associated with American film genres. The repeated use of newspaper headlines to signify the topicality of key events to the audience is for example a technique lifted from 1930s Hollywood gangster films such as *Angels with Dirty Faces* (Michael Curtiz, 1938), and the association with this genre is made explicit by overt references to 1930s Chicago by characters in the film itself. The narrative structure, meanwhile, follows the generic conventions of heist films such as *The Asphalt Jungle* (John Huston, 1950) and *The Killing* (Stanley Kubrick, 1956), by aligning the audience with the robbers on an epistemological level to dwell on the logistical aspects of the main crime, which is then divided up into segments detailing the stake-out, the execution and the violent aftermath.

On a more substantial level, *Banditi a Milano* registers broader preoccupations with the rapid changes wrought on Italian society in the preceding decades. The film's prologue provides a stream of lamentations around the pace of transformation. The young police commissioner says that even he has seen Milan change before his eyes, while an ex-convict explains that his generation was more gentlemanly and less likely to engage in violence than modern-day criminals, who lack moral fibre and use violence too readily, because their outlook has been formed by reading too many comics.[4] An example of such modern-day criminality is then represented, with a nightclub being vandalised by a protection racket. Smashing glass and ricocheting bullets from the diegetic criminal violence provide the scene with its soundtrack, but the images that play over this are cells from a Batman comic, implicitly linking the loss of the old systems of criminal honour with Americana. The film's negotiation with American influence is therefore communicated on a more indirect level than simply making use of Hollywood reference points, since this prologue also dwells on how Italy has changed as it has charged headlong to embrace US-led modernity. As we shall see in Chapter 3, such a projection of the transformations in Italian society onto the criminal underworld would become a recurrent feature of Italian crime films in the 1970s.

The arguments that follow throughout this book will draw significance from such recurrences, and will relate them to the contextual factors so far outlined in this chapter. It is, however, important to avoid the easy assumption that such thematic duplication necessarily amounts to a meaningful socio-political intervention, since there is another crucial context to consider. The industrial conditions of the *filone* production model – through which the majority of Italian crime films were made – will prove to be pivotal to my arguments throughout this book. These were defined by rapid and concentrated repetition of profitable formulae with incremental variations on a theme. The haste of these films' production schedules is self-evident when we observe that Umberto Lenzi directed twelve crime films (be they *poliziotteschi*, *gialli* or vigilante films) between 1973 and 1979, or that Stelvio Massi directed thirteen between 1974 and 1979. Unsurprisingly, interviews with those who took part in the production process of these films are usually replete with anecdotes about the imperative to churn them out as quickly as possible. Actor Richard Harrison, for example, recalls that the standard practice in Hollywood studios in the 1970s was to schedule three or four camera set-ups per day of shooting, in stark contrast to his experience on *filone* film sets where the schedule was 120 per day (Malloy 2012). Writer Claudio Fragasso similarly recalls: 'The films had to be made, printed and distributed onto screens within a certain period of time, or you screwed up the schedule . . . We signed this contract and we started working. The turnaround was very quick' (Malloy 2012).

There was an obvious reason for such concentrated and repetitive production schedules, since *filone* cinema was supplying a high-demand market. Christopher Wagstaff has charted the material conditions of the *filone* system's distribution and consumption, arguing that 'the production sector, rather than relaying valuable social discourses, was simply tailoring a product to a protected and subsidized market' (Wagstaff 2013: 39). Taking the *terza visione* sector (of 'third-run' cinemas, often in remote areas) as an emblematic example, he paints a vivid picture of the target audience:

> The viewer (generally he) went to the cinema nearest to his house (or in rural areas, the only cinema there was) after dinner, at around ten o'clock in the evening. The programme changed daily or every other day. He would not bother to find out what was showing, nor would he make any particular effort to arrive at the beginning of the film . . . People would be coming and going and changing seats throughout the performance . . . The audience of a particular cinema was being offered a nightly appointment where it could receive a series of discrete gratifications that were part of a longer-term sequence. (Wagstaff 1992: 253–4)

Clearly, such consumption habits render assumptions that *filone* films should be read as intentional ideological interventions highly problematic, since products tailored to this market would have no clear need (or time) for philosophical sophistication. Wagstaff thus criticises a scholarly insistence that 'it is possible to deduce from the themes of films that successfully sold tickets what social needs were being met of the consumers who viewed them' (Wagstaff 2013: 39).

Wagstaff's argument that the logic of the *filone* production system was purely an economic one must therefore be taken into account, so as to avoid the trap of assuming popular cinematic trends in Italy to be straightforwardly reflective of their target audiences' socio-political concerns. Indeed, the iterative, 'serial' nature of the *filone* product will be a central factor in the analyses that follow. Wagstaff's approach is, however, of the kind diagnosed by Barbara Klinger as being 'stuck in synchrony', whereby scholars focus narrowly on the moment of a film's initial circumstances of production, exhibition and reception (Klinger 1997: 111). Klinger advocates an approach that also takes into consideration a film's 'diachronic' reception patterns – its changing meanings over time – so as to assess how its 'multiple historicities' exist in an interpretative continuum (Klinger 1997: 107). In other words, there are other contexts to be considered when analysing these films, beyond the intentions of their production companies and the viewing habits of Italian audiences, since the films analysed in the coming chapters do not solely reflect the tastes of those watching them upon their initial releases. Accordingly, though the next three chapters will focus on the immediate contexts of the Italian market at the time of these films' production and domestic releases, Chapter 5 will consider their subsequent international reception patterns. It is to be hoped that this will provide a more complete account of the various Italian crime *filoni* in relation to their multifarious audiences.

The question of whether the concerns of local target audiences should be the primary point of reference when considering *filone* cinema raises the issue of cultural specificity. Tim Bergfelder identifies a widespread critical assumption that, while US cinema is polysemic, open and international in appeal, European cinematic forms exist within discrete national categories, demanding culturally 'competent' viewers. In such a diasporic, supranational arena of distribution and consumption as Europe in the second half of the twentieth century, he argues, notions of national 'belonging' should instead be recalibrated to take account of the fluidity of cultural identities (Bergfelder 2005: 325). Italian crime films of the 1960s and 1970s should accordingly be examined as documents for Italy's globally oriented outlook, which simultaneously addressed local concerns. This is not to disavow the importance of nationhood in the discourse that surrounds the films, but instead to raise questions relating to national belonging in an approach akin to what Will Higbee and Song Hwee Lim dub a 'critical transnationalism'. This 'interrogates how ... film-making activities negotiate with the national on all levels – from cultural policy to financial sources, from the multiculturalism of difference to how it reconfigures the nation's image of itself' (Higbee and Hwee Lim 2010: 18).

Such a perspective is particularly germane when we consider the inherently transnational nature of the *filone* system, from which the Italian crime film's most prolific period arose. This production model can be roughly charted from the phenomenal success (both in Italy and abroad) of the classical epic *Le fatiche di Ercole / Hercules* (Pietro Francisci, 1958),[5] until the decline in film revenues and the television boom of the late 1970s. During this period, a succession of rapidly produced film cycles flourished, turning the Italian film industry into one of the world's most prolific.[6] It is, however, by no means obvious how 'Italian' *filone* cinema actually was. Many of these films were the result of international co-production – most frequently with Spain, West Germany or France – meaning that their production processes were attuned to the tastes and trends of numerous export, as well as domestic, film markets. Additionally, many *filoni* emerged in response to the popularity of American film genres, and all of them existed in a constant state of tension or dialogue with the influence of US cinema.

For example, the 'peplum' (classical epic) *filone* that followed in the lucrative wake of *Le fatiche di Ercole* was simultaneously a resurrection of early Italian cinema and a response to the increased investment of the USA in the local film industry during the 1950s. Its creative use of classical mythology revived the cinematic universe of such foundational epics of Italian national cinema as *La caduta di Troia / The Fall of Troy* (Giovanni Pastrone, 1911), *Gli ultimi giorni di Pompeii / The Last Days of Pompeii* (Mario Caserini 1913), *Quo Vadis?* (Enrico Guazzoni, 1913) and *Cabiria* (Giovanni Pastrone, 1914). Its emergence in the late 1950s, however, was a response to the large numbers of American actors and directors who had decamped to Roman studios to make such epics as *Quo Vadis* (Mervyn LeRoy, 1951), *Helen of Troy* (Robert Wise, 1956) and *Ben Hur* (William Wyler, 1959), utilising local crews and Italy's ready-made industry infrastructure in the phenomenon known as 'Hollywood on the Tiber'. Both the peplum and the Spaghetti Western that would subsequently eclipse it attest to a production model born from a globalised outlook and a keen eye for the rapid exploitation of multiple markets.

The majority of Italian crime films were not in fact international co-productions, but were instead produced solely by Italian companies. Such films' profit imperative was therefore largely predicated on domestic sales, and their overt focus on local events sets them apart from other, more obviously international, *filoni*. These are not, however, grounds to overlook the constant dialogue with global cinematic forms that takes place in these films. For example, the plot of *Milano trema – la polizia vuole giustizia / The Violent Professionals* (Sergio Martino, 1973) explicitly parallels the assassination of Chief Inspector Luigi Calabresi in May 1972 and the execution of the *strategia della tensione*, but simultaneously provides clear evidence for the influence of US cinema. In this film, a rogue cop uses his own violent methods of law enforcement in defiance of an impotent legal system, which is failing in its duty to uphold the rule of law. Only the hero's uncompromising methods are proved to work until, disgusted with the system he has defended, he discards his police-issue revolver, in a clear nod to the final sequence of *Dirty Harry* (itself lifted from Fred

Zinnemann's Western *High Noon* (1952)). To put it another way, this film – which was not an international co-production – replicates the narrative and ideological tropes of Siegel's Hollywood blockbuster, even while it represents decidedly local concerns.

It is not therefore a contradiction to insist on the relevance of a transnational theoretical framework, even while situating these films in a specific Italian backdrop. It is instead to acknowledge that the events of Italy's 1970s took place in a global as well as a local context, analysis of which cannot be confined purely to the concerns of the nation state. Andrew Higson has argued for the inadequacy of national borders as the primary means of demarcating cultural output, since 'the degree of cultural cross-breeding and interpenetration, not only across borders but also within them, suggests that modern cultural formations are invariably hybrid and impure. They [are] always re-fashioning themselves, as opposed to exhibiting an already fully formed identity' (Higson 2006: 19). Alan O'Leary and Catherine O'Rawe have identified 'versions of "Italian-ness"' in popular forms that are conventionally overlooked or denigrated in discourses surrounding Italian national cinema (O'Leary and O'Rawe 2011: 115). Accordingly, the Italian crime film's international aspects document a certain version of Italian-ness – one in the throes of continuing cultural and political upheaval – and reveal complexities and instabilities within the specific national, local and subcultural contexts that surrounded them.

Silences and Cultural Traumas

This chapter began by holding *Il cittadino si ribella* up as an emblematic case study for the contextual factors that have since been appraised. This film was directed by Enzo G. Castellari: a typically versatile filmmaker of the *filone* system, whose ability to adapt to prevailing trends saw him direct eight Spaghetti Westerns and five crime films between 1967 and 1977. As befits such a directorial background, Castellari has since been candid about his transatlantic inspirations, stating in a documentary on his film's DVD release:

> Come regista sono un filo americano. Ciò, io sono crescuto con il cinema americano. Quindi, il fatto stesso che a suo tempo potesse usare la formula americana era veramente un grande regalo che è stato una gioia straordinaria.
>
> As a director, I am of the American kind. That is, I grew up with American cinema. So, the very fact that I was able to use the American formula was a great gift and a great joy. (Gregory 2013)

He goes on to clarify his meaning that his crime films are modern-day Westerns, but this particular film's vigilante plot has drawn another comparison. Bondanella argues that *Il cittadino si ribella* owes 'an obvious debt to the impact of *Death Wish*' (Bondanella 2009: 475), though Castellari claims in the DVD's commentary that his film came out before Michael Winner's. In fact, *Death Wish* was released in July 1974, two months before *Il cittadino si ribella* in September 1974. To give Castellari the benefit of the doubt, his film did marginally precede the Italian release of *Death Wish* in October of that year.[7] Typically for a film emerging from the *filone* system, its relationship with US cinema was immediate and intimate, but not straightforward.

In the same interview, Castellari claims that the crimes depicted in the film's opening few minutes were all based on true events taken from news reports, and that his intention was to chronicle the sense of unease felt by normal Italians amidst such violence (Gregory 2013). I have already argued that, behind this clear authorial intent, lies an implicit preoccupation with the War years through which this critique of the present is executed, and which is symptomatic of broader processes of resurfacing memory in the 1970s. That the War and the contested legacy of the Resistance possessed a singular cultural–political significance after 1968 is a well-established premise. David Ellwood dubs the ongoing debates over the memory of the partisan struggle the 'never-ending liberation' (Ellwood 2005) while, as already discussed, the Resistance years, and the memories and silences that surrounded them, are a key example in Foot's study of 'Italy's divided memory' (Foot 2009: 147–82). Moreover, Dominic Gavin has examined how Italian cinema of the 1970s repeatedly used the Resistance years as a forum for critiquing the present in such films as *Corbari* (Valentino Orsini, 1970) and *1900* (Bernardo Bertolucci, 1976). As Gavin explains, the 1970s are 'well known as a period when issues of historical memory intersected with present-day politics, most notably in the discourses of Fascism and antifascism' (Gavin 2014: 156), and his case study films thus reflect 'the collective desire to interrogate the national past in the wake of the student protests of the late 1960s and the civic tensions of the following years' (Gavin 2014: 157).

My concern in this volume, however, is not with films that were set in the 1940s in order to make explicit political commentary through comparisons with contemporary events. It is instead with implicit, often inadvertent traces and residues of this same preoccupation with the past, which arise from production decisions taken in films that are set in the 1970s present. It is, indeed, the very obliqueness of these references to the past that makes my case studies significant.

Discourses around 'collective' or 'cultural' trauma can help to illustrate this point. Ruth Glynn has analysed the ways in which Italians have experienced, responded to and remembered the violent events of the 1970s as being consistent with a traumatic response, due to a 'collective drive to inhibit recollection and silence discussion' (Glynn 2013: 9) in the years that followed:

> The long unacknowledged persistence of the *anni di piombo* in the collective psyche suggests that Italian culture developed in relation to the political violence and terrorism of the 1970s a defensive amnesia symptomatic of an experience of psychological trauma or wound. (Glynn 2006: 318)

For Glynn, this prolonged silence, followed by an obsessive resurfacing of the events in late 1990s media coverage of renewed terrorism,[8] corroborates the work of psychiatrist Judith Herman around collective responses to political violence, whereby 'entire communities can display symptoms of Post Traumatic Stress Disorder, trapped in alternating cycles of numbing and intrusion, silence and reenactment' (cited in Glynn 2013: 8).

When we consider the preoccupation with the past that was characteristic of 1970s Italy, such an approach can also be extended back in time to position the Years of Lead as part of a larger cycle of traumatic silence and re-emergence: a symptom of prior traumas, as well as a cause of subsequent ones. The extent to which concepts within individual psychology can be seen to correspond to processes of collective or cultural trauma is a subject of ongoing debate. Neil Smelser, for example, has warned against drawing too precise parallels with Freud's notion of 'psychological incubation' – 'a repressed, highly charged, under-the-surface force ready to break into the open at all times' (Smelser 2004: 51) – due to the variations between different historical contexts. Nevertheless, patterns of collective amnesia and denial are commonly identified when analysing devastating shocks to a collective identity. For example, Bernhard Giesen, writing about the aftermath of the Holocaust, diagnoses an 'inability to mourn' and a 'tacitly assumed coalition of silence' that characterised the German national response in the post-war years. For Giesen, this trauma at first manifested itself through the genocide being transposed into a realm of nightmares that only occasionally found expression through cultural representations. 'Only later on, after a period of latency, can it be remembered, worked through, and spoken out' (Giesen 2004: 116, 113).

Italy in the 1970s seems a prime candidate for consideration within this sociological terrain, not only because of violence both past and present, but also because of the bewildering pace of socio-cultural change in the preceding decades. In his sociological study of the impact a devastating flood in Buffalo Creek, West Virginia had on the local community, Kai T. Erikson offers the following definition for 'collective trauma':

> A blow to the basic tissues of social life that damages the bonds attaching people together and impairs the prevailing sense of communality. The collective trauma works its way slowly and even insidiously into the awareness of those who suffer from it. (Erikson 1976: 154)

Piotr Sztompka develops this idea to outline how such collective trauma can emerge, not only from specific events, but also from the kind of far-reaching socio-cultural change commonly associated with processes of modernisation, globalisation or 'Americanisation' (Sztompka 2004: 162). This applies to change that is 'prolonged and cumulative but eventually reaches a *threshold of saturation* beyond which it turns out to be fundamentally, qualitatively new. It suddenly appears to be unbearable, produces a shock of realization about something that was ignored before' (Sztompka 2004: 158; emphasis in original).

In addition to the resurfacing of memories from the 'shared silence' (Foot 2009: 168) around the physical violence and social fracturing of the War, the Resistance and the *resa dei conti*, we can therefore also consider the broader sense in which Italy was taking stock of the profound transformations that had occurred up and down the peninsula in the intervening years. This informs a reading whereby the cultural–political shifts of the recent past – both seismic and incremental – were pervasive in attempts to make sense of the present, across a wide spectrum of cultural and political discourse.

It is a central argument in the coming chapters that these preoccupations with the past emerge for analysis but remain covert and mostly unintentional in Italian crime films. It is not, however, my intention to draw equivalence with Freudian readings of 'incubation' or unconscious repression. Rather, studies of collective or cultural trauma are useful here for how they conceptualise traumatic responses as socially mediated and culturally constituted, rather than intrinsic to particular events. Jeffrey Alexander explains that trauma arises from imagined events as well as real ones, and that the experience of trauma is indistinguishable between the two:

> Traumatic status is attributed to real or imagined phenomena, not because of their actual harmfulness or their objective abruptness, but because these phenomena are believed to have abruptly, and harmfully, affected collective identity ... It is the

meanings that provide the sense of shock and fear, not the events in themselves. (Alexander 2004: 9–10)

Glynn similarly considers the mediated nature of cultural trauma. She relates the Years of Lead to sociological studies showing that violent events can traumatise people who were not directly involved, with exposure through media coverage alone being enough to elicit symptoms of post-traumatic stress in the cases of the 1995 Oklahoma bomb and the attacks of 11 September 2001: 'It is the exceptional quality of the *impact* of the event, rather than the event itself, which constitutes the trauma' (Glynn 2006: 320, 319; emphasis in original).

Such approaches as Glynn's are of great importance because the events of Italy's 1970s were mediated sites of contested political memory from the moment of their occurrence. To assess how surrounding cultural preoccupations manifested themselves within *filone* cinema is not, as Wagstaff's accusation holds, to assume that the films straightforwardly reflected Italian audiences' interpretations or concerns (Wagstaff 2013: 39). It is instead to acknowledge that the processes of mediation, interpretation and response that developed alongside the events were inseparable from, and entwined within, the events themselves. We will see in the next chapter how the attribution of meaning to acts of violence during the Years of Lead was an integral and organic part of those acts. The swift turnaround of the *filone* production format therefore not only provided a rapid response to contemporary incidents; it also constituted a collection of cultural artefacts embedded in their historical, political and economic moment. These films were industrial commodities, whose production decisions were made within a concentrated schedule that necessitated the efficient anticipation of their target audiences' levels of prior knowledge. The decisions made to facilitate this shorthand construction of a story world tell us much about the assumed preoccupations of the 'here and now'.

The central yet hardly mentioned presence of the framed manifesto on Carlo's wall in *Il cittadino si ribella* is akin to what Pierre Macherey calls 'a certain absence': a silence in the text whose traces reveal latent preoccupations in the surrounding discourse. Macherey argues that we should ask of every cultural artefact 'what it tacitly implies, what it does not say . . . It is this silence which . . . informs us of the precise conditions for the appearance of an utterance, and thus its limits, giving its real significance' (Macherey 2006: 95, 97). Accordingly, the underlying historical conditions facilitating the text's emergence show through in such small details as Carlo's father's manifesto. This document bespeaks an assumption, which barely requires articulation: that the motivation to fight for one's beliefs in contemporary 1970s Italy arises from the unfinished business of the War years, which stand as an implicit moral guide. In the next chapter, I shall explore two related categories of *filone* cinema that invest heavily in such unspoken assumptions about the past to build their diegetic worlds: the 'conspiracy' strand of the *poliziottesco*, and the vigilante film.

Notes

1. *Stragismo* (literally, 'massacre-ism') is the label given to the indiscriminate campaign of neofascist violence that followed the Piazza Fontana bombing. Anna Cento Bull has argued that it was the legacy of this campaign of terror, rather than the association with Mussolini's regime, that most discredited Italian far-right politics into the early twenty-first century (Bull 2005).
2. At the start of 1946, Italian films were receiving only 13 per cent of box office receipts in Italy. In the same year, American films took 75 per cent (Wagstaff 1998: 75; Wagstaff 1995: 108).
3. In 1955, the UK was still Europe's largest market, with 1,182 million cinema tickets being sold compared to Italy's 819 million. By 1960, Italy had overtaken the UK, with 745 million tickets to the UK's 501 million (Wagstaff 1998: 74).
4. The actual line is 'Questi di oggi invece, essendo maturati troppo in fretta, leggendo quei fumetti . . . cosa vuole . . . vanno a far le rapine e dicono . . . beh, male che va noi spariamo, e sparano' ('These criminals today have grown up too fast, reading those comics. What can you do? They commit robberies and they say: "if something goes wrong we shoot, and they shoot"').
5. *Le fatiche di Ercole* and its sequel *Ercole e la regina di Lidia / Hercules Unchained* (Pietro Francisci, 1959) each grossed almost 900 million lire in Italy at a time when tickets cost as little as 600–1,000 lire. On its US release, *Le fatiche di Ercole* earned a $5 million profit from a $120,000 investment (Bondanella 2009: 167).
6. Italy's cinematic output outnumbered Hollywood's by 242 films to 174 in 1962, 241 to 155 in 1963, 270 to 181 in 1964, 245 to 168 in 1966 and 258 to 215 in 1967 (Eleftheriotis 2001: 105).
7. The success of *Death Wish* on the Italian market (as *Il giustiziere della notte*) is indicated by the weekly rankings for Milanese cinemas in the *Corriere d'Informazione* of 1 October 1974, which lists it in second place (with 12,121 viewers) after *The Exorcist* (William Friedkin, 1973) (with 56,840 viewers). *Il cittadino si ribella* appears in the same list, in eighth place with 5,694 viewers (*Corriere d'Informazione*, 1 October 1974, p. 13). The same newspaper's ranking later in the same month shows *Death Wish* commanding an enduring popularity in third place (with 11,195 viewers that week), while *Il cittadino si ribella* no longer appears (*Corriere d'Informazione*, 22 October 1974, p. 13).

8. The persistence of the Years of Lead as a significant setting in subsequent cultural discourse has also been investigated in Barbara Pezzotti's recent study of Italian crime fiction of the 1990s and 2000s. Pezzotti argues that, in this period, such formats as the literary *giallo* gave voice to the victims of terrorism through their historical representations of the 1970s (Pezzotti 2016: 169–236).

CHAPTER 2

Corruption and Conspiracy in the *Poliziotteschi* and the Vigilante *Filone*

District Attorney Ricciuti: 'Lei ha un'idea precisa Commissario?'
Commissioner Bertone: 'Ah no, niente di preciso, soltanto vaga ma . . . certo che tutto questo: puzza molto di fanatismo.'

Ricciuti: 'Do you have a clear idea Commissioner?'
Bertone: 'Ah no, nothing precise, just a vague idea, but . . . one thing's for sure: all of this stinks of fanaticism.'

The above exchange from *La polizia ringrazia / Execution Squad* (Stefano Vanzina, 1972) takes place as the police arrive at the scene of a summary execution on the banks of the River Tiber. Bertone's words encapsulate a conflicted outlook on the era's intrigues: at once certain of the indelible link between contemporary violence and the fascist past, and unable conclusively to articulate that link's precise nature. The odour of Italy's traumatic history indeed permeates the film as an unmistakable cause for the events depicted, but its political identity cannot here be named. Instead, Bertone alludes to it obliquely, telling Ricciuti: 'sembrerebbe un'esecuzione in piena regola, come una volta' / 'it looks like a full-scale execution, like in the old times'. He avoids the word 'fascista', which weighs heavily by its very absence.[1]

The plot of *La polizia ringrazia* makes clear (if linguistically covert) reference to contemporaneous events of neofascist violence and the political intrigues that surrounded them. This chapter examines how these tropes were replicated and renewed in a number of films, which I shall divide into two categories. Firstly, I shall examine tales of policemen battling against institutional corruption from within, which make explicit reference to recent *coup d'état* plots in Italy and show these plots being 'unmasked' by the protagonist. Secondly, I shall analyse films whose protagonists are vigilante private citizens driven to fight against criminal syndicates, and who in the process become caught up in labyrinthine webs of intrigue.

Figure 2.1 Ricciuti (Mario Adorf) and Bertone (Enrico Maria Salerno) debate the politics of violence in *La polizia ringrazia* (Stefano Vanzina, 1972).

These two *filone* strands are often conflated under the generic umbrella of '*poliziottesco*', or occasionally '*poliziesco*',[2] in critical and scholarly literature. In its original usage, the word '*poliziottesco*' was a pejorative term, used to denote films 'considered to be lowbrow capitalizations on a more "dignified" tradition of the "poliziesco" or police/crime story' (Burke 2017: xxii). My use of the same word is intended as a more descriptive way of denoting the modes of production and consumption that characterised the *filone* system of the 1960s and 1970s: rapid production schedules and concerted exploitation of markets, as distinct from the more celebrated 'political' crime films of (among others) Francesco Rosi, Damiano Damiani or Elio Petri. The problem with the word '*poliziottesco*' is that, though it is usually understood to describe 'cop films', it is also commonly applied to mafia, vigilante or heist narratives, and has therefore become something of a catch-all for Italian crime films.[3]

There are entirely justifiable reasons for this conflation of seemingly diverse strands, which are testament to the innate nebulousness and hybridity of *filone* categories in this era of Italian cinema. They all emerged from the same Italian studio system of rapidly produced films responding at short notice to perceived shifts in public taste. They were produced and directed by the same personnel, and the two strands discussed in this chapter often have similar plot structures, with protagonists being set against complex criminal syndicates that steadily begin to point to the heart of government, the judiciary or the secret service. However, since my concern here is with identifying relatively small subsets of Italian crime *filoni*, I shall try to be cautious with my use of such broad categorisations. For my purposes, the word '*poliziottesco*' will refer to the large trend of police films emerging from the *filone* system in the 1970s (from which many well-known titles will not appear here, since it is not my purpose to conduct a broad genre survey). The two smaller strands I am analysing in this chapter will be called the 'conspiracy' subset of the *poliziottesco*, and the 'vigilante film'.

The films that constitute the 'conspiracy' *poliziottesco* emerged in the wake of *La polizia ringrazia*. They are similarly characterised by an emerging realisation on the part of a protagonist employed by the police force, who gradually comes to see the political machinations at work beneath the surface of the violence that surrounds him. As we shall see, scholarly discourses on the cinema of and about the Years of Lead have often situated such filmmaking as the manifestation of a collective desire: a desire to seek explanation for the traumas, to offer a semblance of coherence where confusion reigns, and to see through the opaque webs of intrigue that characterise the national memory of the 1970s. Certainly, the fascination with this period in the nation's cinematic output to this day attests to the events' ongoing capacity to confound comprehension and to inspire historical investigation. However, films produced during the period itself, such as the 'conspiracy' *poliziottesco*, show us that such an approach was just one available register for the interpretation and mediation of Italy's political surroundings. This *filone* strand demonstrates a divergent register of political address: one that seeks, not to explain or 'make sense' of the era's intrigues, but instead to enact a ritual recognition of innate suspicion, pervasive corruption and assumed distrust. This chapter therefore appraises these films for their immediacy rather than their coherence, as documents of confusion rather than of investigative rigour.

The vigilante films also betray deep-seated assumptions on the part of the filmmakers that historically constituted political corruption is the default state of affairs, but (like Commissario Bertone) they stop short of naming the precise nature of this corruption, since they mostly avoid specific historical or contemporary reference points. They therefore diverge from the 'conspiracy' *poliziotteschi*, which – while doing so in a confused and inconclusive manner – do make direct reference to real-life attempts at *coup d'état*. The overt theme of many of these vigilante films is a determined but futile battle against labyrinthine corruption within a faceless system. Though their implicit links to contemporary intrigues are clear, their lack of historical specificity results in an all-pervasive sense of futility in an inevitable and enduring web. The assumed ubiquity of corruption in these films manifests itself in scene-setting details beneath the purposeful exposition, which expose preoccupations with the nation's traumatic past and the historical continuity of systematic institutional brutality.

I am purposefully starting my analysis with the *filone* that most directly and clearly refers to the contemporaneous *anni di piombo* and *strategia della tensione* (that is, the 'conspiracy' *poliziottesco*), to highlight how even these films betray historical preoccupations, lying behind their immediately obvious commentary on their time and place. By their very contemporaneity, the films analysed in this chapter demonstrate an awareness of their position in a historical continuum, at this national moment of 'taking stock'. The assumptions they make in passing, which occasionally burst through into the diegesis, attest to decades of ideological conflict.

'Conspiracy' *Poliziotteschi*

My focus in the first half of this chapter is on police films that explicitly depict official collusion in acts of politically motivated violence, and that use this to portray the exposure of authoritarian coup plots. Each of *La polizia ringrazia*, *Milano trema – la polizia vuole giustizia / The Violent Professionals* (Sergio Martino, 1973), *La polizia sta a guardare / The Great Kidnapping* (Roberto Infascelli, 1973), *La polizia accusa: il servizio segreto uccide / Silent Action* (Sergio Martino, 1975), *La polizia ha le mani legate / Killer Cop* (Luciano Ercoli, 1975), *Poliziotti violenti / Crimebusters* (Michele Massimo Tarantini, 1976) and *Il grande racket / The Big Racket* (Enzo G. Castellari, 1976) ostensibly provides a revelatory denouement concerning official culpability or authoritarian conspiracy. Yet such a reading overlooks an important point about political discourse in this era: that such assertions of institutional corruption were not necessarily 'revelatory' to an Italian public whose cognisance of political intrigue was incomplete, but growing. I will therefore examine the epistemological status of this 'conspiracy' subset of the *poliziottesco* within these cultural, historical and political contexts.

These films demonstrate immediate responses to numerous acts of far-right political violence, and the intrigues and reprisals that surrounded those acts when evidence began to surface that the secret service and other state institutions were supporting the attacks in an effort to spread fear and promote authoritarian *coup d'état* (the phenomenon that became known as the *strategia della tensione*). As Roberto Curti has illustrated, *La polizia accusa: il servizio segreto uccide* in particular constitutes a veritable encyclopaedia of transparent references to specific events. This film's search for incriminating tapes pointing to a subversive secret service plot against the state displays clear parallels with the Borghese coup plot of 1970, with the discovery of the secret neofascist organisation *Rosa dei Venti* in 1973, and with the actions of Guido Giannettini (a far-right secret agent of the SID (*Servizio Informazione Difesa*, the Italian Secret Service), who had been exposed in 1974). When Commissario Solmi (Luc Merenda) hunts the conspirators down to a paramilitary training camp in the mountains, the reference to the discovery of a neofascist camp at Piano di Rascino in the aftermath of the Brescia bombing of May 1974 is similarly explicit (Curti 2013: 149). Furthermore, the drive-by murder of Solmi in the film's final scene replicates the details of the assassination of Commissioner Luigi Calabresi at the hands of far-left militants in 1972 (an event that is also represented in *Milano trema – la polizia vuole giustizia*, with the killing of Del Buono) (Curti 2006: 151). *La polizia ha le mani legate* takes such direct referencing to actual events a step further. Not only does this film's depiction of a bombing in Milan that implicates secret services and politicians provide a clear reference to the Piazza Fontana attack in December 1969, the film also incorporates archive footage of the actual Piazza Fontana funeral (Curti 2013: 139).[4]

On the most obvious and direct levels, these tales of rogue cops in contemporary urban Italian locales, who both fight violent crime and unmask the power structures lurking behind it, are contemporaneous representations of, and responses to, these events. As we have seen, both left- and right-wing violence informed the broader discursive construction of an Italy spiralling out of control. Both contexts are therefore important for this study of cultural and ideological processes of representation, as is the prominent position of these years' emblematic events in the Italian media and, by extension, the popular imagination. The films under scrutiny here predate the moment of greatest tension that followed the Moro kidnapping in 1978 and heralded the conceptualisation of the '*anni di piombo*' as a traumatic and contested period of Italian history, which has ever since had a lasting impact on the country's political and cultural memories. My intention here is therefore to examine these films as documents of a formative period in this larger discourse of national trauma.

As the previous chapter has argued, while such local specificity provides the main contextual focus of this study, it is also important to take account of the globally oriented aspects of this cultural moment, to recognise the outward looking, rather than strictly 'national', nature of Italian identities. Many *poliziotteschi* interweave their local political backdrops with cinematic and cultural contexts that register the international influence and reach of US cinema. The 'police procedural' paradigm possessed a rich heritage, not in Italy, but in Hollywood; yet it provided an apt model for Italian filmmakers to dramatise their concerns around the individual's relationship with institutional justice and societal power structures. From *G-Men* (William Keighley, 1935) onwards, through *Where the Sidewalk Ends* (Otto Preminger, 1950) and *On Dangerous Ground* (Nicholas Ray, 1951), to *Bullitt* (Peter Yates, 1968), the American cop film repeatedly brings into question the legitimacy of codified law and state power, negotiating a constant tension around the 'social contract' whereby citizens relinquish freedoms to centralised mechanisms of law and order. As Thomas Leitch explains, the figure of the 'rogue' law enforcer who is compelled to break the law in order to uphold an alternative moral code in defiance of 'the system that has failed them and the society they are sworn to protect' was by the 1960s an archetype of Hollywood social commentary (Leitch 2002: 229).

It is easy to see how such an ideologically charged genre model as this could be transposed to the machinations of 1970s Italy, and little surprise that its latest manifestations might find a receptive audience there. As Christopher Barry has outlined, the *poliziottesco*'s proliferation in the early to mid-1970s, while clearly a response to local events, was also indebted to the arrival on the Italian market of internationally successful Hollywood cop thrillers such as *Dirty Harry* (Don Siegel, 1971) and *The French Connection* (William Friedkin, 1971) (Barry 2004: 78–82). These products of Nixon-era neuroses over social breakdown and urban violence in the US, with their depictions of maverick crime-fighters refusing to play by the rules, proved to be highly influential. As we have seen, the anticipation and exploitation of the next cinematic craze was a characteristic pattern of Italian *filone* cinema from the 1950s to the 1970s. Such cycles would burgeon in an incremental balance between repetition and innovation, with an eye firmly trained on the perceived whims of the popular market. The Italian release of *Dirty Harry* in January 1972 followed by *The French Connection* in March of that year accordingly had a notable impact upon both the *poliziottesco*'s recurrent plot devices and its ideological outlook, with filmmakers selectively adopting narrative schemas from these Hollywood blockbusters, and localising them. The marketing strategies that accompanied the American films in Italian cinemas markedly emphasised their apparent endorsement of draconian law enforcement techniques. *The French Connection* became *Il braccio violento della legge* ('The violent arm of the law'), while *Dirty Harry*'s Italian release (as *Ispettore Callaghan: il caso Scorpio è tuo!*) was accompanied by the sensational tagline 'Non risolve i casi di omicidio . . . li annienta!' ('He doesn't solve murder cases . . . he annihilates them!')

Clearly, such transatlantic influences are important factors when considering the success and proliferation of the *poliziottesco*, but we should not overstate the case. *La polizia ringrazia* – commonly seen as this *filone*'s 'founding text' – was released in February 1972, just a few weeks after the arrival of *Dirty Harry* on the Italian market. This certainly points to a shrewd release strategy on the part of the producers. Yet the outlooks on contemporary politics in this film and in the conspiracy *poliziotteschi* that followed it should not be conflated with those emanating from the USA. As Curti has written, the attitude to the state to be found in the *poliziottesco* clearly distinguishes it from the Hollywood format (Curti 2006: 96). In the films considered in this chapter, legal and governmental institutions are not weak and toothless, as they are in *Dirty Harry*. Instead, they are all-powerful and actively malicious, pointing to a widespread unease in Italian society over the culpability for the events of the *anni di piombo*. A persistent opacity surrounding the instruments of state fed strong (and justified) suspicions that the secret service was either aiding atrocities or covering up their culpabilities, or both. We have seen in Chapter 1 that *Milano trema – la polizia vuole giustizia* replicates narrative tropes from *Dirty Harry*, but this film conspicuously diverges from the US model with its revelatory denouement. Its 'twist' ending comes as the chief of police reveals himself to be the hidden crime boss, manipulating the violence as part of an authoritarian *strategia della tensione*. Such investment in notions of high-level conspiracy is a recurrent feature within the *poliziottesco*, with the lone hero similarly unmasking conspiratorial coup plots involving retired police chiefs (*La polizia ringrazia*, *La polizia sta a guardare*) lawyers (*Poliziotti violenti*, *Il grande racket*) and members of the secret service (*La polizia accusa: il servizio segreto uccide*).

Such a transatlantic cultural context therefore exists alongside these films' decidedly local focus, serving to illustrate the globally attuned nature of Italian cultural practices in this era. Through their negotiation with US genre convention, these films can be seen in a number of ways as documents of their time and place. Firstly, by turning to a signifier of American popular culture as a conduit for local political oppositions, they register an Italy in the midst of continuing cultural change, in which such reference points were instantly recognisable. Furthermore, due to their tendency to utilise such tropes as the 'twist' ending to lay bare notions of state complicity, they have been discussed as films that seek to attach coherent, understandable narratives to an era of extreme cultural–political uncertainty. Peter Bondanella, for example, aligns the *poliziottesco*'s social concerns with those of Italy's famed political auteurs such as Francesco Rosi, Gillo Pontecorvo, Elio Petri and Marco Bellocchio (Bondanella 2009: 453). The appeal of these more critically lauded filmmakers' 1970s conspiracy thrillers is identified by Mary P. Wood as lying in their 'attempt to impose order on a world which is perceived as difficult to understand, complex, mysterious, controlled by people who mask their control behind common sense assumptions, coercion, and ritual' (Wood 2003: 153). Wood also places the *poliziottesco* within this spectrum of cultural output that 'attempts to establish the causes and attribute blame. Cinematic narratives of police investigations were . . . part of this impetus to give concrete form to fears and anxieties, and to understand what was happening in society' (Wood 2012: 29).

Christian Uva also identifies in the *poliziottesco* a desire to understand or to make sense of the era's intrigues, positioning this *filone* within a broader cultural trajectory in which cinematic images shaped popular perceptions of the events of the 1970s, to the extent that the divide between cinema and reality was at times imperceptible. Uva uses the opening sequence of *Sbatti il mostro in prima pagina / Slap the Monster on Page One* (Marco Bellocchio, 1972) – a film depicting a fictional right-wing newspaper, which manipulates the events of the era to scapegoat the left – as an emblematic example of this trajectory, in which 'la realtà entra nel cinema ed il cinema nella realtà in uno scambio osmotico in cui i confini dell'uno e dell'altra sembrano svanire' / 'reality enters cinema and cinema enters reality in an osmotic exchange, in which the boundaries of each seem to vanish' (Uva 2007: 9). Bellocchio's film begins with archive footage of the 1972 funeral of militant communist activist Giangiacomo Feltrinelli in Milan, and then seamlessly progresses into a dramatised representation of the street battles that were taking place around such events.

Uva's argument raises pertinent questions over the ontological status of archive footage. There are, for example, clear parallels between the manipulation of such material in *Sbatti il mostro in prima pagina* and the footage of the Piazza Fontana funeral that appears in *La polizia ha le mani legate*, pointing to an equivalent attempt to interrogate the ways in which these events were being represented through the mass media. Uva thus advances a wider methodology in Italian film studies that analyses archival manipulation as a strategy of negotiating and defining this period's memory. See, for example, Catherine O'Rawe's work on more recent films such as *Pasolini: un delitto italiano / Who Killed Pasolini?* (Marco Tullio Giordana, 1995) and *La prima linea / The Front Line* (Renato De Maria, 2009), which posits their incorporation of archive footage as 'a determination to make visible the events of the past' (O'Rawe 2011: 110), emphasising how the 1970s remains a pivotal moment in the ongoing negotiation of Italian cultural identities.

The diverse and important studies on the cinema of and about the *anni di piombo* outlined above therefore offer valuable insights into how the period has served as a locus for a search for meaning within a range of cinematic and political registers up to the present day. Uva situates the *poliziottesco* within these larger discourses, and frames it as a reflection of the popular imaginary and a way of processing and understanding the realities of the era's complex events. The *poliziottesco*, he argues, functions as 'un cinema inteso come riflesso, ma anche come elaborazione di un immaginario di massa che muta con il modificarsi della realtà sociopolitica da cui emerge' / 'a cinema understood as a reflection, but also as an elaboration, of a mass imaginary that changes with modifications in the socio-political reality from which it emerges' (Uva and Picchi 2006: 63). Since my focus here is on a relatively small subset of the larger *poliziottesco* category, however, I wish to pursue an alternative approach for the specific analysis of these 'conspiracy' films, because they pose problems for notions of cinema offering explanation or coherence, or providing a filter for 'reality'. This point becomes clearer when we consider the complexities of the relationship between acts of physical violence and their modes of representation in this cultural–political moment.

In Chapter 1, I argued that the events of Italy's 1970s were from the moment of their occurrence sites of contested political memory across numerous strata of cultural and political discourse. Violent acts from the far left and those from the far right, though emerging from the same trajectory of residual historical conflict, differed markedly in both their modus operandi and their strategies of self-representation. As we have seen, the left was assigned the role of a convenient scapegoat for the Piazza Fontana bombing, while the right enjoyed the covert protection of state institutions. These facts are closely related to the ways in which publicity was either sought or eschewed on each side, which are fundamental to an understanding of the *anni di piombo* as an evolving unit of discourse. The imperative amongst left-wing militant groups to 'be noticed' should be seen as a counterpoint to right-wing attempts at invisibility.

The passage taken by certain leftist protest factions from the mass mobilisation of the late 1960s to the clandestinity of armed struggle in the early 1970s is a notoriously contentious topic. Sidney Tarrow argues that, from the moment the bomb in Piazza Fontana exploded on 12 December 1969, 'death and violence became contested symbolic terrain around which the political class reconstituted its unity and over which various elements of the extraparliamentary left competed for supremacy' (Tarrow 1991: 43–4). Political activists, state institutions and the mainstream press were immediately competing to confer their own meanings on both the act itself and the events that followed (such as the suspicious death in custody of suspect and anarchist Giuseppe Pinelli). While the *Corriere della Sera* and the police laid the blame for the bombing on leftist anarchists, the militant left-wing journal *Lotta Continua* mobilised to expose neofascist culpability and a secret service cover-up. Tarrow's analysis of the months that followed depicts a 'spiral of competitive tactical innovation' (Tarrow 1991: 43), whereby clandestine leftist groups competed with each other to make not only their methods of activism, but also the significance they attached to those methods, prominent in the popular consciousness.

This imperative amongst leftist extraparliamentary groups to 'be noticed' in this era also informs the analysis of David Moss, who examines the strategies necessary for them to 'disambiguate the otherwise politically meaningless language of violence' (1989: 8), by using a variety of cultural registers: videos, leaflets and banners, as well as longer political tracts or treatises. *Lotta Continua*, for example, attracted a broad readership by investing in overtly sensationalised reportage, in competition for attention with other revolutionary leftist outlets. Much scholarship has also focused on the decisions made by left-wing armed factions such as the BR, the *Formazioni Comuniste Combattenti* (FCC) and *Prima Linea* to undertake newsworthy forms of activism (such as bank robberies and kidnappings), to maximise the dissemination of the political meanings they ascribed to their own activities. Donatella Della Porta writes that between 1970 and 1983, 783 acts of violence committed by the BR, *Prima Linea* and the FCC were justified by their perpetrators as propagandist activities aimed at gaining support, while 263 were for purposes of self-defence and 219 were intended as acts of 'anti-repression' (assaults on the police or judiciary) (Della Porta 1995: 120). Well over half were therefore aimed solely at communicating the validity and efficacy of violent methods.

Far-right terrorism was on the other hand marked by wilful opacity and impenetrability, which was aided and abetted by the official cover-ups. Consequently, a sense of growing certainty that agents of the state were sponsoring atrocities in the surrounding discourse was coupled with a paradoxical inability to pin down the precise culprits. Pier Paolo Pasolini famously encapsulated these feelings in the *Corriere della Sera* in November 1974: 'Io so tutti questi nomi e so tutti i fatti (attentati alle istituzioni e stragi) di cui si sono resi colpevoli. Io so. Ma non ho le prove. Non ho nemmeno indizi' / 'I know all these names and all the events (the attacks on institutions and the massacres) that they have been guilty of. I know. But I have no evidence. I do not even have any clues' (Pasolini 1974). It is this enigmatic form of far-right terrorism that is addressed by the 'conspiracy' *poliziottesco* and – as Commissioner Bertone's words in the epigraph to this chapter demonstrate – these films' modes of address are correspondingly shaped by this discourse of partial knowledge and elusive culpability.

Even such a partial summary of the emergence and development of politicised violence in this era as is provided here makes two important things clear. Firstly, as has been argued in Chapter 1, rather than viewing films as filtering or reflecting interpretations or realities of the period, we must recognise that the very processes of mediation that grew around the events were inseparable from, and entwined within, those events themselves. The act of interpreting violence perpetrated by both the left and the right was an organic and active agent – indeed, a cognitive battleground – in the developing discourse of 1970s terrorism. Secondly, these processes of mediation manifested themselves in a wide variety of cultural and political registers. The investment in this cultural moment to be found within the *poliziottesco*'s conspiracy mode is accordingly more complex than an attempt to explain or impose order on the material conditions that surrounded the films. This mode of address was not a route towards 'making sense' of the world, but instead a site of ritual, spectacle and emotional release.

To explore this argument, I shall turn to where many critiques of the *poliziottesco* (including this chapter) begin: with *La polizia ringrazia* (1972). On the surface, this film adheres to a straightforward detective / mystery narrative structure whereby key plot information is withheld from, and then incrementally revealed to, the audience. This is akin to the model identified by Bordwell and Thompson as depending 'on our curiosity – on our desire to know . . . what forces lurk behind certain events' (2010: 83). The film's protagonist, Commissioner Bertone, embarks on a pursuit of armed robbers, but his efforts are frustrated by media and bureaucratic mechanisms that seem to favour the criminals. Bertone is then provided with a succession of hints that a clandestine right-wing organisation is using the violence to influence public opinion and to take control until, finally, it is revealed that a cabal of politicians, industrialists, bankers and the former police commissioner (who has acted as Bertone's mentor throughout the film) is seeking to overthrow the state and instigate a dictatorship. Similar 'twist' endings, unmasking high-level neofascist *coup d'état* plots and thus making direct reference to the cover-ups surrounding the *strategia della tensione*, are also to be found in *Milano trema – la polizia vuole giustizia* (1973), *La polizia sta a guardare* (1973), *La polizia accusa: il servizio segreto uccide* (1975), *La polizia ha le mani legate* (1975), *Poliziotti violenti* (1976) and *Il grande racket* (1976). The clear concordances between such plots and the real-life intrigue of 1970s Italy cause Christopher Barry to identify 'accurate coverage' of this political backdrop, offering 'oppressed citizens an opportunity to see on the screen what newspapers at that time did not dare show' (Barry 2004: 85, 82).

However, the extent to which such a plot device can be taken at face value, by seeing it as providing a truthful revelation regarding the films' political surroundings, is doubtful. Diegetically, it is true, an audience is aligned with Bertone, and hears of the intrigue lying behind the events incrementally as the protagonist articulates his gradual awakening. For example, his response to the scene of a summary execution on the banks of the River Tiber with the aforementioned observation that the crime 'puzza molto di fanatismo' / 'stinks of fanaticism' is followed in the next scene by his theory that a radical group is seeking to undermine Italian democracy. This is not, however, to say that the viewer is necessarily aligned with Bertone on an epistemological level, or that s/he undergoes an equivalent realisation. Alex Marlow-Mann takes a more nuanced approach than accounts that offer literal readings of the political content of *poliziotteschi*, arguing instead that the ideological messages of such films are less important than the emotional investment or catharsis on offer to the viewer. Using *Il grande racket* as a case study, Marlow-Mann applies the ideas of moral philosopher Robert Solomon to illustrate how emotional responses are integral to processes of supposedly 'rational' cognition. Further, he argues that in the *poliziottesco*, whose *raison d'être* is the triggering of such emotional responses, 'the viewer must be consciously aware of the sociological and political tensions the filmmaker mobilizes and engage with them in order to respond fully on an emotional level' (Marlow-Mann 2013: 140). In other words, rather than being passively granted the 'opportunity to see' hidden political depths, as Barry claims, specific audiences bring specific levels of prior knowledge into the viewing experience. Moreover, particularly given the imperative for rapid profit that characterised the Italian *filone* model, this suggests that filmmakers would seek to work within the level of prior knowledge assumed to be shared by their immediate target market.[5]

This point becomes clearer, and conceptions of these films offering political revelation more problematic, when we further place the conspiracy *poliziottesco* within the cultural–political framework of 1970s Italy. Despite sustained cover-ups, information about attempts at subversion and state-sponsored terror was in the public domain. The foiled coup orchestrated by General De Lorenzo in 1964, for example, had been made public by *L'Espresso* journalists in May 1967. As already mentioned, far-right culpability for the Piazza Fontana bomb, along with the cover-up orchestrated by the secret service, was exposed by investigative journalists affiliated with *Lotta Continua*, whose book *La strage di stato* sold over 100,000 copies between 1970 and 1972 (Lumley 1990: 123). Another abortive coup, led by the head of the neofascist party *Fronte Nazionale*, Prince

Valerio Borghese, and supported by sections of the armed forces, was then made public in March 1971. Such instances of far-right violence, official cover-ups and suspicious judicial acquittals would continue throughout the decade, entering into the public consciousness to varying degrees (for example, the bombing at Peteano in 1972, and the investigation into the *Rosa dei Venti* group's covert activities in 1974, which led to the arrest of the secret service head, Vito Miceli).

Anna Cento Bull (2007) offers a comprehensive analysis of both contemporaneous and subsequent investigations into these events, detailing what was and what was not known at the time. The involvement of the Central Intelligence Agency (CIA) and North Atlantic Treaty Organization (NATO), for example, would remain hidden until the 1980s, as would the existence and links to right-wing terrorist organisations of the Masonic lodge P2 (whose membership comprised senior politicians and police officers, along with heads of the army, navy, air force, judiciary and secret service). The picture that emerges is therefore one, not of certainty or clarity, but one of hearsay, innuendo, diffuse unease and inchoate suspicion that subversive intrigue was afoot within the Italian state (Bull 2007: 59). While it is true that the full extent of state culpability has never been revealed, one thing is apparent: the notion that senior officials from the secret services, the army, the police force and the judiciary might be conspiring to topple the liberal-democratic status quo and curtail a perceived communist encroachment by sponsoring neofascist violence – though not yet understood in a concrete sense – was a plausible and accessible outlook in Italy by the mid-1970s.

The films that comprise my chief focus here were released on the Italian market between 1972 and 1976 and, through their recourse to ostensibly revelatory denouements, provide documents of this period's confusions. They simultaneously register the assumption of a corrupt state and the incompleteness of concrete knowledge about this corruption, through their simplified depictions of conspiracy. Each film adopts a 'detective' narrative structure similar to that outlined above in the case of *La polizia ringrazia*. Each similarly presents a protagonist who undergoes a realisation leading him to look beneath official explanations of events to unmask shady and disturbing truths about state complicity. Yet, in each case, the viewer's alignment with this protagonist is ambiguous.

This point can be illustrated on a relatively obvious level by the opening sequence of *La polizia accusa: il servizio segreto uccide*, in which a series of captions frame the deaths of senior army personnel (see Figures 2.2–2.7). The circumstances around each death are depicted in detail, to either suggest or explicitly reveal that we are witnessing a murder rather than an

Figures 2.2 to 2.7 Each assassination (left column: 2.2, 2.4, 2.6) is accompanied by an inadequately informed media report (right column: 2.3, 2.5, 2.7) at the start of *La polizia accusa: il servizio segreto uccide* (Sergio Martino, 1975).

accident or a suicide. Each death is immediately followed by an explanatory headline superimposed over a whirring printing press, and in each case the headline's inadequacy or inaccuracy creates an epistemological dissonance between what the viewer has just witnessed and what public explanation is being presented. The spectacular car crash on a Milanese *autostrada* (Figure 2.2) is preceded by close-up shots inside the vehicle, of Major Lorusso suddenly realising that his brakes are malfunctioning: a clearly suspicious death that is explained as a 'spaventoso incidente' / 'frightening incident' in the accompanying headline (Figure 2.3). The demise of Colonel Scanni is even more explicitly shown to be the work of criminals, who knock him unconscious and manipulate the scene to resemble a suicide (Figure 2.4). Unsurprisingly, the headline announces a 'suicidio ... inspiegabili' / 'unexplained suicide' (Figure 2.5). Finally, the circumstances surrounding the death of General Stocchi are described as 'misteriose' / 'mysterious', but the accompanying question 'delitto o suicidio?' / 'crime or suicide?' (Figure 2.7) has already been answered for the viewer, who has seen the unconscious General being carefully placed on a train track (Figure 2.6). The full significance of these deaths will only unravel to the viewer as the planned military coup is divulged through the course of the film, but the premise that murderous intrigue is afoot, and remains hidden from public knowledge, is a given from the start. The film's hero Commissario Solmi then enters the narrative in a state of ignorance and incrementally comes to discover the truth, placing the audience at a remove from him: one step ahead, and waiting for him to catch up.

With reference to *La polizia accusa: il servizio segreto uccide*, Alan O'Leary argues that the *poliziottesco*'s conspiracy mode was, for Italians consuming these films amid the turmoil of the era, performing a ritual function, whereby the hero witnesses 'the criminality and degradation of the contemporary Italian city on behalf of the spectator [and assumes] the vain burden of struggle against it' (O'Leary 2011: 100). Thus, for O'Leary, the hero operates as 'a scapegoat and fantasy representative who assuages or avenges the spectator's sense of social and economic insecurity or political impotence' (O'Leary 2011: 103). If we develop this argument into an appraisal of the narrative strategies deployed in these films, the identification of a ritual function further illuminates the 'revelatory' insight on offer to the spectator: one akin to Aristotle's concept of *anagnorisis* (Aristotle 2008: 19–21). This word, referring to a change from ignorance to awareness, is usually translated from the Greek as either 'discovery' or 'recognition'. Northrop Frye outlines how the latter usage denotes dramatic plots in which the moment of revelation is a shock for the central character, but not for the audience, who have known what is coming all along (Frye et al. 1985: 353).

Furthermore, scholarship around the concept of *anagnorisis* in relation to ancient Greek drama has long debated the extent to which it does not refer solely to audience knowledge obtained from what a plot has shown up to that point in the diegesis, but can also denote a broader cultural awareness of, and familiarity with, the dramatic ritual being enacted on stage. In contextualising the myriad references (both mythic and topical) contained within Sophocles' *Oedipus at Colonus* (*c*. 406 BC), Andreas Markantonatos refers to a 'spectator's encyclopaedia', or 'the reservoir of knowledge and presuppositions that each member of the audience brings with him [*sic*] in order to make sense of the performance' (Markantonatos 2002: 24). Roger Herzel counters Aristotle's suggestion that only the informed few possessed intimate knowledge of the myths being represented on stage, by pointing to the efforts made by the playwrights 'who take great pains to inform the audience in advance of what will happen ... The most ignorant spectator will see in the actual event the *re*-enactment of what he [*sic*] already knows' (Herzel 1974: 503; emphasis in original). This highlights a crucial point. Whether an audience's prior knowledge of the on-stage ritual is actually present or not is less important than the extent to which the text itself is shaped by the dramatist's assumption that it is present. As Emily Allen-Hornblower argues: 'we must understand every speech, gesture, or scene in light of what the dramatists presupposed to be the audience's knowledge and past experience of a given scene or myth' (Allen-Hornblower 2016: 14).

Such a debate seems an appropriate way of examining the 'revelatory' performance of conspiracy on show in the films considered in this chapter: the unmasking of culpability operating as a ritual recognition of already accepted political tenets. To appraise this point, it is necessary to move beyond analysis of such narrative devices as the dramatic irony outlined above in the case of *La polizia accusa: il servizio segreto uccide*, and consider the extent to which the viewer's level of cultural recognition is presupposed to be already in a privileged position over the *commissario* hero. Approaching these films on their own terms, as it were, we can see that they do not function to explain, investigate or illuminate the finer details of the intrigue and its culpabilities. They instead use an already pervasive corruption as a backdrop, stage and forum for an unfocused but assumed *dietrologia*[6] that does not require sophisticated analysis or articulation.

For example, the ending of *La polizia ringrazia* – even while it unmasks former chief of police Stolfi as complicit in the intrigue – ultimately obfuscates the precise culpabilities for the coup conspiracy. The denouement makes it clear that Bertone's suspicions of an elite cabal seeking to manipulate public opinion and overthrow the democratic order were correct. Stolfi's calm declaration that nobody will discover the true culpability for the murder of Bertone or the larger plot because he knows how to manipulate any resultant investigations puts a seal on the film's broader accusations that governmental and civic institutions were complicit in the cover-ups that accompanied the strategy of tension. It should also, however, be seen as a self-reflexive gambit. The film's viewer, of course, does know of the conspiracy's finer details, having just heard Bertone and Stolfi talking at length about its mechanisms and then having witnessed its dastardly ruthlessness in the revelatory act of betrayal. As District Attorney Ricciuti vows to continue Bertone's investigation, however, he is challenged by a man who is clearly a high-ranking official, but whose precise identity is hidden from the viewer thanks to conspicuous *mise en scène* that conceals his face behind a car door frame as the film draws to an end.[7] The implicit suggestion appears to be that a level of complicity, to which the viewer is finally not party, exists above Stolfi. Far from offering lucid analysis or explanation, the outlook that emerges here recalls Bertone's earlier musings on the banks of the Tiber: certainty that high-level intrigue is afoot, coupled with a literal inability to unmask its agents or to pin down its precise nature.

The persistence of neofascist anonymity on display here is echoed in *La polizia ha le mani legate*, in which the only on-screen appearances of the coup's perpetrators come through silhouettes, shots filtered through glass prisms, close-ups of hands, or long shots that deny the viewer a detailed cognisance of facial features. Such framings act as a visual manifestation of Pier Paolo Pasolini's frustrations, cited earlier in this chapter, that the culprits' identities seem within one's grasp, but remain tantalisingly out of reach. They also adhere to a broader pattern in Italian cinema of the era identified by Alfio Leotta, whereby right-wing radicals are depicted as 'monodimensional characters, mysterious or sometimes invisible hit men who do not display any emotion and are dangerously ubiquitous' (Leotta 2013: 149).

In the case of the *polizottesco*'s treatment of conspiracy, this tentative representation of an all-pervasive neofascism is also tangible in the films' omissions and oversimplifications. *Milano trema – la polizia vuole giustizia*, for example, presents its protagonist with a convoluted riddle that does very little to clarify the political situation. Here, a hippie commune (decorated in Campaign for Nuclear Disarmament (CND) symbols and 'flower power' iconography) is implicated in the web of intrigue that leads his investigations through a politically motivated assassination, an organised crime boss and his gang of hoodlums, their professed determination to spread chaos and influence public opinion, and the ultimate revelation that the police chief is the puppet master of all the turmoil. This unmasking of the hero's erstwhile ally should firstly be recognised as an opportunistic and familiar *filone* echo of *La polizia ringrazia*, whose box-office success had pointed to the lucrative potential of such repetition the year before. Secondly, the crime network and political motivations depicted in this film do not in any way render the era's confusions coherent. On the contrary, they make these confusions manifest, by unproblematically conflating leftist agitation with a right-wing strategy of tension in a reductive framing of 'political violence' per se.

My point is not to denigrate these filmmakers' understanding of political or historical processes. Rather, it is to argue that *La polizia ringrazia* and *Milano trema – la polizia vuole giustizia*, and the 'conspiracy' *poliziottesco* strand of which they are part, take corruption and conspiracy as an accepted and assumed starting point and therefore offer little pretence towards complex analysis or investigation into its precise political motivations. To approach these films trying to find such insight, or to be disappointed when we fail to do so, would be to overlook the cultural coordinates of the *poliziottesco*'s industrial milieu. These films' progression towards their 'revelatory' unmasking of official culpability instead offers something akin to what Christopher Wagstaff describes as *filone* cinema's 'pay-off' (Wagstaff 1992: 253): an anticipated thrill or gratification whose repetition characterises a given formula or strand. Once the archetype is established in *La polizia ringrazia*, the ritual performance of the hero's revelation and the 'confession' of a high-powered ringleader asserting the need to foment chaos in society so as to topple the democratic status quo offer such catharsis, as a formulaic ending repeated in all but one of the films discussed so far in this chapter.[8] Though each film positions this act of 'unmasking' as its pivotal moment, the revelation on offer is less an epistemological one of being informed that arms of the state might act as covert sponsors for terror, and more a cathartic one of witnessing a variation on a familiar *filone* trope: the hero eliminating the ringleader (*Milano trema - la polizia vuole giustizia*, *La polizia sta a guardare*, *Il grande racket*), perishing in his heroic attempt to do so (*La polizia ringrazia*, *La polizia accusa: il servizio segreto uccide*) or both (*Poliziotti violenti*).

We can better understand this process of repetition with variation by thinking of these films, not as discrete, standalone pieces offering closure or enlightenment to a viewer, but instead as something akin to what Frank Kelleter terms 'popular seriality' (Kelleter 2017). This is not to say that these films are 'serialised' narratives in the sense of regular episodes comprising a single long-form storyline or existing in a unified story world; indeed, this was not a particularly common occurrence in *filone* cinema.[9] The relevance of this approach instead pertains to the inherent nature of the *filone* as a category of filmmaking that is characterised by repetition and intertextuality, rather than films operating independently from each other. Kelleter's conceptual framework is particularly illuminating to understand this point, and warrants citation at some length:

> Setting up conclusions is only part of what stories do. The other part has to do with uncertainty about final outcomes, with the postponement of a definite end, the promise of perpetual renewal. Even finished tales seek to continue and multiply themselves... Commonly, [serial genres] provide smooth endings, but what paradox is inherent in the fact that they do so again and again, without a redeeming overall conclusion to their perpetual acts of narrating?
>
> ... Anyone looking at this issue with an exclusive interest in completed individual stories (as literary scholarship has taught us with its concentration on works of art) loses sight of the fact that the tension curve rises again after a story has ended: What might be different in the next monster movie[?]. (Kelleter 2017: 8–9)

The term 'perpetual renewal' efficiently describes how the process of '*anagnorisis*' at work in the 'conspiracy' *poliziottesco* serves to replicate the *filone* strand: a ritual recognition of familiar and assumed tenets in a serial text that 'prepares its own variation and renewal in another text that does not yet exist' (Kelleter 2017: 17).

This is certainly not a new way of framing *filone* cinema. As already mentioned in the previous chapter, Wagstaff has long argued that the 'popular' cinematic product in 1960s and 1970s Italy should be appraised for its patterns of serial repetition, whereby a cinema audience was being offered 'gratifications that were part of a longer-term sequence' (Wagstaff 1992: 254). In the same article, Wagstaff rejected the relevance for this production milieu of traditional Film Studies methodologies that have 'seen the individual film as the unit to be studied, and have assumed that the object of the spectator's attention is that unit in its integrity' (Wagstaff 1992: 253). Indeed, such conventional methodologies of textual analysis do tend to overlook the material circumstances that produce and consume formulaic or serial artefacts, which are in Kelleter's words 'commodities [that] do not usually try to cover up their economic conditions' (Kelleter 2017: 10).

Despite Wagstaff's influential exhortation to the scholarly field, this point warrants re-articulation, since there remains in Italian Film Studies a tendency to judge the *poliziottesco* according to the standards of more 'respected' works of *cinema d'impegno* (politically 'committed' films). Brunetta states that this *filone* 'began with the films of [Elio] Petri and [Damiano] Damiani' (Brunetta 2009: 210), while Bondanella includes Damiani alongside Fernando di Leo (whom he dubs 'King of the B's') and Umberto Lenzi as the *filone*'s leading auteurs, in an overview chapter entitled 'The Poliziesco' (Bondanella 2009: 459–72). For Bondanella, Damiani's films (such as the internationally award-winning *Confessione di un commissario di polizia al procuratore della repubblica / Confessions of a Police Captain* (1971)) are 'among the best examples of explicitly political spin on the *poliziesco*' (Bondanella 2009: 470).

Doubtless, there are interesting routes of influence to be drawn between *poliziotteschi* and the more critically lauded works of such directors as Damiani and Petri (as well as their even more critically admired contemporary, Francesco Rosi). Petri's *Indagine su un cittadino al di sopra di ogni sospetto / Investigation of a Citizen Above Suspicion* (1970), for example, examines the hard-wired eagerness of the authorities to overlook evidence pointing to high-level culpabilities for violent crime, and it preceded the onset of the 'conspiracy' *poliziottesco*. In turn, Rosi's *Cadaveri eccellenti / Illustrious Corpses* (1976) has been analysed for its indebtedness to this *filone* trend (O'Leary 2011: 83–91). Damiani's *Io ho paura / I Am Afraid* (1977), too, has a narrative affinity with the 'conspiracy' *poliziottesco* through its plot of a policeman uncovering links between a terrorist attack and a planned secret service coup. Each of these films can be broadly placed in a 'police procedural' generic framework, and each therefore provides a valuable case study to appraise the cultural–political outlooks that surrounded this *filone* strand.

The problem comes when, like Bondanella, one attempts to apply ill-fitting auteurist value judgements of artistic 'quality' to films whose internal logic and material industrial conditions operated according to a different set of rules. The films of Damiani, Petri and Rosi occupy a divergent mode of political address to the *filone* films under discussion here, offering considerably more sophisticated analyses of the era's cover-ups with varying degrees of philosophical examination into the distinction between left- and right-wing terrorism, as well as the authorities' efforts to frame leftist extremists. Mary P. Wood identifies in both *Indagine su un cittadino al di sopra di ogni sospetto* and *Cadaveri eccellenti* a thematic analysis of ideology and power coercing and indoctrinating the populace into acceptance of the state's operations (Wood 2012: 36–7). *Io ho paura*, meanwhile, features a fraught discussion between Brigadiere Ludovico Graziano (Gian Maria Volontè) and Judge Cancedda (Erland Josephson) over whether a train bombing was carried out by extremists on the left or on the right. In this film, the implications of this issue are foregrounded, as links between acts of violence and the secret services become apparent.

No such detailed analysis exists in the *poliziotteschi* under consideration here, in which 'public opinion' is repeatedly presented by the plotters as a self-explanatory entity to be straightforwardly manipulated by spreading violence. Arguably the most sophisticated of the 'conspiracy' *poliziotteschi* in this regard is *La polizia ha le mani legate*, which does feature discussions concerning the distinction between left- and right-wing terrorism, when passengers on a tram argue over a recent bombing. After one man has condemned the atrocity as the actions of fascists, a woman responds by saying 'secondo me sono rossi' / 'I think it was the reds'. At this, another man puts down his newspaper and interjects: 'chi mette le bombe è fascista' / 'fascists are the ones who plant bombs'. The woman then says: 'ci vorrebbe un governo con un pugno di ferro . . . In quei vent'anni queste cose non succedevano' / 'We need a government with an iron fist . . . these things didn't happen during those twenty years [of the Fascist period].' Clearly, this is not a detailed or particularly insightful discussion of ideology or history. Rather, it aids the broader construction of a believable backdrop for the film's plot: one in which people animatedly discuss the news and debate their political alignments on public transport, and thereby demonstrate the continuing burden of the Fascist past on everyday consciousness. Rather than decrying this lack of sophistication, my concern here is to chart how these *filone* films document a particular political register: one of innate suspicion and assumed distrust, rather than incisive critique, investigative rigour or intellectual insight. Indeed, the backdrops that emerge from filmmakers' efforts to create such verisimilitude are precisely where historical silences are most often given a voice in these films.

Alan O'Leary identifies in the representation of the Moro kidnapping *Piazza delle cinque lune / Five Moons Plaza* (Renzo Martinelli, 2003) an address to an international viewer, who is assumed by the filmmakers to be ignorant of the events the film interrogates: 'This makes it difficult, perhaps, to insert unproblematically into the tradition of the *cinema d'impegno*: the spectator is addressed by this text as a *consumer* . . . something perhaps incompatible with the address to a *citizen*' (O'Leary 2009: 56; emphasis in original). The 'conspiracy' *poliziottesco* seems to complicate this notion of incompatibility, since it addresses its viewers as both 'consumers' (of what Kelleter terms 'commercial storytelling . . . a network of cultural practices rather than a set of distinct structures' (Kelleter 2017: 12)) and 'citizens' (whose knowledge of the local events being referred to is assumed). It is in the nature of these assumptions that their mode of political address diverges most meaningfully from more respected forms of *cinema d'impegno*. Their ritual performance of conspiracy, their *filone* production values, their oversimplifications and their investment in spectacle all serve the primary task of constructing a credible backdrop for the films' action sequences and cathartic unmaskings, rather than attempting to offer detailed analysis. It is therefore through analysing the unspoken assumptions that make up those backdrops – which often manifest themselves in the *mise en scène*, in seemingly inconsequential asides or in scene-setting moments – that we can most meaningfully appraise these films' significance.

Returning to my earlier argument that the events of the 1970s were inseparable from the processes of mediation that grew around them, we can therefore place the *poliziottesco*'s conspiracy mode within the evolving historical discourse that would later become known as Italy's *anni di piombo*. I have argued that the filmmakers assumed their audiences' familiarity with corruption, intrigue and collusion with terrorism on the part of the state. It remains to explore in more depth how these assumptions were historically constituted. The sense of 'pastness' that infuses these films will be further illuminated by examining a closely related *filone* strand of vigilante films.

The Vigilante *Filone*

In the wake of the significant box-office success garnered by *Il cittadino si ribella / Street Law* (Enzo G. Castellari, 1974),[10] a relatively small cycle of films emerged between 1974 and 1977 that similarly depicted private citizens taking it upon themselves to fight back against corruption or violent crime. Such a 'vigilante' strand had in fact been in evidence in Italian studios before Castellari's film, with *Città violenta / The Family* (Sergio Sollima, 1970), *Ricatto alla mala / Summertime Killer* (Antonio Isasi, 1972) and *Revolver / Blood in the Streets* (Sergio Sollima, 1973). Though, as we shall see, these three films have much in common with the larger vigilante strand, all three make extensive use of settings outside Italy, and all three were international co-productions. *Il cittadino si ribella* was produced solely by a Roman studio (Capital Film), and was the first film of this strand to embed its action in an entirely Italian locale. It is therefore justifiably seen as a template for the films that followed, each of which is specifically focused on Italian society.[11] As with many *filone* categories, the boundaries here are porous, but the spate of such films that followed *Il cittadino si ribella* include *La città sconvolta: caccia spietata ai rapitori / Kidnap Syndicate* (Fernando Di Leo, 1975), *Roma violenta / Violent City* (Marino Girolami, 1975), *Il giustiziere sfida la città / Syndicate Sadists* (Umberto Lenzi, 1975), *L'uomo della strada fa giustizia / Manhunt in the City* (Umberto Lenzi, 1975), *Vai gorilla / The Hired Gun* (Tonino Valerii, 1975), *Roma, l'altra faccia della violenza / Rome: The Other Side of Violence* (Marino Girolami, 1976), *Torino violenta / Double Game* (Carlo Ausino, 1977) and *No alla violenza / Death Hunt* (Tano Cimarosa, 1977).[12]

Alex Marlow-Mann argues that the commonplace conflation of these films with the larger *polizottesco* category is a mistake, because 'the pleasures they offer the viewer are not the same ... [the vigilante's] very presence reminds the viewer of the ultimate failure of the professional class of lawmaker to tackle the wave of crime sweeping the country' (Marlow-Mann 2013: 137). Indeed, this is a more nebulous *filone* strand than the 'conspiracy' *poliziottesco*, mostly because these films' protagonists are not so consistently occupying one particular role in society. The Italian titles of the films I have listed in the above paragraph are strikingly different to those analysed in the first part of this chapter, since the word '*polizia*' (or its derivations) does not appear in any of them. This points to a broad sense in these films that institutional law is either ineffectual or absent, and this can be seen as a generic prerequisite for a 'vigilante' strand (which requires such a backdrop so as to necessitate the hero's vigilantism). The diverse identities of these films' central characters include engineers (*Il cittadino si ribella* and *L'uomo della strada fa giustizia*), a doctor (*Roma, l'altra faccia della violenza*) and a hitman (*Città violenta*), while *Torino violenta*'s Ispettore Moretti is in fact a policeman, who moonlights as the mysterious '*giustiziere*' to pass death sentences on criminals where the law dares not.

What unites these films is that their protagonists' consistent obsession with battling criminality emerges from a personal code of honour or a desire for revenge rather than professional duty. One of the most recurrent motivations for such obsession provided in these narratives is a preoccupation with a traumatic past, often relating to the loss of a family member. *Ricatto alla mala* is the story of a son avenging his father's violent death, while *La città sconvolta: caccia spietata ai rapitori*, *L'uomo della strada fa giustizia* and *Roma, l'altra faccia della violenza* all depict fathers hunting down the murderers of their children. As we have seen, *Il cittadino si ribella* also demonstrates an underlying fixation with honouring the memory of a family member, as a decisive factor in the protagonist's decision to fight back.

It is with this recurring theme of a traumatic past that this *filone* strand is most closely aligned with a broader, international 'vigilante' genre. Scholarly analysis on vigilante films released across a wide variety of cultural and temporal contexts frequently coalesces around consistent themes of memory, cultural trauma and nostalgia for a recent past that predates rapid socio-economic change. James Scorer, for example, examines how *Un oso rojo / Red Bear* (Israel Adrián Caetano, 2002) responds to political and economic shifts in 1990s Argentina around post-Cold War globalisation and the attendant urban fragmentation and governmental state corruption (Scorer 2010: 142–5). For Scorer, this film's focus on urban fear and on vigilante revenge as a potential solution to social ills registers the long-drawn-out collapse of Argentinian civic identity at the end of the twentieth century. This sense that vigilante narratives have functioned as responses to a tipping point brought about by rapid globalisation in the late twentieth century is similarly identified in a Russian context by Anthony Anemone. In his analysis of Aleksei Balabanov's trilogy of vigilante films, *Brat / Brother* (1997), *Brat 2 / Brother 2* (2000) and *Voyna / War* (2002), Anemone identifies a response to the breakdown of institutional law in post-Soviet Russia coupled with a rejection of Americanised consumerism. *Voyna*'s vigilante protagonist is thus seen to be a receptacle for 'nationalist values, xenophobic discourse, and nostalgia for the lost power of the Soviet State' (Anemone 2008: 131). These processes of cultural trauma identified in such films recall Sztompka's analysis (cited in

Chapter 1) of cumulative changes in a society that reach a 'threshold of saturation' to produce a shock of sudden realisation (Sztompka 2004: 158).

To cite yet another context for such discourse, twenty-first century American vigilante films have been analysed as responses to the trauma of 9/11. Claire Sisco King examines how the rhetoric of trauma in *The Brave One* (Neil Jordan, 2007) 'construct[s] and make[s] sense of national history and identity, framing 9/11 as a culturally traumatic event akin to Vietnam in its destabilization of the politics of visibility and gender'. For King, the personal traumas of the film's female protagonist operate as 'a synecdotal frame for understanding the perceived wounds of the nation' and participate in a cinematic history whereby 'genre films (and vigilante films, in particular) have long been understood as managing cultural memory' (King 2010: 112–13). In a related study, Lisa Coulthard analyses the implicit advocacy of vigilantism in *Mystic River* (Clint Eastwood, 2003) through the lens of nostalgia for a time of moral certainty, which characterised the 'War on Terror' in the wake of the trauma of 9/11 (Coulthard 2011).

Across diverse contexts, there is therefore a consistent identification of the vigilante film's 'citizen taking control' trope as being symptomatic of a nation having taken a wrong turn, with the protagonist's obligatory obsession with a traumatic past (often characterised by flashbacks or memories that motivate the need for vigilante justice) acting as a symbol for a resultant social malaise. Vigilante films are analysed for how they emerge at times of national crisis, when a state's ability to ensure the security of its citizens is being brought into question across wider cultural–political discourses. As discussed in Chapter 1, the American example of most direct relevance to 1970s Italy is *Death Wish* (Michael Winner, 1974), which Kirby Farrell diagnoses as a manifestation of an emasculated nation seeking renewal at the end of the Vietnam War: a reprisal of 'the *fin de siècle* dread that civilization has sapped "manliness," suggesting that purgative violence can free the "pitiful, helpless giant" from its crippling inhibitions' (Farrell 1998: 291). For King, too, American cinematic vigilantism has similarly operated as a 'perform[ance of] national resilience', as the individual's reassertion of his or her agency redresses the nation's perceived weaknesses in the face of devastating traumas (most pertinently, Vietnam and 9/11) (King 2010: 123).

Clearly, then, the Italian vigilante strand can be appraised within this larger discourse of national crisis. Its emergence in a moment of civic fragmentation and urban fear at the culmination of a process of rapid modernisation is consistent with the above analyses from other cultural contexts. There is, however, a marked difference between how the above

American examples frame the individual's relationship to society, and how some of the Italian films do so. Far from reasserting the agency of the lone citizen as a corrective to a dysfunctional polity, the endings of the Italian films repeatedly provide nihilistic assertions of the futility of fighting against a corrupt, faceless system. In *Revolver*, for example, ex-cop Vito Cipriani (Oliver Reed) embarks on a quest to expose and fight an opaque syndicate, which seeks to silence the petty criminal Milo Ruiz (Fabio Testi) for what he knows about the murder of a high-ranking official. After every level of officialdom has actively frustrated Cipriani's pursuit of justice, he is eventually driven to capitulate, lamenting that 'we're up against something far bigger than ourselves' before shooting Ruiz in the back to save his kidnapped wife. As Cipriani is then forced to betray all he has fought for by playing along with the cover-up and falsely testifying to the police, the film's final shot – a freeze-frame with a close-up of his tearful face in the foreground, and his horrified wife backing away from him in disbelief (Figure 2.8) – encapsulates the powerlessness of the individual subject in the face of systemic criminality.

Revolver's depiction of impenetrable labyrinthine corruption is consistent with the political themes in a number of director Sollima's previous films. His Westerns – most notably *La resa dei conti / The Big Gundown* (1966) and *Faccia a faccia / Face to Face* (1967) – similarly depict the struggles of powerless individuals caught up in societies run by ruthless, murderous cabals,[13] while his earlier vigilante film *Città violenta* ends on a comparable note of nihilism. In the latter film, the protagonist

Figure 2.8 Vito Cipriani (Oliver Reed) capitulates to the corrupt system in *Revolver* (Sergio Sollima, 1973).

Jeff Heston (played by Charles Bronson) eliminates the mob boss Weber (Telly Savalas) and hunts down his former lover and a corrupt lawyer, both of whom have manipulated Jeff so that they can gain control of Weber's corporation. Having achieved his goal and uncovered the intricate layers of criminal intrigue that surround him, he sits on a rooftop in weary resignation, and tells the policeman who finds him to kill him there and then.

Yet this is not a trope that can simply be ascribed to the political views of one director, since time and again, the protagonists of this *filone* strand find themselves ultimately rendered impotent in the face of insurmountable and inevitable corruption, even when they successfully kill the people they have been hunting. The ending of *Il cittadino si ribella*, for example, echoes that of *Revolver*, as Carlo's investigation into connections between the police and the criminal underworld comes to nothing, and he is finally forced to capitulate by signing a false statement that his accusations against the police were made under duress. In *Ricatto alla mala*, the virtuous cop (played by Karl Malden) who has hunted the vigilante avenger throughout the film finally lets him go free upon realising that his own paymasters are corrupt, and is consequently gunned down by those same paymasters in the final scene. In *L'uomo della strada fa giustizia*, the avenger Vanucchi (Henry Silva) hunts down and kills the gang he has been pursuing, but it turns out he has been manipulated to kill the wrong people by a fanatical neofascist organisation. Similarly, though Luc Merenda's hero in *La città sconvolta: caccia spietata ai rapitori* ultimately kills the people who murdered his son, the process of finding them reveals underlying and inherent power structures. He infiltrates multiple levels of a criminal syndicate in an attempt to unravel the truth and unmask its head, but constantly finds another level of command leading all the way up to corporate boardrooms and government.

The depiction in many of these films of a determined but ultimately futile attempt to uncover the intricate machinations connecting organised crime to corporate capital or branches of government therefore situates them firmly in their immediate contexts of the *anni di piombo* and the *strategia della tensione*. It is primarily for this reason that they warrant analysis alongside the 'conspiracy' *poliziottesco*, since the two strands share similar outlooks on contemporary Italy's political intrigues and consequently operate on equivalent epistemological levels. I have previously argued that such films as *La polizia ringrazia* and *La polizia accusa: il servizio segreto uccide* assume their audiences to be a step ahead of their protagonists, so that the moment of revelation is not one of realising that corruption exists, but is instead a ritual catharsis of witnessing the central character's awakening to this fact. The opening few minutes of *Il cittadino si ribella* deploy a similar strategy to *La polizia accusa*, with a montage of targeted killings on the streets of Genoa providing the audience with an impression that acts of violence are being coordinated, before the main character enters the narrative and tries to unravel that fact for himself. *Revolver* also opens with an indication for the viewer that the culpability for an assassination is being covered up, when a police inspector expresses satisfaction that the identification of the supposed murderer's body will avoid unwanted complications, before Cipriani enters the film. This points to an equivalent level of assumption on the part of the filmmakers that corruption and intrigue are the default setting, rather than an epistemological revelation for the audience.

What distinguishes the films of the vigilante strand from those of the 'conspiracy' *poliziottesco*, apart from the professional status of their protagonists, are the ways in which they utilise real-life reference points. As we have seen, 'conspiracy' *poliziotteschi* make extensive and unmistakable references to specific recent events such as the Piazza Fontana bombing, the assassination of Commissioner Calabresi, the activities of the *Rosa dei venti* and the military training camp at Piano di Rascino. In the vigilante films, on the other hand, acts of violence and the opaque intrigues that surround those acts accumulate through repetition to establish a general sense of unease. This is not to say that these films were not based on actual crimes (we shall, for example, see that the high-profile 'Circeo massacre' of 1975 provided one such source of inspiration). The explanations given for their conception by their makers, however, often followed a consistent and revealing theme. Fernando Di Leo claimed that the idea for *La città sconvolta: caccia spietata ai rapitori* came because 'kidnappings were a hot topic back then' (Curti 2013: 137), and Tonino Valerii provides a more detailed explanation for the same year's *Vai gorilla*:

> I saw a newspaper with a big headline about a wealthy Italian industrialist, who claimed that he was tired of living in such an anarchic and dangerous country, and that he was moving abroad for fear of being kidnapped. I though [sic] it was a situation which perfectly captured the troubled historical moment we were living in. (Curti 2013: 133)

It is telling that the specific news stories in question are not named. Instead, repeated (and therefore 'serial') themes in *cronaca nera* (newspaper crime reports) are taken as an inspiration for a broad-brush backdrop of a violent society spiralling out of control. *Cronaca nera* themselves often appear in the films as part of this scene-setting strategy, helping to advance the plots of *Il cittadino si ribella*, *Roma, l'altra faccia della violenza* and *Torino violenta*. In *L'uomo della strada fa giustizia*, newspaper headlines – 'Bomba inesplosa' ('Unexploded bomb'), 'Sparatoria a Sesto S.G.' ('Shooting in Sesto San Giovanni'), 'Bomba a Milano' ('Bomb in Milan') – make clearer reference to real-life events and tie the film to its Milanese setting, but they appear only fleetingly, as one component in the construction of a believable *mise en scène*.[14]

Enzo G. Castellari's claim (cited in Chapter 1) that the crimes contained within the opening montage of *Il cittadino si ribella* were based on true events taken from news reports is therefore particularly revealing, since he also does not specify which events he had in mind. Instead, his stated intention is to evoke a sense of general unease being felt by Italians with 'un serie di fatti di cronaca che determina realmente il pericolo che il cittadino aveva in quel momento' / 'a series of news stories that showed the real danger the citizens had to deal with at that time' (Gregory 2013). As I have already argued, the measures taken to construct a believable backdrop for this film's plot also extended to the *mise en scène*, with Carlo's framed manifesto conveying an unspoken preoccupation with the moral lessons of the past. By assuming an all-pervasive sense of enduring corruption rather than explicitly dwelling on specific contemporary events, these films can thus be seen tacitly to invite their viewers to 'think historically', by contemplating the continuity of systematic institutional brutality. Crucially, this preoccupation with a historical continuum is rarely made explicit; instead, a taken-as-read ubiquity manifests itself in scene-setting details and off-guard moments of background exposition.

Chapter 1's broad picture of 'unfinished business' surrounding the War years, the Resistance and the *resa dei conti* – of lingering bitterness having been shelved back in 1945 and lurking beneath the national psyche – means that, for the cultural historian, such inexplicit or hidden manifestations of wartime memory become particularly revealing. Giacomo Lichtner has examined various strategies by which Italian cinema has dealt with the historical memory of the Fascist past since the War ended. For Lichtner, this past is paradoxically 'both ubiquitous and only partially retold':

> In few sites of memory can the symbiotic existence of memory and forgetfulness be more clearly evident . . . The concept of silence dissects the relationship between memory and forgetting . . . and serves well the need to distinguish between what is genuinely forgotten and what is deliberately left unsaid. (Lichtner 2013: 189)

Silences and 'unsaids' are therefore of utmost importance when analysing traces of the Fascist past in Italian cinema, since amnesia was a key part of Italy's post-war memory. When we place the vigilante films in this cultural backdrop, their 'historicity' becomes apparent. As I have said, they can be seen to contemplate the historical continuity of institutional brutality, implicitly placing their critiques of contemporary Italy within a broader continuum. The lack of explicitness surrounding this engagement with history means that it acts instead as a 'silence' in the text: one that emerges from a process of serial repetition, is woven from the assumptions that construct the films' backdrops and only occasionally bursts through to the surface of the narratives.

These backdrops manifest themselves in a variety of minor scene-setting details and seemingly inconsequential asides. Individually, each of these moments is of secondary interest to a viewer whose attention is being steered towards the action of each film's plot. I have, however, already argued that we should view such films not as standalone pieces of carefully wrought narrative coherence, but instead as a series of repetitions being created in a rapid production cycle and responding at short notice to contemporary events. From this perspective, the recurrence of these moments reveals off-guard assumptions of corruption in the surrounding polity that are deemed not to require overt articulation, but that acquire meaning by their very accumulation. One such repeated scene-setting trope frames the physical landscape of urban modernity as a taken-as-read space where criminality and big business intertwine, with cinematography working to diminish the vigilante figure in comparison to architectural edifices. In *Città violenta*, for example, the mob boss Weber points Jeff's attention to a skyscraper he owns, to explain how far he has come in his career, and a low-angle point-of-view shot frames the tower to emphasise its scale. Similarly, near the beginning of *Ricatto alla mala*, an establishing tilt shot of a daunting New York skyscraper is used to introduce the organised criminals against whom the vigilante Ray must fight.

This shot construction is repeated in *La città sconvolta: caccia spietata ai rapitori*. Here, the hero Colella arrives at the headquarters of the syndicate that killed his son, and another tilt shot charts the scale of their imposing office block. In this shot, the building is itself an icon of Italy's march towards post-war modernity: the Torre Velasca in Milan, which was completed at the height of the Economic Miracle. We will see in the next chapter that this framing device extended beyond the vigilante film, and into the mafia *filone*, with another tilt shot – again of the Torre Velasca – being used for an identical narrative purpose in *Milano calibro 9 / Calibre 9* (Fernando Di Leo, 1972). In both of these cases, Di Leo's choice of building implicitly links Italy's rapid economic and cultural progress to violent corruption. Indeed, all of the shots mentioned above efficiently and wordlessly situate modern office blocks as natural and accepted settings for organised crime: a premise that is also repeatedly presupposed by representatives of the law in the films' plots. The police commissioner in *La città sconvolta* explains to Collela that kidnappers are just businessmen with their own jargon and advanced modern power structures, in an exasperated tone that suggests this should be common knowledge. In *Revolver*, a lawyer's matter-of-fact approach to a political assassination is described by Cipriani as 'a bureaucratic adjustment, like a cross in a register by a name, not like somebody bleeding to death in the street'. In response, the lawyer similarly explains the ways of the world to the vigilante protagonist, overtly conflating political violence and the bureaucratic institutions of state: 'society has many ways of defending itself: red tape, prison bars, and the revolver'.

It is when we look closely at such asides – seemingly minor pieces of throwaway dialogue whose function is to establish a backdrop for the main exposition – that we can most tangibly detect inadvertent or 'silent' assumptions that inform the construction of a believable story world. Often, these register a resigned certainty that the police are either corrupt or incapable of keeping people safe. For example, in *Roma, l'altra faccia della violenza*, Dr Alessi tries to assure a flower seller that the police will protect him if he testifies to seeing the faces of his daughter's murderers. The vendor's brief mocking response – 'what the fuck are the police going to do?'[15] – dismisses that notion as obviously absurd, and not even warranting consideration. Similarly, in *Revolver*, when Milo Ruiz is preparing to escape from the prison hospital having been beaten up by Cipriani, we hear a guard and the doctor casually discussing 'the usual problem: a prisoner fell down the stairs' in the background. This matter-of-fact line is not dwelt upon, but instead helps the filmmakers to build a milieu in which police brutality is an accepted norm (and its sense of verisimilitude is surely aided by the implicit association with the 'accidental' death of Giuseppe Pinelli in police custody in December 1969).

Another repeated feature of such asides is an explicitly articulated awareness of how this sense of inevitable corruption exists in a historical continuum, either because it arises from past conflict, or because it is a sign of the changes wrought on Italian society by the onset of modernity. *Il giustiziere sfida la città* implicitly frames the dangers of the present moment as part of a downward historical spiral when the barman says to the vigilante hero Rambo (Tomas Milian): 'Each passing day it [crime] gets worse.'[16] In *Città violenta*, too, Weber repeatedly laments that times have changed ('It was different in the old days . . . young people, they're all cynics. They don't care about anything and they don't show respect'), and links the pace of progress to the closer marriage between organised crime and big business ('Sometimes I get homesick for the old days . . . You see that bank? The first time I went in there I had an automatic rifle . . . Now I own it. I've got to preside over the board meetings'). In *Revolver*, an even more overt conflation of national progress with increased criminal sophistication is asserted by the snitch Grappa, who tells Cipriani that the people who want Ruiz won't be the mafia, but instead contract killers who come up from the south and then disappear without leaving a trace: 'They're professionals, home-grown gunmen. We used to be a backward country, but now we're moving up fast.'

Weber's lament at a new generation of reckless young criminals lacking respect is far from an anomaly in Italian crime films (indeed, we will see in Chapter 3 that this trope is widespread in the mafia *filone*). A similar theme of generational conflict and youth delinquency also plays a central role in *Roma, l'altra faccia della violenza*, where it points to the vigilante strand's most direct and explicit reference to a contemporary event. It is telling that the event in question was itself an infamous symbol of 1970s Italy's inability to escape its fascist past. Both Marlow-Mann and Curti emphasise that the film's gang of three young, decadent aristocratic murderers is a clear reference to the perpetrators of the 'Circeo massacre' (Marlow-Mann 2013: 134; Curti 2013: 190). This notorious case of rape, torture and murder occurred in 1975, and a sentence of life imprisonment was passed on the trio of upper-class neofascist culprits in July 1976: just one month before the release of *Roma, l'altra faccia della violenza*. This film, alongside others released in the same year that similarly exploited the Circeo massacre's high media profile such as *I ragazzi della Roma violenta* (Renato Savino, 1976) and *I violenti di Roma bene / Terror in Rome* (Segri and Ferrara, 1976), was therefore a prime example of *filone* cinema reacting rapidly to surrounding events. Moreover, as Curti explains (Curti 2013: 188), this particular event had become embroiled in the broader context of resurgent neofascist violence, which was a prominent presence in *cronaca nera*. A number of high-profile violent crimes by far-right street gangs such as Rome's *Pariolini*, Turin's *Cabinotti* and Milan's *Sanbabilini* were seen in 1975 and 1976. The latter gang's war against left-wing students was the subject of another 1976 film: Carlo Lizzani's *San Babila ore 20: un delitto inutile / San Babila 8 pm*. *Roma, l'altra faccia della violenza* was therefore part of a wider discourse around the persistent pathology of fascist machismo, as a symbol of 1970s Italy's inability to escape the traumatic schisms and open wounds of the nation's past.

In fact, the representation of clandestine gangs or organisations whose political alignment is at least implicitly on the far right had been a repeated trope in the vigilante *filone* the year before *Roma, l'altra faccia della violenza*, appearing in each of *L'uomo della strada fa giustizia*, *Roma violenta* and *Il giustiziere sfida la città* (all 1975). In *L'uomo della strada fa giustizia*, the father seeking to avenge his daughter is recruited by a vigilante organisation run by a lawyer and an army lieutenant, whose remedy for the inability of the state to punish criminals is to send a gang of thugs out to mete summary justice. In *Roma violenta*, a cop who has been sacked for excessive brutality is similarly recruited as the head of a vigilante squad that has been assembled by a wealthy lawyer, while in *Il giustiziere sfida la città* Rambo's friend Pino is employed by a private police force, to fight the crime wave in the absence of an effective state. Though the lawyer in *L'uomo della strada fa giustizia* does opine a decidedly right-wing political vision, the specifically neofascist significance of such organisations at this time is not overtly dwelt upon through any detailed discussion of ideology in these films. Rather, it seems to be assumed (with some justification) that this political reference point is unmissable at this cultural moment. To recall the words of *La polizia ringrazia*'s Inspector Bertone, the mere presence of these vigilante squads 'stinks of fanaticism'.

La polizia ringrazia, of course, is another film that revolves around the activities of a neofascist vigilante gang. Curti argues that, though Vanzina claimed his film's primary inspiration to be the Brazilian death squads, the most direct influence is Leonardo Sciascia's novel *Il contesto* (1971) (Curti 2013: 57). Sciascia's book was famously adapted for the screen in Francesco Rosi's 1976 film *Cadaveri eccellenti / Illustrious Corpses*. Rosi's film is the tale of a police inspector who is investigating the murders of powerful judges, and who comes to realise that the killings are being blamed on the communists and the revolutionary youth movements in order to facilitate a neofascist *coup d'état*. As O'Leary argues, *Cadaveri eccellenti* must be understood through its explicit references to specific political events of its era, regarding both the coup plot and the final scene's depiction of the communists capitulating to the cover-up:

> At a fundamental level, the film is a fable about the Strategy of Tension as well as being a kind of polemic against the Historic Compromise, implicitly criticized . . . as playing into the hands of the ruling DC [Christian Democrat party]. (O'Leary 2011: 85)

The partial plot parallels with *La polizia ringrazia* are self-evident, and Vanzina's film must of course also be considered in the immediate contexts of the *strategia della tensione*. However, its engagement with its political moment is less detailed than *Cadaveri eccellenti*'s, since particular political parties and protest movements are not so overtly represented. It is for this reason that *La polizia ringrazia* bookends this chapter as an emblem for my key arguments, since its political reference points are more of an unspoken and assumed backdrop than a carefully interrogated object of analysis. As Bertone's words suggest, the silent but unmistakable odour of the traumatic past infuses this film's construction of the present.

The films analysed in this chapter are all embedded in their present moment through their responses to contemporary events, and it is through that very immediacy that their preoccupation with the past becomes apparent. This is not to claim that these films are individually 'about' the past. Instead, it is to argue that they should be viewed as an iterative set of serial repetitions and that when we view them thus, the historical silences and preoccupations in the surrounding discourse – what Pierre Macherey calls 'the precise conditions for the appearance of an utterance' (Macherey 2006: 97) – are shown to manifest themselves in the films' taken-as-read backdrops. The historical significance of their present moment reveals itself in off-guard moments of 'taking stock', reflecting on the rapid social, political and economic changes of the preceding decades, on how far Italy had come since the War, and on the lingering vestiges of wartime conflicts that had never been resolved or even fully acknowledged. The next chapter will explore a related, but considerably larger, set of films whose fixations with the past are altogether more explicit.

Notes

1. The English dub of this line on the 2011 Colosseo Film DVD sees fit to make the historical reference explicit, with Bertone describing the crime as 'very much like an execution in old Fascist style'. This was presumably deemed necessary for an anglophone audience, who might otherwise miss the culturally specific implications of Bertone's words.
2. Peter Bondanella, for example, analyses these (and many other) crime films in a chapter called 'The Poliziesco' (Bondanella 2009: 453–94).
3. For example, the wide-ranging and fan-maintained 'Grindhouse Cinema Database' (which describes itself as 'the classic-international exploitation & cult film encyclopedia') lists eighty-nine films under the '*poliziotteschi*' umbrella, including police, mafia, vigilante, heist and gangster films.
4. This clear association with real-life events makes the film's fictitious disclaimer – 'I fatti e i personaggi di questo film sono imaginari. Ogni riferimento alla realtà è da ritenersi puramente casuale' ('The events and people in this film are imaginary. Any reference to reality is to be considered purely coincidental) – disingenuous in its adherence to industry legal practices.

Similar text appears in the credit sequences of *La polizia ringrazia*, *La polizia accusa: il servizio segreto uccide*, and *Milano trema – la polizia vuole giustizia*.

5. As Chapter 1 has discussed, it is not universally the case that this imperative for rapid profit was focused on local audiences, since a high proportion of *filone* products were international co-productions and were consequently designed in part for export markets. The logic of my claim here should not therefore be assumed. In the case of the *poliziottesco*, however, the majority of these films (including *Milano trema – la polizia vuole giustizia*, *La polizia accusa: il servizio segreto uccide*, *Il grande racket* and *Poliziotti violenti*) were made solely by Italian production companies. This particular production milieu was therefore one with a focus on domestic profits.
6. I use this word (which commonly denotes a peculiarly Italian refusal to believe official explanations for events), not to make broad claims about Italian audiences' actual outlooks, but instead to identify the assumptions that were being made about those audiences' attitudes by the filmmakers under consideration.
7. One's interpretation of this man's precise identity might depend on which dubbed version one watches. A careful listener to the English dub on the 2011 Colosseo Film DVD will identify the character's voice as that of the Interior Minister encountered earlier in the film (though the scene's visual construction wilfully obscures this realisation). The Italian version on the same DVD, however, gives the Minister and this mysterious figure noticeably different voices.
8. The exception to this is *La polizia ha le mani legate*, in which the ending shows Commissario Rolandi continuing the hunt for the ringleaders, having identified Attorney Bondi as their go-between. The postscript hints that Rolandi kills Bondi eight days later, suggesting that the ritual has merely been put on hold.
9. There are of course exceptions to this claim. The success of *Mark il poliziotto / Blood, Sweat and Fear* (Stelvio Massi, 1975), for example, led to a sequel following the further adventures of 'Mark the Cop', with *Mark il poliziotto spara per primo / Mark Shoots First* (Stelvio Massi, 1975) being released just four months later. As Curti points out, however, the third film in this series – *Mark colpisce ancora / Mark Strikes Again* (Stelvio Massi, 1976) – changes the central character's surname and demeanour (Curti 2006: 183). This points to an opportunistic attempt to exploit the commercial appeal of the previous films' protagonist rather than a coherent continuation of his storyline, and this was a common feature of *filone* filmmaking. The Spaghetti Western *Django* (Sergio Corbucci, 1966), for example, inspired around fifty 'sequels', the vast majority of which were rebrandings of unrelated films in particular markets, in response to *Django*'s success (see Fisher 2013).
10. *Il cittadino si ribella* made 1,723,405,000 lire in domestic gross profit. This compares favourably with other influential Italian crime films of the period,

such as *La polizia ringrazia* (1,696,360,000 lire), *Milano trema – la polizia vuole giustizia* (1,162,424,000 lire) and *La polizia incrimina la legge assolve* (1,625,825,000 lire) (Curti 2013: 122, 56, 102, 85).

11. Of the vigilante films that followed in the wake of *Il cittadino si ribella*, all were solely Italian productions, except for *Roma, l'altra faccia della violenza*, which was an Italian–French co-production.
12. Aficionados of the Italian vigilante film might reasonably object that *Un borghese piccolo piccolo / An Average Little Man* (Mario Monicelli, 1977) is absent from this list. As an internationally acclaimed entrant at the Cannes Film Festival, however, this film's production context and cultural capital place it at a remove from the *filone* products that are my focus here.
13. For more on the politics of Sollima's Westerns, see my previous book, *Radical Frontiers in the Spaghetti Western: Politics, Violence and Popular Italian Cinema* (Fisher 2011: 96–115).
14. Newspaper headlines are also used for the purpose of constructing a believable backdrop in the aforementioned tram scene in *La polizia ha le mani legate*. As we have seen, however, this film's broader relationship with specific real-life events is considerably more explicit than is evident in the vigilante films.
15. The line in the Italian soundtrack is: 'Ma che cazzo protegge la polizia?' ('But what the fuck are the police going to protect?').
16. This is my translation from the Italian soundtrack's 'ogni giorno che passa andiamo peggio'. Intriguingly, a set of fan-produced English language subtitles for *Il giustiziere sfida la città* (from www.opensubtitles.org) translates this line as: 'Things were better in the war during the occupation.' I am unaware of an alternative soundtrack to the film that might corroborate this wording, but I would not dispute the subtitler's interpretation of the barman's underlying implication. This would be a surprisingly literal manifestation of an 'unsaid'.

CHAPTER 3

Nostalgic Gangsters and the Mafia *Filone*

On 10 May 1978 – the same day on which Aldo Moro's dead body was found in the boot of a car in Rome – Milanese newspaper the *Corriere della Sera* reported that a bomb had exploded near the small Sicilian town of Cinisi, on the Trapani to Palermo railway track, killing one Giovanni Impastato. The headline read: 'Ultrà di sinistra dilaniato dalla sua bomba sul binario' / 'Leftist fanatic blown up by his own bomb on the railway line' (S.V. 1978: 13). It took twenty-two years for the truth – that Impastato had in fact been beaten, tortured and dumped on the track with dynamite strapped to his body by local *mafiosi* – to at last be confirmed courtesy of a parliamentary commission in December 2000.

John Dickie cites the above story as an illustration of how 1970s Italy's national preoccupation with politically motivated violence 'helped to drown out concerns about the mafia's re-emergence, and about its day-to-day regime of terror in western Sicily' (Dickie 2007: 347). The original investigation, it emerged, had unquestioningly fallen for the killers' efforts to make Impastato's demise appear to be the result of a bungled terrorist attack. This was the latest manifestation of a considerably larger pattern of silence, opacity and *omertà*[1] that had surrounded the activities of the Sicilian *Cosa Nostra*[2] since its inception in the 1860s. This fostered the myth that the word 'mafia' did not denote a carefully structured organisation, but instead an intangible notion of chivalric honour and 'a vestige of traditional Sicilian society, inextricable from its wider socio-cultural milieu' (Merlino 2014: 112).

Since my focus on the 1970s has so far been on acts of terrorism and the political intrigues that surrounded them, such a silence around mafia activity has existed in this book as well, and it is my intention to redress that fact in this chapter. The historical schisms that lay behind the events of the *anni di piombo* are of course crucial to an understanding of this period, but unspoken assumptions of lethal political corruption have long possessed more ingrained meanings in Italian national discourse. Though media outlets and institutions of state frequently overlooked it, mafia violence ran parallel to the more famous events of the Years of Lead (indeed, the 1969 Viale Lazio massacre in Palermo, which marked the resumption of *Cosa Nostra* activity after the Catanzaro trials, coincidentally took place just two days before the Piazza Fontana bombing in Milan). It is therefore worth noting that, though the words of Commissioner Bertone that opened the previous chapter refer to the elusive nature of neofascist terrorism, they also evoke a well-known phrase that encapsulates the deep-rooted but similarly intangible presence of organised crime: 'puzza di mafia' / 'smell of mafia'.

This silence around mafia activity in the 1970s is also in evidence when we look at popular discourses concerning *filone* cinema. As has been discussed in the previous chapter, the word '*poliziottesco*' has become an umbrella term for a diverse array of 1970s Italian crime films, many of which do not have the activities of law enforcers or the terrorist atrocities of the era as their main focus. Around forty films whose narratives instead revolved around mafia activity emerged from the *filone* production line between 1968 and 1981, peaking in 1973 (with eleven releases) in opportunistic response to the Italian release of *The Godfather* (Francis Ford Coppola, 1972). As we shall see, these films engage with specific historical, political and cinematic discourses in both Italy and the USA, which require that they be considered apart from other crime *filoni*. Nevertheless, they also possess clear areas of continuity with 'conspiracy' *polizotteschi* and vigilante films, since they too betray pervasive assumptions of state corruption. On the surface, they also appear to demonstrate a preoccupation with the changes wrought on Italian society in the preceding decades. As we shall see, however, this latter aspect is not so much a socio-political intervention, as a set of production decisions making opportunistic use of pre-existing cinematic reference points.

To begin my analysis of how these films engaged with such themes, I shall turn to the work of the most revered director of this mafia *filone*, Fernando Di Leo. Such an auteurist[3] methodology may seem out of place in a book whose self-proclaimed remit is to return time and again to the 'seriality' of the Italian studio system, but taking Di Leo as a starting point raises a number of important issues, to which I shall return. Why does he occupy a privileged status in critical and fan discourses? What does his status tell us about the various types of mafia film produced in Italy? Where does he sit on the discursive spectrum that so often pits 'committed' *impegno* cinema against the seriality of the *filone* production line? For now suffice to say that, after Sergio Leone, his work has attracted more grandiose claims than any other *filone* director. Maitland

McDonagh, for example, adopts the quintessential language of auteurist adulation in *Film Comment* magazine: 'Di Leo was more than a cog in the machine of Italy's ruthlessly au courant cinema of international appropriation ... [His films demonstrate his] ability to take superficially conventional crime stories and invest them with near-operatic emotional impact' (McDonagh 2013: 44, 46). Di Leo's *oeuvre* has also been given the honour of a lovingly compiled two-volume DVD box set for the US market – Raro Video's 'Fernando Di Leo: The Italian Crime Collection' – complete with 'extra' documentaries, in which the director himself indulges in further auteurist self-aggrandisement.[4] This elevated status is, I suggest, due less to the stylistic and textual features of Di Leo's filmmaking or his abilities as a director, and more to the afterlives of his films in anglophone markets. I shall return to this point in more depth in Chapter 5, exploring the drive-in and grindhouse distribution patterns of Italian crime films. Bondanella's epithet for Di Leo – 'King of the B's' – is notable for how it frames him, not in the Italian studio system, but in the North American distribution context of double-bill 'B' features (Bondanella 2009: 459).

The most overt theme of Di Leo's mafia films is one of mob corruption being imbricated within every facet of Italy's civic, political and religious life. An obvious point of continuity with other crime *filoni* comes in the consistent depiction of toothless or corrupt legal structures, crooked cops and politicians in the pockets of gangsters. This is most vividly depicted in *Il boss / The Boss* (Di Leo, 1973), when the Sicilian mob boss Don Corrasco (Richard Conte) collaborates with the corrupt Commissioner Torri (Gianni Garko) to enact politicians' desires in the sanctuary of a cathedral. The scene's dialogue, setting and soundtrack work together to emphasise the extent of mafia influence, both in Italian (and Papal) institutions and abroad. Firstly, a cardinal says to Don Corrasco: 'Thank you for the offerings of your American friends, and for your generosity. Make yourself at home.' Then, church organ music punctuates the conversation as Corrasco reveals the full extent of his influence to Torri:

> Don Corrasco: 'When someone does something for me, I show my appreciation. I'll have you promoted. There are deputies who owe me a lot, and some are there because I got them there.'
>
> Commissioner Torri: 'Right now the authority of the state depends on order, and you appreciate order Don Corrasco. That is why your parliamentary friends and I don't consider you an outlaw. We consider you a collaborator.'

Such an assertion of insidious, far-reaching mafia infiltration had a concrete basis in fact. Dickie's research into the history of *Cosa Nostra* charts in great detail how the organisation took on the attributes of a shadow state, by controlling territory and ruling its subjects, and by infiltrating the various mechanisms of the legal state with its tentacular reach (a common nickname for the mafia is 'la piovra' / 'the octopus') (Dickie 2007: 2).

However, as was the case with the 'conspiracy' *poliziottesco*, it would be a mistake to assume that these connections were being presented as revelatory. As we have seen, in 1970s Italy the notion that instruments of state might be in cahoots with criminal elements was far from a shocking premise, and can instead be approached as an assumed truism. The finer details of the mafia's operations would not become public knowledge until the Falcone investigation in the 1980s, but these films were produced within the same atmosphere of innate distrust as were those analysed in Chapter 2. The above scene's position within this broader epistemological discourse is well illustrated by the accounts of those involved in the production of *Il boss*. Di Leo himself explained (in Gomarasca and Pulici 2011b) that the character of the Cardinal was intended as a reference to the former Archbishop of Palermo Cardinal Ruffini, who had infamously turned a blind eye to the existence of an organised 'mafia' in 1964, publically describing them as 'nothing more than an insignificant minority of criminals' (Merlino 2014: 111). When the dialogue of another scene in *Il boss* named one *mafioso* character 'Gioia', the real-life Christian Democrat politician Giovanni Gioia threatened to sue over the implication that he was involved in mafia activity, but then dropped the case because (as one of the film's actors Pier Paolo Capponi told it), 'you can only sue if it's a lie. There's proof. Everyone knows it. Everyone is talking about it' (Gomarasca and Pulici 2011b). Such a depiction of widespread corruption is therefore in itself entirely unremarkable: more a ritual rehearsal of familiar tropes than a sign of any exceptionally insightful 'understanding of . . . sociopolitical forces' (McDonagh 2013: 46) on Di Leo's part.

Of more interest for the purposes of this book are the ways in which Di Leo's characters repeatedly demonstrate an overt preoccupation with the past. Time and again, the viewer is presented with older *mafiosi* lamenting the passing of a more honourable age, as bygone codes of honour are disregarded by young punks who have no respect. In *Milano calibro 9 / Caliber 9* (Di Leo, 1972), the blind old man Don Vincenzo states: 'They call it the mafia, but today they are just gangs fighting each other . . . The real mafia does not exist any more . . . The real mafia is dead' (Figure 3.1). Don Corrasco in *Il boss* objects to a proposed merger with drug-dealing Calabrian criminals because 'our family is strictly Sicilian . . . The mafia

Figures 3.1 and 3.2 Don Vincenzo in *Milano calibro 9* (Fernando Di Leo, 1972) and Don Corrasco in *Il boss* (Fernando Di Leo, 1973) lament the debasement of modern criminality.

has existed for centuries, and survives because we are Sicilian through bonds of blood, kinship and marriage . . . We can't let them in our family' (Figure 3.2). In a more comedic vein, in *I padroni della città / Rulers of the City* (Di Leo, 1976) the old-timer Napoli lectures a young criminal about his years of training to be a pickpocket, but is mocked because bag-snatching from a scooter is a more modern form of street crime. He later rants that the fun has gone out of being a criminal nowadays, because modern thieves and kidnappers are idiots.

As we shall see, these representations of mafia dons articulating romantic nostalgia for old codes of honour have their roots in a network of pre-existing discourses and well-worn myths from both sides of the Atlantic Ocean. Simultaneously, their fixations on the past are embedded in the immediate concerns of 1970s Italy. In this latter respect, what is striking about the narratives of these films is the kind of events that are lamented as signs of this debased criminality. On top of the elegiac reflections on the passing of a bygone era of close-knit family networks and respect for old values, these *mafioso* protagonists are deployed to bemoan changes that have visited the nation of Italy more broadly since the economic boom of the 1950s.

Milano calibro 9 contains a plot strand that overtly ruminates on the state of contemporary Italy throughout the film, in the ongoing argument between two detectives – one right-wing (played by Frank Wolff), the other left-wing (Luigi Pistilli) – that runs alongside the film's main 'mafia' narrative. A persistent topic of their dispute is the traumatic social change that has been brought about by rapid economic growth, in particular the migration of impoverished southern Italians to the more developed north of the country. The caricatured communist sympathiser Mercuri (Pistilli) sees this as a chief cause for the current crime wave in Milan, repeatedly attacking the reactionary views of his Commissioner (Wolff). When Mercuri is at last punished for his insubordination by being transferred to Basilicata, his parting shot explains his point of view:

> The Americano [the film's head *mafioso*] and the criminals from the south are an effect [rather than a cause] ... The masses of southerners coming to live up north do the most menial jobs, that no one else will do. They're badly paid, they have bad housing and no social benefits. No wonder they turn to crime.

Commissioner Torri in *Il boss* also focuses on this issue, when he says that Sicily's mafia bosses are being forced to move north and are leaving idiots to fill the power vacuum, thus causing chaos in Palermo.

This debate co-exists with other signs that contemporary Italy has been corrupted by socio-economic developments of recent decades. The growing influence of corporate transatlantic power bases is one recurrent manifestation of modernity in Di Leo's mafia films. The plot of *La mala ordina / The Italian Connection* (Di Leo, 1972) depicts the power of global crime syndicates, as a mob boss operating from a New York skyscraper sends representatives to Italy to enforce his orders, effectively relegating the Italian mafia to become an outsourced branch of a multinational corporation. This theme is also visually rendered in *Milano calibro 9*, when Ugo decides to visit the villain known only as 'the Americano', and the camera tilts to register the modernist edifice (Milan's Torre Velasca, as discussed in Chapter 2) in which the crime boss resides.

The laments of Di Leo's old-timer *mafiosi* are also aimed at more recent developments, presented in the films as signs of a licentious young generation with no respect for tradition or family ties, such as the growth of student militancy that had started in 1967. In *Il boss*, the kidnapped daughter of Don Daniello reveals herself to be a student anarchist, as well as a drug addict, an alcoholic and a nymphomaniac, admitting to sleeping with professors and criminals, and ecstatically cavorting with her captors while her honourable elderly *mafioso* father struggles to set her free. *Milano calibro 9* contains Di Leo's most vivid reference to contemporary political strife, when a double bombing occurs at a crowded train station, and the police file on one of the bombers shows that he is a former student protester. Though this is clearly a scene that was produced with the extremist atrocities of the *anni di piombo* in mind, such a parallel is in fact problematic. These 'bombings' are shown not to be the result of political terrorism, but instead of betrayals within criminal underworlds spilling over almost by accident into public arenas. The explosions come from packages that have been exchanged by criminals who are unwitting pawns in the mob war, rather than political fanatics. What is taken by the police to be an act of terror is therefore not the main point of the film, but is instead present as a subordinate narrative device to illustrate the larger theme of a debased new generation of criminals whose lack of respect for old codes of honour leads to reckless violence.

Di Leo's mafia dons, through their concerns with key changes that had visited Italian society since the Second World War – rapid economic growth, increasing American influence, student militancy and the emergence of indiscriminate acts of public violence – therefore stand in as mouthpieces for an Italian polity, with national anxieties transposed onto the mob. This is a revealing choice, perhaps documenting once more how links between criminal organisations and the state were being assumed by *filone* filmmakers in the 1970s. The subtext of Di Leo's films appears to be that the mafia and the state of Italy are intertwined to such an extent that analysis of this point is not required. It is instead a given, and simply a starting point for a broader preoccupation with the 'taking stock' of the 1970s and its historical position. This sense of reflecting on the rapid changes since the Economic Miracle and the tensions of the past thirty years underlies all of the depictions of gang-on-gang violence in these films.

This said, while the assumptions of deep-seated corruption I have diagnosed above were operating within an equivalent world-view to those analysed in Chapter 2, it is important to distinguish the historical specificity of mafia criminality from that of neofascism. The commonplace notion that the mafia is entwined within the Italian state is unsurprising when we consider that the mafia and the Italian nation were born side-by-side, both emerging in the 1860s from the turmoil and aftermath of the *Risorgimento*. With this in mind, Dana Renga argues that the mafia is unlike other national traumas in Italian history, such as the First World War, the Fascist period, the Second World War or the Years of Lead. In each of these cases, a period of latency after the event itself allowed a trauma discourse to emerge in the public sphere, creating a space 'for the psychological impact of traumatizing events to be understood and articulated' (Renga 2013: 4). The permanence of the mafia, however, has meant that no such space for understanding and articulation has existed around it. Instead, Renga diagnoses a process of 'perpetual melancholia' in cultural representations of the mafia, whereby it has been internalised and prolonged, rather than overcome (Renga 2013: 15).

This sense of permanence is at the heart of Di Leo's cinema of assumed corruption, which inherits, recycles and perpetuates a number of pre-existing popular myths about the mafia. In particular, Don Corrasco's claim in *Il boss* that 'the mafia has existed for centuries' is more than simply an example of historical inaccuracy on the part of the filmmakers. This line recycles a long tradition of misconceptions that emerged alongside the mafia itself in the 1860s, when the Kingdom of Italy's ruling classes assumed that it must be a residue of rustic, medieval backwardness in Sicily, rather than a new and highly organised criminal business venture (Dickie 2007: 24). Indeed, Di Leo's broader strategy of deploying *mafiosi* as repositories for elegiac nostalgia has a rich heritage, both at home and abroad.

Hollywood's Mafia Nostalgia

A pivotal sequence in *The Godfather* (Francis Ford Coppola, 1972) begins with Michael Corleone (Al Pacino) greeting old family friend Don Tommasino (Corrado Gaipa) at Michael's Sicilian hiding place. Michael asks how things are in Palermo, and Tommasino replies: 'Young people have no respect anymore. Times are changing.' Two devastating events – the news that his brother Sonny has been assassinated back in New York, and the death of his new wife Apollonia in a car bomb – then befall Michael, and precipitate his return to the USA, where he will pursue revenge on Don Barzini, the culprit for both killings. The fade-out that follows the car bomb then fades back in to a tilt shot emphasising the scale of a downtown New York office block, in which Barzini (Richard Conte) is chairing a meeting of the five New York mafia families. When Don Vito Corleone (Marlon Brando) expresses his opposition to the families entering the narcotics business, Barzini responds: 'Times have changed. It's not like the old days, when we could do anything we want.'

It does not require a huge leap of faith to extrapolate from the above description – which spans less than five minutes of screen time – a line of influence from *The Godfather* (released in Italy in September 1972) into the filmmaking of Fernando Di Leo. The lament at a young generation's disrespect, the tension between an 'old' mafia code of family honour and a 'new' pragmatic move into the lucrative world of drug-dealing, the power of the modern American mob being symbolised by the imposing edifice of a New York office building and – most obviously – the presence of Hollywood gangster film veteran Richard Conte as an old don reflecting on how times have changed all add up to a litany of transatlantic similarities. As this mirroring of Don Corrasco and Don Barzini suggests, *Il boss* (released in February 1973) bears the hallmarks of Coppola's internationally lauded film in a particularly marked fashion. Even Di Leo's symbolic implication of the Catholic Church in mafia activity has a precursor in *The Godfather*, when Michael's final acts of revenge are spliced with the baptism of his nephew in Little Italy's Old St Patrick's Cathedral. The brutal on-screen killings occur as the organ music and the priest's catechism build to an unsettling crescendo, tying the rituals of Catholic piety to those of mafia vengeance.

None of which should come as a surprise to anybody with an understanding of the production practices of Italian *filone* cinema during the 1960s and the 1970s. The oft-quoted line, attributed to Luigi Cozzi, that 'in Italy, when you bring a script to a producer, the first question he asks is not "what is your film like?" but "what *film* is your film like?"' (Hunt 1992: 66) is amusing, pithy and possibly apocryphal. Either way, it emphasises the important role played by Hollywood films that succeeded at the Italian box office as catalysts for the proliferation of *filone* cycles. As already discussed, *Dirty Harry* (Don Siegel, 1971) and *Death Wish* (Michael Winner, 1974) are two notable examples of Hollywood films that gave Italian filmmakers indications of where lucrative returns would likely lie for a given period after their Italian releases. As has also been discussed, however, neither film can straightforwardly be said to have initiated a *filone* cycle, since both the *poliziottesco* and the Italian vigilante film were already in the pipeline prior to their arrival. In much the same vein, the situation under consideration in this chapter is more complex than Di Leo and others simply imitating Coppola's film. Firstly, a number of mafia films had emerged from the Roman studio system prior to *The Godfather* (*Milano calibro 9*, for example, was released in February 1972, a month before *The Godfather*'s US premiere). Secondly, *The Godfather* itself emerged from and responded to pre-existing traditions of representation and stereotyping.

The cultural figure of 'the Italian American' had been a repository for tensions around acculturation and assimilation in US national discourse since before the opening of New York's Ellis Island as a gateway for European immigrants in 1892. Approximately five million Italians, mostly from southern Italy and Sicily, migrated to the US between the 1880s and the beginning of the First World War. Linguistic barriers, along with the persisting absence of a unified Italian national identity, meant that these immigrants tended to live and work in clusters based on their native geographic regions, leading to perceptions that they were peculiarly clannish, insular and averse to assimilation into US society (Warner and Riggio 2012: 212). Fred L. Gardaphé records that these immigrants were slow to represent their own cultures to the American public, 'which enabled others publicly to present Italians any way they pleased' (Gardaphé 2006: xiv). Media stereotypes therefore abounded of a backward, superstitious people whose attachment to their traditional ethnic customs – known as *la via vecchia* ('the old way') – surpassed any desire to partake in the enterprising modernity on offer from US citizenship.

Another stereotype of Italian immigrants that flourished in these years concerned this ethnic group's supposed propensity to violence and organised crime. Bondanella traces cinema's indulgence in such associations back to 1891 New Orleans, when a group of Italians were acquitted of murdering a local sheriff. The rising economic power of the Italian community in the city's docks had led to suspicions, incited by local businessmen, that these immigrants were involved in criminal networks, and the men were lynched amid a wave of anti-Italian press coverage across the USA. Bondanella explains:

> When the American cinema soon afterward began to portray various kinds of emigrants arriving in the urban centers of the North . . . the association of Italian emigrants with the Mafia had already been made and was assumed to be true. Hollywood merely looked to the popular press for its subject matter. (Bondanella 2006: 19)

Warner and Riggio suggest that such stereotypes as the Italian-American crime boss were likely based on the labour agents, known as *padrones*, who provided jobs, housing, and financial and linguistic support for newly arrived Italian immigrants in the late nineteenth and early twentieth centuries (Warner and Riggio 2012: 213). While some of these figures were indeed exploitative, most became respected and loved community leaders, and were referred to as *pappas*:

> The *pappas* played an important part in fostering a more unified Italian-American identity, and a sense of allegiance to the United States. Indeed, some *pappas* believed that the mutual aid societies were created to serve two goals: As one Italian-American leader, Pappa Paolo Russo of New Haven, Connecticut, said, 'We organized mainly for the purpose of promoting our [American] citizenship and preserving at the same time a love for the [Italian] motherland'. (Warner and Riggio 2012: 212)

Even the very act of trying to foster a community identity that allowed for assimilation into US society while retaining links to the Old World was therefore feeding already extant stereotypes of close-knit ghettoes with a propensity for criminality.

As Bondanella points out, such pre-existing modes of representation fed directly into cinematic narratives when they took up the immigrant tale in the first two decades of the twentieth century. Carlos E. Cortés describes such early 'immigrant films' as *The Organ Grinder* (George Melford, 1912), *The Italian* (Reginald Barker, 1915), *Tony America* (Thomas N. Heffron, 1918) and *My Cousin* (Edward José, 1918) as films that portrayed 'people with odd, quaint, humorous customs, but customs that could be "cured" with the proper dose of Americanization. In fact, learning to be American became a common subtext of these early immigrant films.' Moreover, in Hollywood's ethnic roll call, Italian Americans became 'not only . . . popular cultural embodiments of their ethnic group, but also . . . symbols for the ethnic experience in general' (Cortés 1987: 108). In other words, issues of acculturation that lay at the heart of the Italian-American experience translated into cinema to such an extent that this ethnic group became early cinematic shorthand for the traumatic struggle to enter modernity by 'becoming American', and to free oneself of the cultural shackles of the Old World.

These very same tensions around the competing pulls of the Old World and the New that ran throughout Italian-American 'immigrant films' would eventually feed directly into the mafia genre. Indeed, for Robert Casillo, the familial rupture between an ethnic past and a corporate present, manifested in a struggle between older first generation immigrants and a younger second generation, is the very definition of a 'mafia film' as a subset of the more generic 'gangster film' (Casillo 2011: 85). The gangster film is usually traced back to a confluence of circumstances at the beginning of the 1930s, with the socio-economic backdrop of the Great Depression and the tail end of the Prohibition era producing sensationalised headlines around organised crime, ripe for exploitation by Hollywood studios. The two most iconic 'founding texts' of the gangster genre – *Little Caesar* (Mervyn LeRoy, 1931) and *Scarface* (Howard Hawks, 1932), both modelled on the career of second-generation Italian-American gangster Al Capone – were also turning points in the representation of Italian Americans on screen. Casillo argues that the hubristic impulsiveness and self-destructive downfalls of these films' protagonists Rico Bandello (*Little Caesar*) and Tony Camonte (*Scarface*) are presented as components of a stereotypically 'Italian' ethnic coding, embodying a 'national megalomania' redolent of Renaissance duplicity and Mussolini's bombast (Casillo 1991: 377).

Certainly, *Scarface* and *Little Caesar* register long-standing prejudices against Italian Americans in the period after the 1921–4 Federal Immigration Laws restricted immigration from southern and eastern Europe amid renewed fears of criminality from such 'undesirable' parts of the world. However, the fatally flawed, over-reaching nature of these films' central characters is also frequently read as a more general critique of untrammelled capitalism. The 'Italian American' figure again stands in as a generic representative of the 'huddled masses' at Ellis Island, in admonitory morality tales of unrestrained individualism leading to a corruption of the American Dream. They thus typify Robert Warshow's seminal analysis of the wider gangster genre as a 'nightmare inversion of the values of ambition and opportunity' (Warshow 2001: 107).

The origins of the 'mafia film' as a discrete subcategory might instead be charted to *The Black Hand* (Wallace McCutcheon, 1906). This short film dramatises the *Mano Nera* extortion rackets that had been imported from Italy, and were reported to be blighting Italian-American communities in the USA around the turn of the century. The criminals in the film are located firmly, if stereotypically, within the Italian immigrant experience in New York through their wine-swilling and their pidgin English (their extortion note to the butcher warns 'Bewar!! We are desperut!'). Bondanella points out that the butcher's actions in response to the threat constitutes a rejection of *la via vecchia* and *omertà*, and an embrace of 'the American way' of reporting crimes to the police like a good citizen (a trope that is repeated in the opening moments of *The Godfather* when Bonasera tells Don Corleone that he also 'went to the police, like a good American', but has been left unsatisfied with the US justice system) (Bondanella 2006: 179).

By Casillo's definition, the mafia genre that flourished in the 1970s is distinguished from the larger gangster genre by its inheritance of this 'immigrant film' conflict between the Old World and the New. Representations of Italians as gangsters persisted throughout the twentieth century, occasionally (as in the case of *The Black Hand* (Richard Thorpe, 1950)) examining the historical roots of this phenomenon. The mafia genre of the 1960s and 1970s, however, is characterised by its specific focus on issues of acculturation through the prism of second-generation Italian Americans. By analysing *The Brotherhood* (Martin Ritt, 1968) as a 'prelude' to *The Godfather*'s supposedly foundational status within this genre, Casillo identifies a common theme of generational conflict setting parental pressure to remain loyal to one's ethnic roots against the attempt to assimilate into US-led modernity. Ritt's and Coppola's films share 'exploration of Mafia familism, tradition, social codes, and Old World origins manifest in a contemporary Italian-American criminal family . . . torn apart by the ultimately irreconcilable claims of the ethnic past and corporate present' (Casillo 2011: 85). Ever since the Senate's Kefauver Committee hearings of 1950–1 had brought the word 'Mafia' back into US national discourse, it had been replete with Old World associations.

The Godfather's cross cutting between a sun-baked Sicily and the muted browns and shadowy interiors of New York renders this generational conflict in stark visual terms. The two-way pull of ancestral roots and vibrant modernity is encapsulated when Michael Corleone has just arrived in Sicily and is framed amid a pastoral idyll of sheep farming, mountains and his father's picturesque home town of Corleone (actually filmed in the hill-towns of Savoca and Forza d'Agrò). Michael's Sicilian companions immediately register their own desire to travel in the opposite direction by stating that the town's menfolk are all dead due to vendettas, and then shouting at passing jeeps full of American GIs: 'take me to America! Clark Gable! Rita Hayworth!' Indeed, the allure of the USA for Europeans weary of conflict and poverty is one of *The Godfather*'s core themes, embodied in the character of Michael's father, Vito. Anthony Julian Tamburri has analysed the costumes worn by Marlon Brando in his portrayal of Vito, observing that his meeting with Solozzo (at which he rejects the offer to become involved in the modern mob's move towards drug trafficking) comprises six men in smart business suits, and Don Corleone 'dressed like any other immigrant grandfather' in a brown jacket and olive green shirt. This, added to the subsequent scene at the fruit and vegetable market, leads Tamburri to argue: 'More than a gangster film, at this juncture, it seems we are viewing an immigrant saga' (Tamburri 2011: 96–7).

The elegiac laments at the passing of a nobler age to be found in the mafia films of Fernando Di Leo are therefore part of a much larger transatlantic discourse surrounding the tension between ethnic or national identity and corporate modernity. The historical facts that *Cosa Nostra* was only just over a hundred years old in the 1970s, or that 'there never was a traditional mafia that then became more modern, organized and business minded' (Dickie 2007: 8), are less relevant here than the myths that had been attached to the mafia since its inception, and that were perpetuated by cinematic representations. Don Corrasco's erroneous claim in *Il boss* that 'the mafia has existed for centuries' should be considered in the context of these ongoing myths. In *The Godfather: Part II* (Francis Ford Coppola, 1974), Kay (Diane Keaton) begins to articulate the very same fallacy, before she is cut off by her husband Michael Corleone hitting her, when she says that their relationship cannot work due to 'this Sicilian thing, that's been going on for two thousand yea . . .'. The 'mafia film' was intrinsically a genre of nostalgia, framing *Cosa Nostra* as a manifestation of ancient 'Old World' traditions.

What is particularly interesting, for the purposes of this book, is to see a cinematic trope that pertained specifically to the experiences of second-generation Italian immigrants to the USA – crises in ethnic loyalty, tensions surrounding acculturation and integration, nostalgia for Old World customs – being appropriated by filmmakers in Italy itself in the 1970s. The Hollywood mafia film is always already a chronicle of cultural displacement and identity crisis. That it was recycled by the *filone* production line in the wake of *The Godfather*'s box-office success was of course an example of what Wagstaff describes as 'tailoring a product to a . . . market' (Wagstaff 2013: 39). Yet this process should not be dismissed as merely fiscal opportunism, since there was already a sporadic tradition of Italian mafia films before Coppola's international blockbuster. Danielle Hipkins explains: 'we might presume that . . . mafia [media] forms are more or less constantly present in Italian daily life, but it is only in particular generic forms and historical moments that they are articulated in its media culture' (Gordon et al. 2013: 226). Such 'moments' therefore require careful examination, if we are to understand the evolution and cultural significance of mafia films in Italy. We have already seen that 1970s Italy can broadly be characterised by an impression that society had changed beyond recognition in the preceding decades. Certainly, the very fact that Hollywood offered a suitable paradigm for an elegiac reflection on ancient Italian customs registers an attendant cultural shift in and of itself, but Italian representations of the mafia had also long invested in discourses around the past.

A Window into Italy's Past

Dana Renga draws a distinction between mafia films made in the USA and those made in Italy by stating that, while Italian filmmakers frequently demonstrate the insidious reach of the mafia into both politics and everyday life, 'American filmmakers . . . tend to glamourize organized crime, and create sympathetic mobsters that many of us would like to invite over for dinner' (Renga 2011: 4). In her introduction to the edited collection *Mafia Movies: A Reader*, Renga thus identifies a repeated pattern in the book's section on US mafia films, whereby '"family" stands out as a key theme [and] generational conflicts are foregrounded'. The section on Italian mafia films, on the other hand, tends to focus on 'directors most well known for their work on political cinema, such as Pietro Germi, Elio Petri, Francesco Rosi, or Damiano Damiani' (Renga 2011: 7).

I do not seek to reject this distinction, since it more or less accurately describes the thematic make-up of two important forms of mafia cinema, but any such binary constructions invite the identification of exceptions. As we have seen, Fernando Di Leo also depicts the mafia's insidious reach to address his nation's contemporary political preoccupations. Yet he simultaneously deploys 'Hollywood' stereotypes of generational conflict and old codes of family honour. He therefore seems to sit uneasily between these two forms. In truth, the boundaries between 'local' politically engaged mafia cinema and 'imported' Hollywood formats were not so clear-cut as the above distinction might suggest. In the previous chapter, I argued that politically 'committed' *cinema d'impegno* and 'serial' *filone* films can be distinguished by their modes of political address and their production contexts, and that the *filone* product should therefore not be judged according to the assumptions of conventional textual analysis. This remains a central methodological argument of this book, and I will be pursuing a related point in the final section of this chapter. This is not, however, to say that these two forms are mutually exclusive where their relationship to Hollywood genre convention is concerned, since such influences are to be found throughout Italian cinema from the post-war era onwards. Dom Holdaway analyses two examples of the mafia *filone* – namely, *I padroni della città / Rulers of the City* (Di Leo, 1976) and *Tony Arzenta / No Way Out* (Duccio Tessari, 1973) – alongside the more celebrated *impegno* film *Lucky Luciano* (Francesco Rosi, 1973). Holdaway takes Di Leo's and Tessari's films as serial examples of 'repetitive consumability', in contrast to Rosi's more analytical attempts to alienate the spectator. He also argues, however, for an underlying equivalence between all three films' complex engagements with the Hollywood gangster genre: 'It is possible to view genre conventions . . . as a more concretized aesthetic instance of commodification which permeates both modes of representation, either via conformity or rejection' (Holdaway 2013b: 44, 133).

Indeed, as has been explored in Chapter 1, a number of Italian crime films whose cultural capital and critical esteem far outstrip those of the *filone* production line have been analysed for their recourse to Hollywood genre conventions. *In nome della legge / In the Name of the Law* (Pietro Germi, 1949) is described by Pasquale Iannone as both 'one of the first Italian sound films to explore seriously the phenomenon of the Sicilian Mafia' and a film that '[draws] on the iconography of the Western genre' (Iannone 2016: 49, 57). Its narrative structure of a lawman arriving in a remote town with the intention of 'civilising' the townsfolk resembles one of the Western genre's most recognisable and enduring tropes, from the silent era (*Desert Love* (Jacques Jaccard, 1920), *Bells of San Juan* (Scott Dunlap, 1922)) to the post-war prestige Western (*My Darling Clementine* (John Ford, 1946)) and beyond (*High Noon* (Fred Zinnemann, 1952)). One particularly striking manifestation of Germi's debt to the Western comes when the mafia boss Passalacqua and his men appear on the horizon on horseback to intimidate the lawman and representative of modern civilisation, Pretore Schiavi. This depiction echoes another recurrent and instantly recognisable trope of the Hollywood genre: that of native tribesmen, framed as if they are an elemental component of the menacing wilderness.

The above comparisons with the Western provide a valuable insight into the visibility and reach of US popular culture in post-war Italy – infusing not only the products of a putative 'mass' culture, but also those of the supposedly inward-looking 'neorealist' trend – but drawing too direct an influence from Hollywood would risk obscuring the local significance of these modes of representation. That *In nome della legge* depicts *mafiosi* as being 'of the land' in a comparable manner to the dominant framing of Native Americans returns us to the widespread misconceptions around the mafia's ancient heritage cited at the start of this chapter. The film's opening voiceover, which accompanies a long shot of the Sicilian landscape, encapsulates a sense that the film's subject matter possesses atavistic roots:

> This land, this boundless solitude crushed by the sun, is Sicily: not only the pleasant gardens of oranges, olives and flowers . . . but also a bare, burnt land of blinding white walls, and men steeped in ancient customs that outsiders cannot comprehend. A mysterious and splendid world, of tragic and harsh beauty.

Accordingly, the *mafioso* natives who later ride over the horizon on horseback are shown to be bound to the fertile Sicilian soil, when Passalacqua explains to Schiavi that the olive harvest has been taking up all of his time.

Il giorno della civetta / Day of the Owl (Damiano Damiani, 1968) inherits the dual identity of Germi's film, by simultaneously utilising tropes from the Western genre while investing in modes of representing Sicily that had a long pedigree on the Italian peninsula. For Piero Garofalo, this film 'transposes the Wild West, with its heroes, villains, and innocent townsfolk onto another fictive world, the indomitable isle . . . defamiliariz[ing] the Mafia tale by making it both recognizable and strange' (Garofalo 2011: 252). As in *In nome della legge*, so in *Il giorno della civetta* a young lawman arrives in a Sicilian town determined to end mafia lawlessness, before encountering the entrenched *omertà* of the local populace. Garofalo also points to other features of the film that evoke the Western besides this narrative structure, such as the cast (Franco Nero, Claudia Cardinale, Lee J. Cobb) and the cinematographer (Tonino Delli Colli), all of whom carried associations with this genre by 1968. Again, the identification of such parallels throws some light on Italy's post-war encounter with US popular culture, though Garofalo does not investigate Hollywood Westerns but instead focuses on those made by Sergio Leone and Damiani himself (most notably *Quién sabe? / A Bullet for the General* (1967)). The attendant risk of seeking out these parallels with the Western, however, is once again one of neglecting the more local significance of the film's representations. Holdaway criticises Garofalo's argument for overlooking the extent to which the depictions of an underdeveloped Sicilian landscape in *In nome della legge* and *Il giorno della civetta* rely on 'a specifically *present-tense* depiction of a complex and morally ambiguous society in order to comment critically upon it', as opposed to the Western's dependence on nostalgia for an imagined pre-industrial past (Holdaway 2013b: 161–2).

Il giorno della civetta's engagement with the Sicilian landscape is indeed rooted firmly in its contemporaneous moment, holding the island's backwardness up as a gauge for Italy's broader pretentions towards modernity. The construction of a new road through the middle of the countryside is the ever-present focal point of the narrative, as both a setting for mafia business interests and a symbol for *Cosa Nostra*'s immutable entwinement within Sicilian culture. The film's denouement comes as Captain Bellodi (Franco Nero), having spent most of the film trying to uncover the truth behind the mysterious disappearance of Nicolosi only to be frustrated by the enduring *omertà* of the townsfolk, orders a section of the new road to be dug up. A body is discovered in the concrete, but Bellodi's assumption that it is Nicolosi is frustrated when the victim's face is turned around to reveal the informer Parineddu. The horrors of mafia violence here literally lurk just beneath the surface of Italy's attempts to modernise its benighted regions, but even the concrete – the physical manifestation of mafia business interests – refuses to give up carefully guarded secrets to the police. *Il giorno della civetta* therefore rejects stereotypes of a picturesque Sicily, only to embrace and utilise other stereotypes: a land of entrenched *omertà*, in which the mafia remains an entity 'at one' with the land even as it scars the landscape with its vast construction sites.

This notion of the mafia being somehow bound up with the Sicilian soil is of course a mythic construction. It does, however, arise from a rich heritage of representation surrounding the southern regions of Italy (known collectively as the *Mezzogiorno*),[5] which had been cast as a window into the primal past of the peninsula since at least the eighteenth century. The Marquis de Sade, for example, reacted with revulsion at the barbarousness of Naples in 1776, but identified therein a 'blessing for Europe' in the fact that 'there are belated provinces like these whose backwardness enables us to measure the progress of the others' (cited in Moe 2002: 64). In 1854, the French journalist Alfred Maury saw himself travelling back in time as he journeyed south:

> As one moves down into Italy . . . the look of the customs and populations takes you back into the past. In Milan and Turin, one finds modern society . . . in Florence it is

like the time of the Medicis . . . In Rome you are immersed in the Middle Ages . . . In Naples, we reenter the pagan era . . . Move from there into Puglia, into the principality of Salerno, and the customs present themselves to you with all the naive simplicity of ancient times. (Cited in Moe 2002: 38)

Such stereotypes became a source of anxiety amongst intellectuals and lawmakers once the Kingdom of Naples had been subsumed into the Italian nation in 1860. The *questione meridionale* ('Southern Question') arose from Pasquale Villari's *Lettere meridionali* ('Southern Letters') of 1875, which called for governmental intervention to alleviate the socio-economic chasm between landowners and peasants in the southern regions. The enduring cultural–political role allocated to Italy's south as a result is described by Dickie as 'the testing-ground of Italy's modernity, the measure of its claims to civility, and the focus of national solidarity' (Dickie 1999: 56).

The discursive construction of 'the south of Italy', then, had long served as a gauge against which the nation would measure how far it had progressed towards Western conceptions of modernity. Though Maury did not include Sicily in his vivid account (the logic of his timeline would presumably have portrayed it as a portal into prehistoric times), Nelson Moe explains that the island was frequently framed 'as the southernmost part of Italy, the "deep" south, if you will, where the southern characteristics not only of the *Mezzogiorno* but of Italy as a whole manifest themselves in their most powerful, essential form' (Moe 2002: 42). In the years after unification, 'mafia' became a component part of this system of representation, whereby a supposed southern propensity toward degenerate violence was to be found in its most savage form at its most southerly point. Dickie has collated a number of sources that equated notions of southern barbarism, agrarian *sicilianità* and mafia. One such example is Alfredo Niceforo's assertion in 1898 that, while northern crimes are usually of a sophisticated inclination (such as fraud), southern crimes instead arise from medieval impulses and involve brutal violence brought about by brigandage or mafia (Dickie 1999: 2). Another is Leopoldo Franchetti's 1876 publication *Condizioni politiche e amministrative della Sicilia*, which diagnosed the rise of the mafia to be a sign of Sicily's failed transition from feudalism to capitalism. Franchetti's sweeping use of the words 'Sicily', 'mafia' and 'violence' as what Dickie terms 'an inverted mirror image' of liberal capitalism led to him being accused of pioneering 'a socioanthropological tradition according to which the mafia is virtually indistinguishable from Sicilian culture per se' (Dickie 1999: 65–6).

Post-*Risorgimento* assumptions that the mafia was an ancient phenomenon (cited at the start of this chapter) were tied to this larger sense of incredulity that Sicily was still a relic of the past. As Dickie explains:

> The interior of Sicily was a metaphor for everything Italy wanted to leave behind. The great estates were worked by droves of hungry peasants who were exploited by brutal bosses. Many Italians hoped and believed that the mafia was a symptom of this kind of backwardness and poverty, that it was destined to disappear as soon as Sicily emerged from its isolation and caught up with the historical timetable. (Dickie 2007: 24–5)

Moreover, Sicily's historical association with banditry and brigandage reached a peak in the immediate aftermath of the *Risorgimento* – at the very time the mafia was emerging – when the Italian army fought a protracted campaign against rural guerrillas in the southern regions. Northern military conceptions of southern brigandage tended to frame the phenomenon as a force of nature, bound up with the land itself: 'everyone says it exists, but no one knows where it is' (Gaetano Negri); 'it is occult, mysterious, absolutely vast, extremely widespread and intangible' (Alessandro Bianco di Saint Jorioz) (cited in Dickie 1999: 33).

Portrayals of the mafia as an elemental force of the Sicilian landscape are therefore not surprising. Rather, the various components of this broad network of stereotyping – the mafia among them – took on the *Mezzogiorno*'s dual role in the national imaginary as a site of archaic residues from a bygone era and a forum for taking stock of the contemporary moment in relation to that benighted past. This is particularly evident in Giuseppe Tomasi di Lampedusa's 1958 novel *Il gattopardo / The Leopard* and Luchino Visconti's 1963 cinematic adaptation, the latter of which is described by Elizabeth Leake as 'an uncontested (and often unacknowledged) prototype for many of the subsequent films that deal with the Sicilian Mafia' (Leake 2011: 234). Taking place in the immediate aftermath of Garibaldi's 1860 invasion of Sicily in the name of a unified Italy, *Il gattopardo* dwells on the historical turning point of its setting by utilising well-worn stereotypes of the island. The aristocrat Don Fabrizio (Burt Lancaster) is self-consciously a representative of both the old order, and of Sicily:

> We are old . . . very old. For twenty-five centuries we have borne magnificent civilisations: all from abroad, none made by us . . . we are very tired, empty, burnt out . . . A long sleep is what the Sicilians want, and they'll always hate those who want to wake them.

Sicily is here framed in its familiar position as both an archaic bulwark against modernity, and a vehicle to examine Italy's historical advancement. Moreover, Leake argues that, though the word 'mafia' is only mentioned once in both the book and the film, the images of Sicily that are propagated by Visconti set the template for subsequent cinematic mafia representations: for example, when the northerner Chevalley is terrified by tales of a person going missing and being returned to his family piece-by-piece; or the figure of Don Calogero, whose shady business interests, nascent property empire and rigging of an election make him a *mafioso* in all but name. As Leake suggests, such tropes 'seem to retroactively legitimate the Siciliano *equals* Mafioso equation' by their assumed entwinement within the fabric of Sicilian society (Leake 2011: 237).

It is particularly telling that one of *Il gattopardo*'s central debates around the island's political upheavals takes place amidst the rugged beauty of the Sicilian countryside, when Don Fabrizio and Ciccio discuss the rigging of the plebiscite, the growing influence of Don Calogero and the implications for the Sicilian aristocracy of Garibaldi's victory. Ciccio reveals the suspicions of murder and corruption that surround Calogero's past from a high point overlooking a grand vista of the mountainous interior. The feudal past, the volatile present and the emergent mafia are thereby intertwined in their association with the landscape. Fabrizio's later attribution of Sicily's volatility to 'this environment, the violence of the landscape, the cruelty of the climate' reinforces this message by rehearsing more age-old stereotypes. In the words of Montesquieu's *The Spirit of the Laws* (1748), 'in northern climates, you shall find peoples who have few vices . . . Draw near the southern climates, and you will think you have left morality itself far behind' (cited in Moe 2002: 24).

This conflation of Sicily's natural environment with the island's culture, politics and history positions them as equivalently primeval, immutable and resistant to change. Fabrizio's son Tancredi (Alain Delon) famously explains his support for the *Garibaldini* by saying that the transition to Savoyard rule is the only way to preserve their aristocratic ways of life in the long term: 'if we want things to stay the same, everything has to change'. On this point, Leake compares Don Fabrizio's speech about the Sicilians' desire for 'a long sleep' with the rallying cry for Sicilian independence uttered by Don Pietro in *Salvatore Giuliano* (Francesco Rosi, 1961): 'Sicily, awaken! Your shameful slumber has lasted far too long' (Leake 2011: 237–8). The cinematography of Rosi's film similarly makes use of the Sicilian landscape: most notably, with a one-and-a-half minute panning shot from a high point in the hills. The voiceover points out the various settlements and the grand mountain range stretching into the distance, before the shot slowly locates and then zooms into the town of Montelepre: '[Salvatore] Giuliano's kingdom, protected by *omertà*, passion and terror.' As the camera scans the maze of tightly packed buildings and narrow streets, it is explained that the *Carabinieri* have been unable to find the notorious outlaw. Indeed, Rosi also denies his audience the chance to locate Giuliano, both here and in the rest of the film, in which the character only appears briefly at the edge of shot or in the background, or as a dead body. The desired effect is to compel the viewer to search for the elusive truth behind the life and death of Sicily's 'last bandit'. In so doing, these shots serve to frame him in a familiar cultural position as an elemental force of nature, hidden amongst the mountains alongside the island's other historical brigands.

Neither *Il gattopardo* nor *Salvatore Giuliano* are 'mafia films' per se, but both frame their subject matter as turning points in Sicily's history in which the mafia played a decisive role (Leake 2011: 238). Moreover, subsequent films that were more directly 'about' the mafia – notably those directed by Damiano Damiani – inherit many of these films' tropes. The untouched beauty of *Il gattopardo*'s scenic shots is doomed to become the mafia-run building sites of *Il giorno della civetta* and *Confessione di un commissario di polizia al procuratore della repubblica / Confessions of a Police Captain* (Damiani, 1971). Both of these films continue to dwell on the Sicilian landscape, even as it is being despoiled.

Confessione di un commissario di polizia (as I shall henceforth abbreviate the title) is set almost exclusively amidst the rapidly changing cityscape of Palermo, whose concrete edifices are shown to contain similarly gruesome secrets to those of the new road in *Il giorno della civetta*. One scene stands out as an exception, when Bonavia (Martin Balsam) takes Traini (Franco Nero) to a remote mountaintop, to tell him a story about a union organiser who fell foul of the mafia ten years previously. The jaded Commissario Bonavia ('haven't you ever had any doubts about enforcing unjust laws?') and the by-the-book District Attorney Traini ('it's not for us to judge the law but to enforce it') go on to discuss the morality of enforcing codified law in the light of this brutal local history. *Perché si uccide un magistrato / How to Kill a Judge* (Damiano Damiani, 1975) almost replicates this scene, when Solaris (Franco Nero) and Antonia Traini (Françoise Fabian) argue over the morality of Solaris's actions in accusing Antonia's late husband of mafia-related corruption, while they stand on yet another viewpoint overlooking a vista of the mountainous Sicilian interior. Both films therefore reproduce *Il gattopardo*'s trope of framing such locations as a common sense setting for the contemplation of Sicilian politics and history.

We can therefore see a pattern of Italian mafia films inheriting dominant modes of representing and stereotyping Sicily and the broader *Mezzogiorno*. Holdaway's argument that comparisons with the Western fall short is predicated upon a lack of nostalgia in these depictions of such underdeveloped regions, which should instead be thought of in terms of the archetypes from *Il gattopardo*, whereby 'the tensions between present and past are at [the] root of . . . continued mafia domination' (Holdaway 2013b: 162). In other words, Italian mafia films' inheritance from Lampedusa and Visconti goes beyond the stereotypes of brutality and corruption surrounding Don Calogero. Sicily's long-established role as a forum for contemplating the state of contemporary Italy in relation both to the past and to prevailing conceptions of modernity also makes the transition into this cinematic genre.[6] Though markedly different in tone to Hollywood mafia films' frequently elegiac emphasis on ancient 'Old World' traditions, generational conflict and acculturation to the modern world, the Italian mafia film remains a genre fixated on the past, even while it is set firmly in its contemporary moment.

The Mafia *Filone*

Perché si uccide un magistrato tells the story of a film director (played by Franco Nero) whose latest release indirectly accuses Judge Traini (Marco Guglielmi) of collusion with the mafia. An early scene shows Traini and his deputy De Fornari (Pierluigi Aprà) watching the film in question with amused detachment, discussing the resemblance of its scenes to actual mafia crimes while observing that the names have been changed. One scene in particular catches Traini's eye, as two policemen enter a parked car. 'Boom!', exclaims Traini, moments before the car bomb explodes. As the screen is then filled with debris, Traini says: 'Avrei giurato che lo facevano rallentatore' / 'I knew they would use slow motion.'

The self-reflexivity of the above sequence is hard to miss. When Traini and De Fornari discuss the extent to which the film resembles real-life events, just three minutes of screen time have passed since *Perché si uccide un magistrato* has itself opened with its own fictitious disclaimer: 'Gli avvenimenti, i personaggi, e i nomi di questo film sono immaginari ed ogni riferimento a persone, cose e fatti della vita reale, è del tutto casuale' / 'The events, characters and names in this film are imaginary and any reference to people or events in real life is accidental.' The fact that Traini is able to act as a cinematic soothsayer, predicting not only the on-screen events but also the manner in which they are filmed, however, suggests a wider critique that Italian mafia films in the 1970s had become predictable and repetitious. Curti speculates that Damiani is here 'critically rethinking the stylistic devices and plot clichés of politically-committed films' (Curti 2013: 136). Whether this accurately identifies Damiani's intentions or not, the broader implication – that predictability, repetitiveness and cliché are undesirable in films dealing with such a 'serious' political subject as the mafia – warrants more detailed consideration in this particular period of Italian filmmaking, beyond the critique of *cinema d'impegno* hinted at by Curti.

As stated earlier, a handful of mafia films had emerged from the *filone* production line prior to *The Godfather*, but the significant success[7] of this film on the *prima visione* circuit upon its release in September 1972 (as *Il padrino*) was accompanied by a sudden upsurge, which lasted for a period of around nineteen months. Table 3.1 shows my attempt to chart this period of proliferation, which will provide the focus for the remainder of this chapter. This list is inescapably subjective, since all three of the descriptors I am using in it – 'Italian', 'mafia' and '*filone*' – are potentially ambiguous. For the purposes of this table, an 'Italian film' is one produced or co-produced by an Italian studio. A 'mafia film' is here one whose narrative revolves chiefly around the activities of organised criminals. This distinguishes these films from the many *poliziotteschi* and vigilante films that feature gangsters as secondary characters or villains, but whose plots are more focused on a protagonist's efforts to fight such crime (such as *Città violenta*, discussed in Chapter 2). At the same time, the category includes *Il poliziotto è marcio* / *Shoot First, Die Later* (Fernando Di Leo, 1974), since this film's policeman protagonist is working for the mafia, whose activities form the main narrative focus. Finally, a '*filone*' film is here loosely defined as one that is exploiting already successful thrills or gratifications in a rapid production schedule to maximise profits, in a manner akin to what Wagstaff describes as a 'pay-off' (Wagstaff 1992: 253). I have omitted the explicit *Godfather* parody *L'altra faccia del padrino* / *The Funny Face of the Godfather* (Franco Prosperi, 1973) from the list, because of its undisguised and programmatic reliance on the source text. This *filone*'s more covert opportunism is better illustrated by films that were largely unrelated to Coppola's blockbuster having the word 'padrino' inserted into their titles, such as *La mano lunga del padrino* / *The Long Arm of the Godfather* (Nardo Bonomi, 1972) (which was released the month before *The Godfather* arrived on Italian screens, demonstrating a canny approach to future profits), *L'amico del padrino* / *The Godfather's Friend* (Frank Agrama, 1972) and *La padrina* / *Lady Dynamite* (Giuseppe Vari, 1973).[8]

Table 3.1 Italian mafia *filone* films, August 1972–March 1974.

Italian release title	English language release title	Director	Italian release date
I familiari delle vittime non saranno avvertiti	Crime Boss	Alberto De Martino	August 1972
La mano lunga del padrino	The Long Arm of the Godfather	Nardo Bonomi	August 1972
Camorra	Gang War in Naples	Pasquale Squitieri	August 1972
La mala ordina	The Italian Connection	Fernando Di Leo	September 1972
Torino nera	–	Carlo Lizzani	September 1972
Afyon oppio	The Sicilian Connection	Ferdinando Baldi	December 1972
L'amico del padrino	The Godfather's Friend	Frank Agrama	December 1972
Il boss	The Boss	Fernando Di Leo	February 1973
Gli amici degli amici hanno saputo	–	Fulvio Marcolin	February 1973
Milano rovente	Gang War in Milan	Umberto Lenzi	February 1973
Baciamo le mani	Family Killer	Vittorio Schiraldi	February 1973
La padrina	Lady Dynamite	Giuseppe Vari	March 1973
La mano nera	The Black Hand	Antonio Racioppi	March 1973
L'onorata famiglia – Uccidere è cosa nostra	The Big Family	Tonino Ricci	March 1973
La legge della Camorra	The Godfather's Advisor	Demofilo Fidani	July 1973
Il consigliori	Counselor at Crime	Alberto De Martino	August 1973
Servo suo	Your Honor	Romano Scavolini	September 1973
Tony Arzenta	No Way Out	Duccio Tessari	September 1973
Anna, quel particolare piacere	Secrets of a Call Girl	Giuliano Carnimeo	November 1973
Quelli che contano	Cry of a Prostitute	Andrea Bianchi	January 1974
I guappi	Blood Brothers	Pasquale Squitieri	February 1974
Crazy Joe	–	Carlo Lizzani	February 1974
Il poliziotto è marcio	Shoot First, Die Later	Fernando Di Leo	March 1974

Returning to my earlier dismissal of auteurist approaches to the filmmaking of Fernando Di Leo, it is only once we place his films in this much broader context of rapidly produced variations on a theme that they can be adequately understood in their industrial and cultural surroundings. The elegiac laments of Di Leo's elderly *mafiosi* bewildered by the rate of change, for example, are best comprehended as constituent parts of a series of repetitions. From Table 3.1 alone, each of *I familiari delle vittime non saranno avvertiti*, *La mano lunga del padrino*, *Camorra*, *Afyon oppio*, *L'amico del padrino*, *Baciamo le mani*, *Il consigliori* and *Crazy Joe* contain scenes of younger generations either disrespecting 'traditional' values or seeking to overthrow their elders to gain control of their mafia 'families'. The utterances of some of these films' old-timers resemble each other so closely as to seemingly merge into one continuous lament:

> He is not one of those young men that we see these days who have no respect, not for their fathers, their mothers or their family (Don Calogero in *Afyon oppio*).
>
> It was better in the old days: more restraint. More respect among the families (Poselli in *L'amico del padrino*).
>
> Young people don't have respect any more. They are impulsive, they take matters into their own hands, and they are convinced that they are always right (Don Santino in *Baciamo le mani*).
>
> You are men of respect. Young people today are very different (Don Antonio in *Il consigliori*).

Picking up where I left off in Chapter 2, this mafia *filone* constitutes another process of serial repetition, whose films operate in constant dialogue with both one another and with a diverse set of external influences, rather than as self-contained narrative units. Amanda Ann Klein and R. Barton Palmer categorise such instances of texts being innately joined to other texts as 'multiplicities', in which the 'reuse, reconfiguration, and extension of existing materials, themes, images, formal conventions or motifs' enable the economies of scale upon which commercial mass media have always relied. Phenomena such as genres, series, remakes, adaptations, cycles and spin-offs thereby facilitate 'the continuing provision of a sameness marked indelibly by difference' (Klein and Palmer 2016: 1, 3). This latter phrase is a particularly apt description for the mafia *filone*'s most fertile period of proliferation (outlined in Table 3.1). These films are often diverse in terms of setting, timescale and *mise en scène* – ranging from 1891 Naples (*I guappi*) and 1900 New York (*La mano nera*), to contemporary Rome (*I familiari delle vittime non saranno avvertiti*), Turin (*Torino nera*), Milan (*Milano rovente*) and San Francisco (*Il consigliori*), as well as the more common Sicilian settings – but they replicate certain themes time and again in a maze of intertextual references.

The sometimes bewildering nature of these films' multifarious routes of influence can be demonstrated on a superficial level through two brief examples. Firstly, in *Afyon oppio*, key roles are occupied by Corrado Gaipa (who played Don Tommasino in *The Godfather*, and would go on to appear in *Il boss*, *Baciamo le mani*, *La mano nera*, *Tony Arzenta* and *Anna, quel particolare piacere*), Fausto Tozzi (who was in the mafia prison film *The Valachi Papers* (Terence Young, 1972), and would later appear in *Quelli che contano*), Luciano Catenacci (who played the main mafia boss in *Confessione di un commissario di polizia*, and would later appear in *Perché si uccide un magistrato*) and Carlo Gaddi (who appears in *I familiari delle vittime non saranno avvertiti*, *La padrina* and *Il consigliori*). The Italian-American protagonist of *Afyon oppio* is named Coppola (an unmissable reference two months after the Italian release of *The Godfather*), while its English-language title ('The Sicilian Connection'), along with its international drug-smuggling plot, is a blatant attempt to cash in on the success of *The French Connection* (William Friedkin, 1971). Moreover, Corrado Gaipa's character is a Sicilian mafia boss with family connections in New York (echoing his *Godfather* role), and is named Don Calogero (echoing *Il gattopardo*).

Secondly, before the credits have even rolled in *L'onorata famiglia - Uccidere è cosa nostra*, we are shown Richard Conte (who would later portray *mafiosi* in *Tony Arzenta*, *Anna, quel particolare piacere* and *Il poliziotto è marcio*) as a mafia boss in Palermo running a Sicilian property development business, and waging a war with another boss over land contracts: a fusion of the actor's previous roles in *The Godfather* and *Il boss*. The rival boss is played by Raymond Pellegrin (who also appears in *Camorra*, *I guappi* and *Il poliziotto è marcio*), and the film's plot partly revolves around the character of Commissario La Manna: a young, eager cop who has asked to be transferred to Sicily to fight the mafia (in an echo of *In nome della legge*, *Il giorno della civetta* and *Confessione di un commissario di polizia*).

The above gives us just a taste of the extent to which these films provide their viewers with a peculiar sense of déjà vu, as a catalogue of echoes and half-remembered recollections from an amalgam of other mafia films, from both sides of the Atlantic and with little heed for supposed *filone / impegno* boundaries. One intriguing example of such repetition comes when the brakes of key characters' cars are tampered with, resulting in frenzied drives through the Sicilian mountains as key 'pay-off' sequences in both *La padrina* and *L'onorata famiglia – Uccidere è cosa nostra*, which were released in the same month (March 1973), by different production companies. This is not therefore simply a case of films imitating other films, so much as a collection of references to mafia activities and myths, which emerged in rapid succession from an industry eager to capitalise on a profitable format.

Of course, the most obvious point of reference for such financial opportunism was *The Godfather*, and the mafia *filone* is naturally well equipped with similarities to and quotations of this film, beyond the aforementioned links through casting and titling. These are occasionally direct and explicit – as when Barresi (Anthony Steffen) walks past a poster for *Il padrino* in the streets of Palermo in *La padrina* – but more often come in the form of allusive echoes, which recall but never quite replicate the source text. For example, early on in *Baciamo le mani*, Don Angelino's flashback to his son Stefano's wedding dance is clearly designed to resemble the opening scene of *The Godfather*. The party takes place in a sun-dappled courtyard, where the elderly head of the family is surrounded by his four sons and his *consigliere*, and greets other *mafiosi* (some of whom will soon betray him) as his guests. This mafia war, however, is caused by land deals and construction contracts in Palermo, making this film the hybrid progeny of Mario Puzo and Leonardo Sciascia (the authors of *The Godfather*'s and *Il giorno della civetta*'s source novels respectively). *La padrina* similarly opens with an overt *Godfather* reference, when the five mafia families of New York declare peace, which is then abruptly shattered by the assassination of Cavallo (who is called 'The Godfather' in the newspaper headline that announces his death). The film then immediately departs markedly from Coppola's saga by centring its entire plot around Cavallo's wife, Costanza. In *Il consigliori*, the character of Accardo (Tomas Milian) develops into a parallel of *The Godfather*'s Michael Corleone – a first-generation Italian-American mafia boss's young protégé, who at first wishes to leave the life of crime, but is forced to flee to Sicily and take refuge with friends of the family by a mob war, only for the conflict to catch up with him – but he is not Don Antonio's son, and is not destined to take over the family.

We therefore need to consider the fact that the generation gaps and the elegiac laments of old *mafiosi* that recur so often throughout the mafia *filone* are also constituent parts of this network of allusions. While these tropes may on the surface appear to register a preoccupation with Italy's recent past, they are more aptly appraised as documents of production decisions and fiscal imperatives. If this *filone* was indeed a melting pot of mafia myths, then the dominance of such themes should come as no surprise, since all of these myths were already fixated on the past in various ways. From the early assumptions that *Cosa Nostra* had ancient origins and the persistence of 'Old World' associations with the Italian-American immigrant experience, to Italian stereotypes of southern backwardness and Sicilian resistance to change, the lament at changing times is a default idiom of the fictional *mafioso*.

This is not to say, however, that we should dismiss the mafia *filone* as a merely superficial exercise in cultural recycling. If the wistful reminiscences of old-timers and the insubordination of young punks provide these films with their most consistent narrative devices, it is the underlying thematic patterns that offer their most interesting features in the context of contemporary Italy's ruminations on the recent past. At the start of this chapter, I examined how Fernando Di Leo used transatlantic mafia activity and the migration of southern Italians to the north of the country as two key elements of a broader focus on the changes that had visited Italian society since the Second World War. Once again, an auteurist approach is found wanting, since these same themes are replicated throughout the mafia *filone* in the period under consideration here. In this industrial context, studying individual films (or the output of individual directors) reveals less than the identification of patterns and trends across the larger spectrum of films released within a short period of time.

For example, I previously argued that the subordinate role played by the Milan mafia – as an outsourced branch of a New York business enterprise – in *La mala ordina* (Di Leo, 1972) is symbolically significant in an era immediately following the most intense period of Americanisation in Italy's economic and civic history. This point becomes more interesting when we analyse the frequency with which the larger mafia *filone* depicted such transatlantic routes of mafia activity, repeatedly locating the mob as a conduit for links between the Old World and the New. *La mala ordina*'s trope of 'fixers' travelling over from the USA to resolve problems in the Italian mafia is replicated in both *Milano rovente* and *Quelli che contano*, both of which overtly position American practices as the epitome of efficient modernity, in contrast to outmoded Italian ways of conducting business. The figure of Tony Aniante in *Quelli che contano* (played by Henry Silva, thus recalling his similar role in *La mala ordina*) was sent to New York to gain an 'education', and the ruthless professionalism he displays on his return to Sicily is complimented as being 'all'americana' by Don Cascemi, who then observes: 'Sicily is ancient: much more ancient than Brooklyn.' Similarly, *Milano rovente*'s Billy Barone (Alessandro Sperli) boasts that his methods are inspired by a man he knew back in Chicago who always caught his prey. Indeed, the transatlantic traffic of *mafiosi* in

Figures 3.3 and 3.4 Tony (Henry Silva) is framed in stark contrast to the overtly Sicilian *mise en scène* in *Quelli che contano* (Andrea Bianchi, 1974).

this *filone* is congested, with other Italian Americans travelling from the USA to Sicily (*Afyon oppio*, *La padrina*, *Il consigliori*), as well as in the opposite direction (*Baciamo le mani*, *La mano nera*, *La legge della Camorra*, *Crazy Joe*).

Of all these examples, *Quelli che contano* depicts the contrast between the Old and New Worlds in a particularly purposeful fashion through its *mise en scène*. When Tony walks through an ancient hill town, his sharp business suit is framed in stark contrast to the rest of the scenery as he passes a donkey (a common symbol for the backwardness of rural Sicily) being led down stone steps by an old man (Figure 3.3). Soon afterwards, a young man wearing a *coppola* (a traditional Sicilian flat cap) plays a *marranzano* (a Sicilian mouth harp) while riding a *carretto siciliano* (an ornate horse-drawn cart and symbol of Sicily) through a field of prickly pears (yet another traditional symbol of Sicily). When the cart is ambushed and the riders killed, Tony intervenes, and takes the cart (laden with drugs) to its intended destination at the mansion of a local *capo*. The overt juxtaposition of Tony, still wearing his suit as he rides the *carretto siciliano* (Figure 3.4), is hard to miss (though his smart attire is soon afterwards mocked by a group of Sicilians in a bar, just in case anybody has).

As we have seen, such contrasts, which symbolically position the USA as a representative of the modern capitalist world set against a benighted, archaic Sicily, arise from a rich heritage of representation. *The Godfather*'s emphasis on 'the immigrant experience' was merely the latest manifestation of this process, but its influence can again be felt in the frequency with which such themes arise in the mafia *filone* in the months after its Italian release. *La mano nera* overtly dwells on the cultural dislocation of the Italian immigrant in its 1900 New York setting, by depicting an Italo-American association whose mission is to maintain ties to 'la nostra patria' (in much the same way as the *pappas*' mutual aid societies). *Crazy Joe* similarly infuses its generation-gap plot with a theme of ethnic identity and cultural estrangement among Italian Americans in New York, when Coletti tells old Don Vittorio that their family needs to adopt modern business and public

Figure 3.5 A mafia hit is framed by a quintessentially Sicilian setting in *La violenza: quinto potere* (Florestano Vancini, 1972).

relations techniques, by exploiting civil rights movements and fighting back against racial stereotypes being used to denigrate Italians.

The flip side of this consistent emphasis on the contemporaneity of the USA is a repeated investment in age-old stereotypes of Sicily as a backward vestige of primal violence, since *Quelli che contano* was certainly not alone in deploying symbols of *sicilianità* as the common-sense *mise en scène* for mafia brutality. Though it does not appear in Table 3.1 due to its February 1972 release, *La violenza: quinto potere / The Sicilian Checkmate* (Florestano Vancini, 1972) partakes in this mode of representation in an early flashback sequence, where a mafia hit is introduced by a picturesque setting of prickly pears in a vast mountain range, with a hill town in the background and the victim on horseback wearing a *coppola* (Figure 3.5). *Afyon oppio* also opens by associating a murder with the natural beauty of Sicily, when a marshal asks too many questions about the contents of a coffin during a funeral (the body is stuffed with drugs), and he is nailed inside it and buried alive. As the nails are being hammered into place, shots of the spectacular coastal backdrop and the empty, ancient streets of the town are spliced with shots of the coffin (Figures 3.6 and 3.7). Similarly, in *L'onorata famiglia – Uccidere è cosa nostra*, a witness to an earlier killing drives past a man on a donkey as a non-diegetic *marranzano* plays on the soundtrack. He is then stopped by shepherds (further emphasising the rustic setting), who turn out to be Don Peppino's hitmen when they gun him down. The witness's wife and child are then hunted by more hitmen, who appear from behind prickly pears before chasing their quarry through a lemon grove (yet another commonplace Sicilian icon). Such symbols are also utilised as cinematic shorthand for Sicily in *Milano rovente* (when a

Figures 3.6 and 3.7 The natural beauty and antiquity of Sicily are conflated with mafia violence by the editing in *Afyon oppio* (Ferdinando Baldi, 1972).

cross-cut to Catania is announced by a sweeping pan shot of Mount Etna and the coastline, complete with prickly pears in the foreground and the ubiquitous sound of the *marranzano*) and *La mano nera* (where Tony's return to Sicily is similarly framed by sun, sea, cacti, *marranzani* and lemon trees).

The deserted streets in *Afyon oppio* (Figure 3.7) also provide a visual rendition of other recurrent modes of stereotyping Sicily in this *filone*. Don Fabrizio's words from *Il gattopardo* that 'a long sleep is what the Sicilians want', along with the associated trope of an intransigent resistance to change, are echoed in the dialogue of numerous examples. For example, Professor Salemi in *La violenza: quinto potere* says that in his Sicilian home town, 'nothing ever changes. It is full of violence and hate, wretched squalor and implacable stagnation.' Costanza in *La padrina* observes that the town where she and Barresi had a tryst many years ago 'still looks the same, as if time had come to a stop', while Rossana in *L'onorata famiglia – Uccidere è cosa nostra* tells La Manna that 'it's like living in the Middle Ages' in Palermo. As Nelson Moe (2002: 42) has explained, such traits associated with Sicily have long been situated as extreme versions of those associated with the *Mezzogiorno* as a whole. Accordingly, the same stereotypes are also applied to Naples in *Camorra* ('Nothing ever changes here, and nothing will ever change', says Tonino (Fabio Testi)) and *I guappi* ('I run things according to the old rules. It's been that way for hundreds of years. You can't change it. It stays the same, until you die', Don Gaetano (Fabio Testi) tells Nicola (Franco Nero)). This latter film contains a particularly striking visual illustration of this point at its conclusion, which enacts a sudden temporal shift of around eighty years. As the camera pulls away from the scene of Nicola's murder in the courtroom in 1891, we suddenly see 1970s clothes, uniforms and hairstyles in the corridor outside, with young men being escorted in handcuffs in a single long take, which then exits the courthouse and tracks through the streets of 1970s Naples, as more young men speed past on scooters. This jarring act of time travel places a clear emphasis on the unending continuity of violence across the centuries, and the continuing weight of the *Camorra*'s history on Naples's present.

The deserted streets of the cliff top town at the start of *Afyon oppio* also function as an efficient depiction of *omertà*, as the murder of the policeman is met with silence and implacable stillness. This, too, is a well-worn stereotype of both Sicily and the broader mafia that is amply indulged in this *filone*. Lawmen are frustrated by an entrenched code of silence in *La mano nera*, *L'onorata famiglia - Uccidere è cosa nostra*, *Tony Arzenta* and *I guappi*. In *Il consigliori*, Garofalo says that nobody will talk about his henchman's dead body, because 'this is Sicily'. Moreover, the henchman in question has just been shot by an unseen sniper in the hills around the remote town of Polizzi Generosa, where Garofalo's enemies Accardo and Don Antonio are hiding. Garofalo's assertion that his adversaries are 'protetti da tutti: uomini, vecchi, bambini, cornuti, cavalli, da tutti quanti' / 'protected by everyone: men, the old, the young, cuckolds, horses, all of them' further affirms the sense that Don Antonio's mafia family are so bound up with these hills that even the animals are on their side. As Don Angelino's despairing cry ('this is not just a piece of land!') before he confronts those who are building on his family's property in *Baciamo le mani* demonstrates, this *filone* recycles another common myth: that *mafiosi* are 'of the land'.

Clearly, there is in these films no shortage of the reductive stereotyping and shorthand conflation of 'mafia' and 'southern-ness' that had bedevilled attempts to foster national unity since the *Risorgimento*. The picturesque savagery of the mythic Sicilian (or Neapolitan) hinterland offered enduring and instantly recognisable tropes, ripe for fresh exploitation in the wake of *The Godfather*. Francis Ford Coppola's focus on generational conflict, acculturation and attachment to the Old World provided the mafia *filone* with another set of profitable archetypes which, when fused with enduring modes of local representation, offered a formula for success. As I have mentioned previously, however, this *filone* is a hybrid of all manner of mafia myths, from both sides of the Atlantic and from various points on the putative *filone* / *impegno* spectrum. For all the patterns of repetition identified above, this is a surprisingly heterogeneous set of films, with a number of subsets within it: not all of them beholden to *Il gattopardo* or *The Godfather*. For example, *La mano lunga del padrino*, despite its titular opportunism, is curiously unattached to specific geographical reference points, its two key settings consisting of generic 'countryside' shots instead of grand Sicilian vistas, and a resolutely generalised and touristic 'Arabic' locale.

Il consigliori, too, defies expectations of such derivativeness, even as it echoes commonplace myths about Sicily and the mafia. If, as I have argued, the character of Thomas Accardo in this film is modelled on *The Godfather*'s Michael Corleone, then his arrival in Sicily from the USA is a purposeful reversal of this parallel. Rather than cutting straight to a picturesque hillside, as does Coppola when introducing Michael's hiding place, Alberto De Martino opts to show us inner-city Palermo at rush hour. This serves literally to locate the story within the concerns of contemporary Italy and its relationship to the USA, rather than *The Godfather*'s framing of a picture book Sicily whose primary purpose is to provide a benighted contrast to New York. When Accardo and Don Antonio subsequently travel into the Sicilian interior, their host Don Vezza continues this process of reversing stereotypical expectations, through an oblique reference to Don Fabrizio's speech in *Il gattopardo*: 'Sicily has begun to wake up after all these years. Oil refineries, hotels, and I invested all the money you sent with care.'

By subverting such well-known cultural associations tying Sicily to Italy's primal roots, this overt focus on the island's contemporary society serves to underscore a tension within the mafia *filone* between the past and the present, and between competing cinematic 'Sicilies'. Don Vezza's words provide a bridge between the ancient splendour of *Il gattopardo* and the despoiled landscape of *Il giorno della civetta* and *Confessione di un commissario di polizia*. Indeed, Damiani's films are another common point of reference in this *filone*. *Baciamo le mani* fuses its *Godfather*-esque thematic focus on family roots, generation gaps and mafia business links to the USA with a plot that revolves primarily around land deals for the construction industry in Palermo. The film ends with Don Angelino's death at the hands of an invisible sniper on his family's land that has been taken over by a rival mafia family's construction firm. The final shots show concrete being poured over his body, returning him to his ancestral land in a clear nod to the ending of *Il giorno della civetta*. Such quotations also exist in *Camorra* (when Tonino and Capece discuss building contracts while overlooking the city from the top of a half-constructed tower block, replicating a scene from *Confessione di un commissario di polizia*), *Il consigliori* and *Crazy Joe* (in both of which more dead bodies are disposed of in concrete).

Such links between the construction industry and organised crime in contemporary Italy are also used as a conduit to explore the presence of the mafia in the north of the country, in both *Torino nera* and *Gli amici degli amici hanno saputo*. These two films depict Sicilians who have been forced to Turin to find work on exploitative mafia-run building sites, and in so doing act as documents for the socio-economic changes wrought on the nation since the War. In the five peak years of the Economic Miracle (1958–63), more than 900,000 southerners emigrated north, transforming major northern cities with rapid population booms. Turin was the most extreme case (increasing its population from 719,000 in 1951 to 1,124,714 in 1967): so much so that, by the end of the 1960s it had become the third largest 'southern' city after Naples and Palermo (Ginsborg 1990: 220). Films within this *filone* whose plots are ostensibly centred on the spread of mafia activity to northern Italy repeatedly dwell on this transformation and its attendant social tensions. *Torino nera*, for example, by exploring the alienation felt by a Sicilian family in their new surroundings, deploys southerners in their age-old role as a gauge for the nation's (lack of) progress towards unity. When the family's two children get into a fight with a local boy, he screams 'questi terroni rimandateli tutti in Africa' / 'these southerners should all be sent back to Africa'.[9]

While such an association does nothing to remedy this *filone*'s problematic conflation of 'mafia' with 'southern-ness', it is in the repeated depiction of such cultural alienation that these films betray their clearest preoccupation with the historical position of contemporary Italy. The figure of the ghettoised southerner, positioned as an outsider looking in at the bounties of modernity on offer in the north, is twice portrayed by Sicilian actor Antonio Sabato, in *I familiari delle vittime non saranno avvertiti* and *Milano rovente*. The former film opens with Sabato's character travelling from Sicily to Milan, and instantly uses this scenario's *mise en scène* to establish the character's alienation from the modern world, as he struggles to do up his seat belt on the aeroplane, and is then taken aback by an automatic door at Milan airport. In *Milano rovente*, Sabato's character Cangemi has moved his elderly mother up to Milan with him, and in one scene socialises with other Sicilians, eating Sicilian cuisine and enjoying Sicilian music. Shots of this joyous occasion are spliced with the brutal murder in the restaurant's bathroom of somebody who had earlier betrayed Cangemi. If this is arguably not a 'mafia film' per se (since the words 'mafia' or '*Cosa Nostra*' are never used), but instead a film about Sicilians struggling to make a living in the north, it invests heavily in stereotypical attributes attached to southern migrants (such as insularity and familism), including those associated with the mafia.

This recurrent subtext pertaining to the rapid social changes in recent Italian history is not always so explicit. Both *Tony Arzenta* and *Anna, quel particolare piacere* contain brief asides that highlight the impact southern migration has had on society. When the Sicilian eponymous hero in *Tony*

Arzenta (played by Alain Delon) hides from the mafia in Milan, he moves into a newly built tower block, and discusses the loneliness of this lifestyle as a pan shot registers row upon row of windows in the huge building. This is positioned in explicit contrast both to the life Tony used to enjoy (before his wife and child were murdered) and to the rustic lifestyle of Tony's parents back in Sicily, passing brief but significant comment on the breakdown of traditional family structures being endured by southern migrants to the north, in the face of an alienating and anonymising modernity. *Anna, quel particolare piacere* tells the story of a small-town girl from Bergamo (near Milan), who leaves her family home behind for the decadent metropolitan world of Milanese organised crime, night clubs and strip joints. Anna (played by Edwige Fenech) is introduced from behind a newspaper carrying stories of mafia violence, with a customer in the café she works in commenting that Milan has become a district of Palermo with all of its recent mafia activity. Later, her abusive *mafioso* boyfriend Guido responds to Anna's protestations about having to work as a call girl by saying: 'Get rid of your provincial mentality. Times have changed.' Once again, the mafia functions as a synecdoche for recent changes in Italian society, as traditional family structures are fractured by mass migration and associated criminality.

The mafia *filone* therefore inherits and repurposes a diverse range of mafia myths, each of which possessed a pre-existing function as a register of national or ethnic identity, a gauge for the historical position of contemporary society in relation to prevailing conceptions of modernity, or a locus for tensions between the past and the present. It would be convenient to assume that the proliferation following *The Godfather*'s Italian release indicated a fixation on that film's tensions around ethnic loyalty, acculturation and nostalgia for Old World customs, in itself registering cultural crises within a nation emerging from a period of profound socio-economic change. Such a convenient conclusion would, however, be found wanting, since these films' mode of delivery is a more significant factor than the narrative contents of any one source.

Returning to the soothsaying spectatorship of Judge Traini in *Perché si uccide un magistrato*, while Damiano Damiani may have lamented it, it is precisely in the repetitiveness of these films that their various genre echoes obtain significance through a process of concentrated accumulation. When viewed as a collection of 'multiplicities' (Klein and Palmer 2016: 1) – texts that are innately joined to other texts – what the mafia *filone* provides most of all is an illuminating document of production decisions and marketing ploys, through which ruminations on the state of contemporary Italy inevitably emerge, given the source material. Alongside their opportunistic quotations from *The Godfather*, the repeated depictions of mafia-owned building sites and explorations of southern migration show these films recycling long-established local discourses that always already frame the south of Italy as a window into the nation's past and a testing ground for its unity.

Notes

1. *Omertà* is the mafia's strict code of silence: an obligation not to speak to the authorities under any circumstances. Dickie suggests that it originates from the Sicilian word *umirtà* ('humility'), denoting respect and devotion to one's mafia sect (Dickie 2007: 42).
2. 'Mafia' (or 'maffia') is a Sicilian dialect word whose original meaning equated to 'bold' or 'self-confident'. It obtained criminal connotations in popular and governmental discourse in 1860s Palermo, but has since become applicable to any number of international organised crime networks (Dickie 2007: 55–60). *Cosa Nostra* ('Our Thing') is the name given to the mafia of Sicily by its own members, and is also used by the mafia of the USA. There are a number of other mafia organisations across Italy: the Neapolitan mafia is known as *Camorra*; the Calabrian mafia as *'Ndrangheta*; the Puglian mafia as *Sacra Corona Unita*; and the Roman mafia as *Banda della Magliana*. Each of these has a history particular to its region, and the use of terminology is therefore important. I shall therefore endeavour to be as precise as possible in this respect, though most of the films I am analysing in this chapter do not specify such regional nuances and just use the word 'mafia' instead.
3. The 'Auteur Theory' emerged from French film criticism in the 1950s and was further championed by the US critic Andrew Sarris in the 1960s. The theory centred on the premise that a select group of filmmakers possessed such sophisticated artistic visions that they had stamped their personalities on ostensibly mass-produced studio products, thus transcending the constraints of industrial film production. See Sarris 1968.
4. In these documentaries, Di Leo is at pains to differentiate himself from the mass of *poliziotteschi*, emphasising his higher-brow 'noir' inspirations from John Huston and Jean-Pierre Melville (Gomarasca 2011). Elsewhere, he describes himself as the 'autore' / 'author' of the most influential early Italian Westerns, including *Per un pugno di dollari* / *A Fistful of Dollars* (Sergio Leone, 1964) (he was an uncredited screenwriter on Leone's *filone*-defining film) (Gomarasca and Pulici 2011a).
5. The terms '*Mezzogiorno*' and 'south of Italy' are of course to be taken with a healthy dose of scepticism, since they serve to homogenise the diverse and distinct regions of Abruzzo, Campania, Molise, Puglia, Basilicata, Calabria, Sicily and Sardinia. The historical stereotypes arising from this discursive construction are the object of my analysis here.

6. For example, Luca Peretti has also demonstrated how *Mafioso* (Alberto Lattuada, 1962) uses the mafia as a vehicle to explore the impact of industrialisation and urbanisation, in the immediate wake of the Economic Miracle (Peretti 2018).
7. *The Godfather* came top of the *prima visione* box office charts for 1972–3 (Rossi 1997: 34).
8. The naked opportunism of these films' expedited release strategies was discussed openly in the Italian press at the time. *La mano lunga del padrino*'s reviews adopt a consistent tone: '*Il padrino* non è ancora uscito in Europa, e già hanno pensato a fargli il verso' / '*The Godfather* has not yet come out in Europe, and it has already been imitated' (Vice 1972c: 9); 'Prima del capostipite, arrivano gli epigoni. Sfruttando la macchina pubblicitaria messa in moto per il film sul "Padrino" . . . i nostri distributori stanno già immettendo sul mercato i suoi succedanei, per un filone ritenuto evidentemente redditizio' / 'Before the progenitor, the imitators arrive. Taking advantage of *The Godfather*'s advertising machine . . . our distributors are already introducing its substitutes onto the market, for a *filone* clearly considered to be profitable' (G.C. 1972: 8). By the time *L'amico del padrino* was released four months later, the impending proliferation of this *filone* was already being identified, with the film being described as 'frettolosamente sceneggiato e realizzato per sfruttare . . . la voga della padrinite' / 'hastily scripted and made to exploit . . . the vogue of "*Godfather*-itis"' (Valdata 1973b: 7). The broader implications of these release patterns will be discussed in Chapter 5.
9. 'Terroni' is in fact a considerably more derogatory word than my translation of 'southerner' suggests: an insult targeted at the supposed backwardness of the agricultural southern regions. A more precise equivalent word in English might be something like 'yokel' or 'redneck'.

CHAPTER 4

Serial Killing and the *Giallo*

La ragazza che sapeva troppo / *The Evil Eye* (Mario Bava, 1963) contains a strikingly self-reflexive scene, which positions itself and other Italian murder mysteries in a subordinate position to anglophone popular culture. When the resourceful central character – a young American woman on holiday in Rome – finds herself under threat, the omniscient narrator reveals her thought process, as she thinks of an ingenious way to repel a crazed killer:

> She appealed to her old friends, her *giallo* novels. She appealed to Wallace, to Mickey Spillane, to Agatha Christie . . . Killers never read *gialli*, fortunately, and . . . the novel that was her inspiration had just been published in Philadelphia. It couldn't have been translated into Italian yet.

As a meta-textual joke, this reference to English-language crime writers highlights the film's debt to the yellow-covered mystery novels (known as *gialli*), launched in 1929 by Mondadori publishers, which were at first translated from English-language sources and later localised by Italian writers such as Leonardo Sciascia. With this gambit, Mario Bava therefore plugs into a rich vein of transnational borrowing in Italy, through which foreign crime narratives had long offered filters for familiar locales. The scene's diegesis goes further still, by presenting an American tourist with a cultural advantage over her Italian pursuer. That she alone has access to the most recent popular artefacts positions the USA as a trailblazer, and the latest trends at a perceptual remove from the Italian-speaking world, which clings on to America's pop-cultural coat-tails. This evokes a sense that Italy is playing catch-up with the anglophone world, bringing to mind Jean Baudrillard's comment that 'American is the original version of modernity. [Europeans] are the dubbed or subtitled version' (Baudrillard 1986: 76).

La ragazza che sapeva troppo is commonly positioned as a precursor to the murder-mystery *filone* that would blossom in the early 1970s, which has itself become known as the *giallo*. This *filone* has since entered the pantheon of exploitation cinema for its memorable generic markers — masked, black-gloved psychopaths, sensuous female victims, elaborately grisly murders, witnesses-turned-amateur detectives — and for its influence on US 'slasher' films of the 1970s and 1980s. Like the *polizottesco*, however, this category is more diverse than such an all-encompassing label suggests. This chapter will not therefore attempt to be a broad survey of the cinematic *giallo* (though I will continue to use the term for brevity's sake). Instead, I will identify a set of particular *filone* strands that are usually subsumed within this large[1] category of films, whose unifying identity broadly revolves around the depiction of serial killing in contemporary Italian locales. Tropes that are characteristic of the wider *giallo* category — investigations piecing together fragments of historical trauma, alongside tensions between contemporaneity and pastness, modernity and tradition, cosmopolitanism and provincialism — are negotiated in particularly revealing ways in the films selected in this chapter, accumulating to provide further insights into 1970s Italy's relationship with the recent past.

These tensions are evident in the critical and scholarly reception that has surrounded the *giallo*. For example, after *L'uccello dalle piume di cristallo / The Bird with the Crystal Plumage* (Dario Argento, 1970) provided this *filone* with its first major success, its director was nicknamed 'the Italian Hitchcock' (Hutchings 2003: 128). By bestowing a normative status on Hollywood filmmaking, this phrase underlines a perception that the *giallo* was an imitative phenomenon: its cosmopolitan *mise en scène* amounting to a dilution of 'national' signifiers in the face of transatlantic narrative formats. Furthermore, David Church points out that the *giallo filone* owed a debt to 'a variety of transnationally circulating texts', such as the West German *krimi* films of the 1960s (Church 2015b: 7). Certainly, the vision of contemporary Italy filtered through the eyes of a foreigner (on display in both *La ragazza che sapeva troppo* and *L'uccello dalle piume di cristallo*, and repeated in many other examples, including *Perché quelle strane gocce di sangue sul corpo di Jennifer? / The Case of the Bloody Iris* (Giuliano Carnimeo, 1972) and *Profondo rosso / Deep Red* (Dario Argento, 1975)) is testament to a resolutely globalised outlook.

However, although the *giallo* is often positioned as a contemporary, cosmopolitan and internationally focused *filone*, a number of films that are usually considered to belong to it deviate from this model by deploying primitive backwater settings or demonstrating an overt focus on parochial superstitions. Such films as *Reazione a catena / A Bay of Blood* (Mario Bava, 1971), *Non si sevizia un paperino / Don't Torture a Duckling* (Lucio Fulci, 1972), *I corpi presentano tracce di violenza carnale / Torso* (Sergio Martino, 1973), *La casa dalle finestre che ridono / The House of the Laughing*

Windows (Pupi Avati, 1976) and *Solamente nero / Bloodstained Shadow* (Antonio Bido, 1978) are united by their representations of a peripheral Italian underbelly, gazing inwardly to invest in a set of discourses pertaining to the nation's past. I shall return to these films – which I shall call 'rural *gialli*'[2] – at the end of this chapter. For now, suffice to say that they were not entirely beholden to international trends: a point emphasised in Sergio Martino's account of his inspiration for *I corpi presentano tracce di violenza carnale*:

> The idea for the technique used by the killer to slice his victims came from a major news story. A man killed his in-laws in an apartment in Rome. Then, he dissected the bodies and brought them day by day out of this apartment . . . There were also movies that inspired our films. With *Torso*, I was inspired by Richard Fleischer's *See No Evil* (1971) and I tried to create a plot that could combine the fascination of this film with the Roman news. (Olesen 2017: 263)

The gruesome crimes to which Martino refers are those of Vincenzo Teti: nicknamed 'lo squartatore' ('the ripper') by the Italian press at the time of his arrest in 1969 (Anon 1969: 12). The director's account of *Torso*'s source material – at once local and international – underlines a tension between cosmopolitanism and parochialism, which lies at the heart of the *giallo*'s efforts to negotiate a path through rapid changes in the country's cultural outlook.

It is therefore necessary to hold the very term '*giallo*' up to scrutiny, since its origin as a subordinate category to anglophone popular culture is not a reliable criterion for definition. Moreover, though the word has become irrevocably associated with gruesome violence, serial killers and the 'slasher' variant of the horror genre in US and UK fan communities, its meaning in Italian popular discourse is closer to 'mystery': a point underlined by Russ Hunter, who highlights the Italian titling of the benign, family-oriented American detective show *Murder She Wrote* as *La signora in giallo* (Hunter 2009: 105). Attempts to define the cinematic *giallo*, indeed, are often problematic, and full of caveats and acknowledgements of ambiguity. As Gary Needham argues, this *filone* constitutes 'a body of films that resists generic definition', so permeable are its perceived boundaries (Needham 2003: 136). Alexia Kannas has similarly examined how the *giallo* is so nebulous that it 'seems to endlessly resist the manageable definitions that genre criticism has sought to achieve'. For Kannas, critique of this *filone* necessitates 'being alive to the kaleidoscope of ambiguities, contradictions and tensions inherent in these films so concerned with the conditions of modernity' (Kannas 2017: 174, 187).

As Kannas's argument hints at, where tentative definitions are attempted, they tend to coalesce around consistent themes surrounding modernity and cosmopolitanism. This *filone*'s settings and locations, for example, have been described as 'fundamentally contemporary and cosmopolitan' (Bondanella 2009: 387), 'modern' (Bini 2011: 63) and 'urban' (Olney 2013: 104). Accordingly, the *giallo*'s thematic concerns tend to be traced back to one of two 'founding texts', both directed by Mario Bava: the tourist-in-urban-Italy model of *La ragazza che sapeva troppo*; and the bourgeois fashion-house chic of *Sei donne per l'assassino / Blood and Black Lace* (Mario Bava, 1964). Such a broad generic umbrella therefore appears to be of limited use if we wish to include the concerns of the 'rural *giallo*', whose rustic settings and preoccupation with archaic superstitions point to an alternative point of origin, also directed by Bava: *Reazione a catena*.

If, however, we put to one side the *giallo*'s heterogeneous *mise en scène*, and consider instead the thematic preoccupations that characterise this *filone*, the 'rural' variant has a role to play within a larger generic identity, by providing a counterpoint to the more celebrated 'urban' examples. Tensions between parochialism and cosmopolitanism, the national and the transnational, and between tradition and modernity, run throughout both the films and the scholarship that surrounds them. Needham (2003), Koven (2006), and Baschiera and Di Chiara (2010), for example, all emphasise the *giallo*'s fixation on notions of travel, tourism and foreignness, and include instances of the rural *giallo* in a broader narrative pattern in which an outsider figure travels to an alien locale where he or she becomes a witness to or investigator of grisly murders. Koven identifies a consistent association of 'jet-set' cosmopolitanism with violent psychoses, and ties this to feelings of ambivalence towards encroaching modernity in post-war Italy, arguing that *gialli* perform a culturally and historically specific 'vernacular' function on behalf of Italy's *terza visione* audiences by registering their own feelings of unease at the rapid changes underfoot in their national culture (Koven 2006: 45–59). For Koven, the rural variant's contrasting depictions of provincial villages whose populations resist the invasion of the modern world provide an introspective manifestation of this same anxiety.

This chapter will partake in this ongoing debate, examining how such themes manifest themselves as tensions between contemporaneity and pastness in a variety of *giallo* subsets, and considering the extent to which these tensions can be said to relate to historical and contemporary preoccupations in Italian society. As Richard Dyer explains, such an undertaking is very common in critical analysis of serial killer narratives:

> Actual serial killing is a phenomenon so rare as to be worth remarking only for its curiosity value. Yet not only is it everywhere in Western culture . . . it is also widely taken to be indicative of its time and place. (Dyer 2015: 3)

Lisa Downing examines how critical discourses have historically sought to frame serial killers – from Pierre-François Lacenaire and Jack the Ripper to Myra Hindley – as symptomatic of surrounding socio-cultural ills, in tension with competing claims of the monstrous exceptionality of their crimes (Downing 2013: 30). Dyer diagnoses the former tendency – such murderers being seen as representatives of contemporary maladies – as being particularly prevalent in serial killer narratives in European cinema (Dyer 2015: 9).

This considered, and given their frequent settings in contemporary Italy, it is notable how seldom the serial killings of the *giallo filone* are analysed in relation to the synchronous events of the *anni di piombo*. Alongside the *poliziottesco*, the *giallo* is one of two large *filone* categories that began to proliferate at the beginning of the 1970s, and then flourished during post-war Italy's most traumatic decade. Both of these *filoni* revolve around amplified levels of violence in contemporary Italian locales, and both frequently narrate attempts to solve or explain the causes of these irrational and perplexing acts.[3] As we have seen, the *poliziottesco* is widely studied for its commentary on the politically motivated violence of its time and place. Such analyses of the *giallo* are relatively rare. Alan O'Leary tentatively suggests: 'perhaps the *gialli* of the period . . . refracted . . . anxieties about the presence of violence in Italian society, perceived as an irrational eruption, as a madness afflicting the collective' (O'Leary 2011: 231). Andrea Bini goes further, arguing for a direct link between the blossoming of this *filone* in the early 1970s and the political tumults surrounding student protest, trade union unrest, the Piazza Fontana bombing and the *strategia della tensione*:

> Argento's unexpected and resounding success, and that of the Italian *giallo* in general, was due to the fact that the repercussions of the cultural changes and escalating disorder in the country could no longer be ignored . . . Argento's films portray the fears of Italians whose cities and communities had undergone such rapid growth and change that they had become unfamiliar and threatening places. (Bini 2011: 64–5)

Bini's proclivity for auteurist adulation ('[Argento's] films are a perfect representation of 1970s urban angst' (2011: 65)) is perhaps incongruous, considering the industrial conditions of *filone* production practices, and his claims of a linear and unproblematic correlation between sociopolitical conditions, violent events and cinematic representations seem rather too convenient. His focus on underlying anxieties surrounding the rapid pace of change in Italian society, however, is pertinent.

For obvious reasons, it is common to focus on depictions of violence when looking at the Years of Lead and their processes of cultural representation. Given that the presence of spectacular homicidal acts is integral to the cinematic *giallo*'s identity, it might therefore seem logical to turn one's attention to this aspect if one is seeking to locate this *filone* in its historical contexts. To ascribe growing unease and insecurity in Italian society purely to the fact that indiscriminate acts of violence were becoming more frequent in the 1970s would, however, be to overlook a broader, underlying sense of disquiet towards modernity and the pace of socio-cultural change in the preceding decades of Italian history. As we have seen in Chapter 2, some *poliziotteschi* overtly represent the terrorist acts and related conspiracies of Italy's 1970s, inviting readings of political or historical significance arising from a direct relationship to the material conditions that surrounded the films. This chapter will argue that, in the case of the *giallo*, Italy's 1970s leave their mark through more indirect tensions pertaining to the historical significance of the present moment in relation to the nation's past, which lay behind the contemporaneous intensification of political violence. Once again, my interest is less with uncovering 'hidden' preoccupations of the filmmakers, and more with investigating how the industrial conditions of *filone* filmmaking demanded production decisions that relied on the assumption that such preoccupations were present in a target audience.

I argued in Chapter 1 that the unfinished business of the Second World War, though papered over by the economic boom of the 1950s and 1960s, acted as an originary trauma for the cultural–political conflicts that burst into the open from 1969 onwards. So far in this book, we have encountered various methods of contemplating the weight of the past upon the present moment within *filone* cinema, yet only *Il cittadino si ribella* has been seen to make explicit reference to the War, through Carlo's father's framed manifesto of resistance. Subsumed within the *giallo filone*, however, is a small group of films whose investment in discourses of trauma are overtly situated within devastating memories of the invasion of Italy, the Holocaust and the *resa dei conti* returning to haunt the present.

Wartime Trauma in the *Giallo*

Nelle pieghe della carne / *In the Folds of the Flesh* (Sergio Bergonzelli, 1970) weaves a confusing (and at times confused) narrative of unreliable historical memory and misidentification within a murderous family, isolated in the grounds of their remote castle. The castle's owner, Falaise, is traumatised by the childhood memory of being raped by her father André, and then killing him. The 'serial killer' narrative at first unfolds as a tale of her revenge against men who remind her of this memory, but the supposed facts of this kaleidoscopic flashback unravel one-by-one. First, André turns up at the castle, and Falaise's vivid memory is altered for the benefit of the film's audience to show that the man she killed was in fact an intruder, whom she misidentified as her father. Then, it is revealed that 'Falaise' is in fact the housekeeper's daughter Esther, who was thought to have been killed in a bicycle accident. It then turns out that the flashback is not even hers at all, but instead belongs to the real Falaise, who has been sectioned (while Esther witnessed the killing, suffering a shock to her subconscious that led to a personality switch). When the real Falaise returns to the castle, it finally turns out that the killer was in fact the housekeeper Lucille, that the 'intruder' was actually Lucille's lover, and that the newly arrived 'André' is in fact a policeman who has come to solve the complex riddle.

It is therefore revealing that, amidst this labyrinth of false memories, Lucille's own originary trauma is revealed in a crystal-clear flashback to the Holocaust, when she was forced to watch her mother and sister being executed in a Nazi gas chamber. Every memory in the film is shown to be unreliable and unstable, except for this one, which is introduced to the viewer by a sudden switch to black-and-white film stock (Figure 4.1). This jarring cinematographic shift, when added to the dimly lit interior presented as the setting for an impending Nazi atrocity, immediately evokes the famously harrowing torture sequence from *Roma città aperta / Rome, Open City* (Roberto Rossellini, 1945), in which the Resistance fighter Manfredi's brutal death is framed through a doorway in a similarly lit office complex (Figure 4.2). By fleetingly alluding to such famous conventions of documentary realism in Italian cinema to signify the one reliable memory in the whole film, Bergonzelli positions the War and its related traumas at a cognitive remove. The film thus insists on the conflict's unique permanence as an immutable presence, weighing heavily over contemporary traumas.

Figure 4.1 Victims of the Holocaust are marched to their deaths in *Nelle pieghe della carne* (Sergio Bergonzelli, 1970).

Figure 4.2 Manfredi is tortured by the Nazis in *Roma città aperta* (Roberto Rossellini, 1945).

This is not to say that *Nelle pieghe della carne* should be aggrandised through comparison with Rossellini's seminal film. Once the narrative returns to the saturated colour of the present day, this Holocaust flashback acts as a device to indulge the film's pseudo-Freudianism and cod psychology. Lucille's trauma has, it transpires, driven her to fit the castle's bathroom out as an impromptu gas chamber, through which she first kills the ex-convict Pascal and then later commits suicide. Such examples of the past's weight on the present are framed in explicitly psychoanalytical terms as the 'return of the repressed' by the film's epigraph: 'what has been remains imbedded in the brain, nestled in the folds of the flesh. Distorted, it conditions and subconsciously impels (Freud)'. Moreover, when Lucille's Holocaust flashback is reprised as a framing device for the present-day bathroom gassings, its nod to neorealist stylistics is discarded in favour of the distorted kaleidoscopic filter that is elsewhere associated with Falaise's unreliable flashbacks of familial trauma. Alexia Kannas identifies the kaleidoscope not only as an oft-utilised stylistic device in the *giallo filone*, but also as its defining symbol:

> In the case of [the] *giallo*, the kaleidoscope metaphor works on two levels: it gestures towards the destabilized and fragmentary conditions of modern life that preoccupies these films, while simultaneously, it describes the often-slippery manner in which film genres like the *giallo* operate. (Kannas 2017: 175)

The brief, jarring appearance of conventions associated with documentary realism amongst such fragmentation should therefore be viewed as a counterpoint to the purposefully splintered, ever-shifting memories that provide many *gialli* (including *Nelle pieghe della carne*) with their stock in trade.

Other *gialli* depicting the traumas caused by Nazi atrocities invest more consistently in this *filone*'s convention of fragmented, kaleidoscopic memories that require piecing together, to construct 'whodunnit' narratives. Both *Ragazza tutta nuda assassinata nel parco / Naked Girl Killed in the Park* (Alfonso Brescia, 1972) and *Il gatto dagli occhi di giada / Watch Me When I Kill* (Antonio Bido, 1977) deploy this strategy to arrive at denouements depicting vengeance being taken on former Nazis or their collaborators. Richard Dyer explains how *Ragazza tutta nuda assassinata nel parco* also opens by using conventions of documentary realism to frame a flashback to the War, 'shot in crisply focused, slightly shadowy black and white, already archaic in the context of the importance of colour and widescreen in 1970s Italian cinema' (Dyer 2015: 191–2). Unlike *Nelle pieghe della carne*, however, this film obscures the full significance of this memory until the finale. At the start of the film, the sounds of an air raid accompany a black and white scene of a man in a Nazi uniform tying up a mother and child in a house, before setting a bomb and leaving his victims to their fate. As the woman and her son try to wriggle free of their bonds, the scene cuts back-and-forth between them and stock newsreel footage of anti-aircraft guns, aerial shots of carpet-bombing, and shots of buildings being destroyed. This footage then becomes saturated with red, to form the backdrop for the film's opening credits. As with *Nelle pieghe della carne*, the film's main diegesis is set in the colour footage of the present day, framing the monochrome opening as a past event that somehow haunts the present. Here too, the inescapable trauma of that past eventually catches up with a plot built on unstable identities. Inspector Huber says that many people had reasons to flee Germany at the end of the War, and that Jonannes Wanterburger – the patriarch of the film's central family, who dies early on in the film – changed his name to hide his diabolical past. This past catches up with the family when Chris – an insurance investigator – turns out to be the young boy who was tied up with his mother in the film's opening scene, now hell-bent on meting terrible revenge on ex-Nazi officer Wanterburger and his family.

The fragmentary nature of traumatic wartime memory being pieced together to explain contemporary crimes is enacted in a very literal sense in *Il gatto dagli occhi di giada* by the audio recording that has been sent as a threat to the serial killer's future victims. This distorted, nightmarish cacophony lurks just beyond cognition for both the audience and the amateur detective Lukas, until he manipulates its frequency in a sound studio, to unlock its various levels of meaning. As the sounds of incinerators, snarling Dobermans and screams of agony reveal themselves, this aural kaleidoscope begins to signify the terror of a Nazi concentration camp. That this meaning is still not immediately apparent to Lukas provides an apt symbol for how the Second World War had resided in the Italian national imaginary since 1945: a lurking yet 'unspeakable' past (Judt 2010: 3), whose traumas had been obscured and ignored. Accordingly, Lukas proceeds to follow a red herring around a recent murder trial in which the victims were all on the same jury. His assumption that the accused man at the trial was the culprit for their murders focuses purely on contemporary crimes and misses the underlying links to wartime trauma. When he then discovers that the victims had also all collaborated with the Nazis during the War, he at last begins to realise the truth, and responds to his friend's dismissive comment that 'it's past history' with a pertinent observation: 'It seems like pretty active history to me.'

As has been outlined in Chapter 1, the wartime Resistance movement provided Italy with a potent reference point for collective remembrance and national pride, but certain unspeakable elements of this history were largely obscured in public discourse, constituting what John Foot has called a 'shared silence' (Foot 2009: 168). In particular, the period of brutal retributory violence against Fascists and Nazi collaborators immediately following the Liberation (the *resa dei conti*) was airbrushed out of the cultural memory of a heroic struggle against oppression. It is therefore revealing that this problematic element of Italian history is repeatedly evoked in implicit terms in this group of *gialli* while never being explicitly named, perhaps betraying the filmmakers' assumptions of traumatic recognition from audiences' personal or collective memories. Lukas's realisation that he is dealing with 'active history' comes when he is told that one of the killer's victims fled Padua for Germany when the Allies approached the city, and in the denouement the judge (whose son is the killer) reveals that all of the film's victims betrayed his Jewish family to the Nazis, condemning them to die in concentration camps. When Lukas asks why this revenge is being taken so many years later, the judge responds that not even a lifetime is enough to make him forget. Both *Ragazza tutta nuda assassinata nel parco* and *Il gatto dagli occhi di giada* therefore reveal their serial killers' motivations to be the unfinished business of hunting down Fascists and Nazi collaborators, while obfuscating the precise historical reference point being evoked for Italian audiences by such a plot device.

The *resa dei conti* is more directly summoned up in *Pensione paura / Hotel Fear* (Francesco Barilli, 1978), which invests heavily in the evocation of traumatic memories and lived experiences from the War. Rarely for a film associated with the *giallo filone*, this is not set in a contemporary locale, but in the midst of the War itself. Its mode of address, however, elicits a shared historical experience amongst Italians of the 1970s, through a series of asides and small details designed to evoke and recall the minutiae of wartime trauma. The film revolves around a young girl (Rosa) waiting for her father to return home from fighting, immediately connecting to childhood memories of absent parents assumed to be shared by a sizeable portion of an adult cinema audience in 1978. Rosa's school has been closed due to bombings, so she is helping her mother Marta run the family's remote hotel, which is proving challenging because, as Marta comments, it is getting harder to find food as supplies dry up. At one point, bombers are heard flying over the hotel, leading to fearful upward glances from the guests, one of whom has been obsessively recounting how his entire family died in a bombing raid and who now starts to scream uncontrollably.

Amidst this broader strategy of historical evocation is Marta's lover Alfredo, who is hiding in the upstairs bedroom for reasons that are at first only obliquely hinted at, as he says that when the war is over 'this will all be annulled'. As the hotel's depraved guests later assault Rosa, a mysterious figure turns up and kills them all. Rosa shouts 'papa!', but the figure is instead a friend of her father's, who informs her that her father is dead. He has come to kill Alfredo who, he says, betrayed their military unit. The implication that Rosa's father was part of the Resistance and that Alfredo is a collaborator with the Fascists means that Alfredo's death can be interpreted as a portrayal of the *resa dei conti*. These historical details are not, however, clarified in the film (indeed, it is never mentioned on which side Rosa's father was fighting). This therefore functions merely as one constituent part of the broader attempt to evoke the experience of living through the final phase of the war in Italy. The *resa dei conti* remains a palpable yet unspeakable presence.

The *filone* strand outlined above provides the most explicit evocations of the War in any of the films analysed in this book (except perhaps *Il cittadino si ribella*). Indeed, such direct references to the historical past are rare in the *giallo*, which is for the most part a resolutely contemporary *filone*. These 'wartime trauma' films are, however, part of a larger trend of *gialli* that overtly focus on past traumas, fragmented memories and the unravelling of supposed facts: most famously, those directed by Dario Argento. Both *L'uccello dalle piume di cristallo* and *Profondo rosso*, for example, revolve around a foreigner in Italy witnessing an assault but missing a crucial detail, which lurks in the recesses of his memory. In both cases, the memory is later replayed to reveal the missing details through zooms, freeze-frames or new camera angles, with *L'uccello dalle piume di cristallo*'s Sam Dalmas (played by Tony Musante) having flashbacks that incrementally take us closer to the truth as he tries to dissect his own recollections. In the denouement of each film, this theme of latent or repressed memories is linked to an explanation for the killer's actions that lies in a past trauma. A psychologist in the closing sequence of *L'uccello dalle piume di cristallo* explains to television cameras that Monica (the killer) had been brutally attacked and suffered severe trauma ten years ago, with her mental disturbance remaining dormant until she saw a painting that depicted the assault.

The superficial psychoanalytical overtones of *Nelle pieghe della carne* (released in May 1970, just three months after *L'uccello dalle piume di cristallo*) are therefore part of a much larger theme within the *giallo*. Another epigraph quoting Freud to underscore the power of humankind's latent desires appears in *Lo strano vizio della signora Wardh / Blade of the Ripper* (Sergio Martino, 1971) and the plot device of traumatic memories resurfacing to inspire a killing spree is repeated in *Il rosso segno della follia / A Hatchet for the Honeymoon* (Mario Bava, 1970), *4 mosche di velluto grigio* / *Four Flies on Grey Velvet* (Dario Argento, 1971), *Cosa avete fatto a Solange?* / *What Have You Done to Solange?* (Massimo Dallamano, 1972), *I corpi presentano tracce di violenza carnale* (1973), and *Solamente nero* (1978), among numerous other examples. So too, the obscure audio recording containing a hidden clue in *Il gatto dagli occhi di giada* is a *filone* echo of similar devices – also standing in as symbols for the fragmentation of memory – in *L'uccello dalle piume di cristallo* and *La casa dalle finestre che ridono*. While an overt focus on history is rare in the *giallo*, therefore, neurotic fixation on a more generic past – be it through the acting out of childhood trauma, the examination of supposed facts that unravel before our eyes or the dissecting of unreliable memories – is repeated time and time again.

This does not in and of itself constitute a historical discourse, but the key concern with the dissipation of secure certainties in a hostile and unfamiliar contemporary Italy lends itself to a critical focus on the nation's rapid economic and cultural development of the preceding years. Kannas, for example, links these very themes to the alienation of the subject in late modernity:

> These are characteristics of a world where nothing is stable, knowable, fixed or finite; people catch late flights, ascend and descend staircases, disappear into cabs that speed away into the distance ... before returning to cold grey urban centres ... Amongst this instability the amateur detective obsessively tries to re-establish a sense of order. (Kannas 2013)

Recalling Bini's observations that *gialli* 'portray the fears of Italians whose cities and communities had undergone such rapid growth and change that they had become unfamiliar and threatening places', and that 'the repercussions of the cultural changes and escalating disorder in the country could no longer be ignored' (Bini 2011: 64–5), this returns me to the concept of collective or cultural trauma outlined in Chapter 1.

'O Tempora! O Mores!'[4]

A key scholarly tendency around the *giallo filone* surrounds the notion that, in its ultra-modern settings and its repetitive focus on cosmopolitanism, tourism, fashion and foreignness, it provides a commentary on the increasingly globalised lifestyles of affluent post-war modernity. Mikel J. Koven, for example, compares this *filone*'s outlook on society with the depiction of a spiritually degenerate contemporary Rome in *La dolce vita* (Federico Fellini, 1960). This film arrived at the culmination of a period of rapid modernisation and urbanisation, which brought with it attendant cultural and economic shifts towards consumerism and individualism. Fellini's satirical depiction of 'the sweet life' of vacuous celebrity and untrammelled hedonism ironically became seen as a constituent part of this very milieu, its international success bringing 'further attention to Rome as an exotic holiday destination, filled with glamour, wealth, and the most beautiful people in Europe' (Koven 2006: 45). For Koven, the *giallo* went a step further, reflecting a marked 'ambivalence toward modernity' in its depictions of urban alienation, licentious sexualities and shifting gender roles, to provide a 'vernacular' address to the audiences of the *terza visione* sector (Koven 2006: 15–16). As we have seen in Chapter 1, such audiences' tastes during the post-war era had historically been attuned, not only to the allure of American cinema, but also to 'symbols of continuity with the past . . . during a period of immense, disorienting social and economic development' (Gundle 1996: 316–17).

There are occasional examples within the *giallo* where sentiments that appear to cater to such outlooks are directly articulated, through laments at the changes wrought on post-war Europe. *Paranoia / A Quiet Place to Kill* (Umberto Lenzi, 1970), for example, is the tale of Helen, an impulsive American woman who travels around Europe in search of more thrills. We are told that her lifestyle has encompassed working in the fashion industry and public relations before she became a racing driver, enjoying the licentious high life of an unattached divorcee. The fact that this film was produced and released at the tail end of the long struggle to introduce the right to divorce in Italy (culminating in official legalisation in December 1970; see Ginsborg 1990: 328) is certainly one important factor to consider when contextualising such a depiction of free-spirited femininity. Accordingly, the behaviour of the bourgeois hedonists who cavort in a Majorcan swimming pool is pointedly condemned as a sign of such decadent times by an old man who remarks: 'questi giovani dolce sono veramente dispomenti' (literally, 'these sweet young people are truly displeasing').

Yet this film, as an Italian, French and Spanish co-production, was not aimed exclusively at Italian audiences, and therefore also needs to be considered in a broader international context (and I shall return to this issue in more detail at the end of this chapter). In the English-language dub, the old man's line becomes 'it's not the same Majorca any more. They've brought it to ruin': a lament focusing more specifically on the changes visited on post-war Europe by the tourist trade. As Koven has pointed out (Koven 2006: 52), this sentiment is echoed in another *giallo* directed by Umberto Lenzi and co-produced with Italian and Spanish money: *Gatti rossi in un labirinto di vetro / Eyeball* (Lenzi, 1975). Here, a tour bus full of

Americans see the sights of Barcelona, as a mysterious killer picks them off one-by-one. The nature of tourist sightseeing as an inherently superficial appreciation of the more attractive elements of a region's history which simultaneously overlooks traumatic aspects of that same region's living memory is overtly dwelt upon, when one tourist (Robby) reminisces about his childhood in Barcelona. His wife tells him she is tired of hearing about the facts that his old school has been knocked down to make way for a bank, his old home for a hotel and his old playground for a parking lot. We later hear that Robby has come back to Spain from the USA to revisit Madrid, where he was wounded in a bombardment during the war (presumably referring to the Siege of Madrid during the Spanish Civil War).

Such overt reflections on how living memories of the recent past had been swept away by contemporary Western Europe's headlong embrace of consumerism and tourism are rare in the *giallo*. They are, however, part of a larger trend in which a preoccupation with the tourist gaze on contemporary European cities merges with these urban spaces being rendered culturally alienating and threatening. As we have seen, this is most obviously realised in the many *gialli* in which the protagonist is a foreigner in a European city. With reference to *La ragazza che sapeva troppo* (which makes ample use of Rome's Spanish Steps, but subverts their touristic association by using them as the deserted and nocturnal setting for an escape from the crazed killer), Baschiera and Di Chiara argue:

> The processes of detection and the constant feeling of danger reinvigorate the touristic elements by offering a view of the city that doesn't make it into travel agencies' brochures ... The mapping of real touristic spaces ... appears here in the *giallo* in order to represent a space that is familiar and distant at the same time – that is, an uncanny space. (Baschiera and Di Chiara 2010: 114)

This is also well illustrated in *L'uccello dalle piume di cristallo*: a film which is mostly set in Rome, but which denies the audience a glimpse of that city's world-famous tourist hotspots until near the end, when an aerial shot slowly zooms out from Sam standing, confused and alone, in a side street. As the camera pulls out, the shot pans across the majesty of the River Tiber, briefly registering the Ponte Giacomo Matteotti in the middle distance and the city's ancient skyline behind it, before zooming back in to focus on nearby flats where, as implied by the editing that follows, Sam's girlfriend Julia is being held by the killer. The celebrated Roman cityscape here acts only as a deadly labyrinth for the tourist to negotiate.

In yet another Umberto Lenzi *giallo* – *Un posto ideale per uccidere / A Quiet Place to Kill* (Lenzi, 1971) – tourism in Italian cities is associated with the licentious moral standards of globalised modernity, when a sexually liberated young hippy couple (Dick and Ingrid) finance their travel around Europe by making pornographic images and then selling them to the throngs of sightseers at both the Leaning Tower of Pisa and Florence's Piazza della Signoria. In the Florence scene, the tourists' gaze at Italy's artistic heritage is framed as a vulgar fascination with the statues' nudity, which announces their interest in Dick and Ingrid's X-rated wares. Firstly, suggestive framings of statues' crotches are spliced with a series of lustful reaction shots from the onlookers. Then, a shot of somebody looking at photos of the statues from postcards and guidebooks pans across the piazza to show another person looking at a pornographic magazine.

In these films, tourism is therefore framed as a tangible manifestation of the rapid changes that have visited Italian (and other European) cities and society in recent decades, and a symbol for how once familiar urban spaces have become corrupted and alienating. Indeed, both *Paranoia* and *Un posto ideale per uccidere* go a step further, linking tourism to a broader framing of modern lifestyles and attitudes, typified by youth countercultures and a marked generation gap. The self-professed mission of Dick and Ingrid – themselves foreigners in Italy – is to express 'youth's innate rebellion against authority figures' and to 'bring the gospel of sexual freedom to darkest Italy'. Their hippy manifesto is ultimately shown to be harmless and naïve, and they become the victims of an oppressive state apparatus when they are falsely accused of murder. As they flee the police, they go swimming in the sea and kiss on the beach, just before driving through a roadblock and then over a cliff to their deaths. The film's final shots – of Dick and Ingrid's dead bodies lying at the bottom of the cliff, and their vintage car burning nearby – recall the infamous ending of *Bonnie and Clyde* (Arthur Penn, 1967), and its attendant commentary on the annihilation of free-spirited youth by a cruel system.

Youth countercultures are represented in more sinister tones in a number of other *gialli* of this period, again standing in as symbols for shifting mores towards a new licentious morality. *Una lucertola con la pelle di donna / A Lizard in a Woman's Skin* (Lucio Fulci, 1971) contrasts the English reserve of a wealthy lawyer's daughter with the wild debauchery of her next-door neighbour, whose London flat hosts round-the-clock drug- and sex-fuelled parties with members of a nearby hippy commune. When the neighbour is killed, the police say that she had it coming due to her licentious lifestyle, and the hippies who saw her murder prove to be useless witnesses because they were tripping on LSD at the time.[5] Other countercultural or sexually licentious communities or cults appear repeatedly in either the primary narration or the backstories of a number of characters played by Edwige Fenech in films directed by Sergio Martino in 1971 and 1972. *Lo strano vizio della signora Wardh* (Martino, 1971) shows Julie (Fenech) to be harbouring fantasies of a historical violent sexual encounter, as she meets the perpetrator at a party that seems about to descend into an orgy, and has a sado-masochistic dream about him. *Tutti i colori del buio / All the Colors of the Dark* (Martino, 1972) has Jane (Fenech) taking part in a Black Mass, which promptly turns into an orgy. In *Il tuo vizio è una stanza chiusa e solo io ne ho la chiave / Your Vice Is a Locked Room and Only I Have the Key* (Martino, 1972), Floriana (Fenech) visits her degenerate uncle having been living in a free-love commune for the last six months, and proceeds to have sex with both the uncle and his wife.

Perché quelle strane gocce di sangue sul corpo di Jennifer? (Giuliano Carnimeo, 1972) brings many of the above strands together. Jennifer (again, played by Edwige Fenech) is a foreigner in Italy, who used to be a stripper and now works as a fashion model. She was once a member of a coercive free-love cult, whose leader now pursues her in an attempt to lure her back. The film revolves around a large inner-city tower block, which acts thematically as an alienating modern urban space in which people live in close proximity to their neighbours, and can therefore hear snippets of each other's private lives through the walls, but never get to know one another. This theme of alienation is set up in the very first scene, when the body of a prostitute is found in the lift, and the stripper Mizar has to point out who she is to her neighbours who live on the same floor. Eventually, these thematic threads lead toward an overt focus on the older generation reacting angrily or violently to this immoral world that has changed around them. The old war widow Mrs Moss says she daren't go outside due to the rising crime rates, and she later shouts at Jennifer for being a whore and a drug addict. The serial killer is then revealed to be old Professor Isaacs, who blames the strippers, models and prostitutes for corrupting his daughter into lesbianism.

As *Perché quelle strane gocce di sangue sul corpo di Jennifer?* demonstrates, the *giallo* operated according to the established conventions of the *filone* production model, whereby a generic world accumulates rather than being carefully constructed, through the rapid repetition and incremental evolution of successful tropes. Richard Dyer identifies the attractions of this *filone* in precisely these terms:

> The anticipation of there being another set piece, another number, to thrill to is itself a serial pleasure, it is what we've come for, what we are waiting for. If the killings are not always serial for the killers, they always are for us. (Dyer 2015: 182)

It is primarily for this reason that I find terminology such as the *giallo* acting as a 'critique' of modernity or a 'commentary' on the Economic

Miracle (Koven 2006: 46, 49) to be problematic. Certainly, the repeated representation of a superficial, licentious consumer society obsessed with surface beauty to be found in this *filone* points to an underlying preoccupation with the rapid cultural and economic changes of the preceding years. Yet this comes packaged with an equally repetitive exploitation of naked female flesh, which positions these films as manifestations, rather than critiques, of such licentiousness. For example, the frequency with which Edwige Fenech was required to take her clothes off in front of the camera tells us as much (if not more) about the production practices and cultural mores of *filone* cinema in the 1970s than do any political or moral evaluations coming from the filmmakers.

This is certainly not to accuse Koven of ascribing a disproportionate importance to authorial intent. Indeed, his most compelling argument is that 'vernacular' cinema such as the *giallo* is defined by an address to its historically and culturally specific audiences within the terms of their own lived experience, opening up a 'discursive space' for those audiences to contemplate their relationship to modernity (Koven 2006: 59). For Koven, such vernacular cinema is of necessity formulaic, repetitive and simplistic, because 'the world the film is situated within needs to be immediately recognizable as the world the audience lives in' (Koven 2006: 39–40). It is therefore more productive here to observe the iterative accumulation of tropes that went into the construction of common sense, assumed or taken-as-read 'modern' settings than it is to seek to identify purposeful commentary.

The repeated use of the fashion world as a symbol for bourgeois decadence or consumerist modernity is a case in point. Mario Bava's *Sei donne per l'assassino* (1964) is commonly seen to be an important early trailblazer for the *giallo filone*: 'the earliest true example of the form' (Olney 2013: 107), which put 'most of the subgenre's features in place' (Hunt 1992: 71) and 'set the structural standards for the subsequent entries in the genre' (Baschiera and Di Chiara 2010: 113). As well as providing a template for some of this *filone*'s most recognisable iconography – most obviously, a masked killer committing a series of grisly murders of sensuous, semi-clad women – this film's setting in a *haute couture* fashion house positions it as a foundational text for one of the *giallo*'s most repeated formulae. The backdrop to its opening credits, in which the key characters stand completely still as they are framed among a collection of mannequins, provides an efficient, wordless commentary on how contemporary consumer society has rendered the human body an inanimate commodity serving the purposes of fetishistic display.

Bava himself reprises this trope in *Il rosso segno della follia* (1970) when John, the psychopathic owner of another fashion house, first 'seduces' one of his mannequins and then invites Alice (one of his models) to put on one of his wedding dresses. As John enters the display room, meat-cleaver in hand, he finds Alice standing still among the mannequins, modelling the dress. Once he has hacked her to death, he kisses her limp body (still in the dress). The link to the earlier kiss of the mannequin is abundantly clear: John has successfully rendered Alice a 'model' of inanimate femininity. As with so many *gialli*, the links to psychoanalysis are as obvious as they are pat and superficial (John spends the film killing women in bridal dresses while reliving the childhood trauma of his mother's death, before awakening to the fact that he had killed her to stop her remarrying), and are not of particular interest in this volume. Of more importance, for my purposes, is how the fashion world reappeared time and again as shorthand for modern lifestyles in the *giallo filone*. To name but a few examples: one of Helen's past professions in *Paranoia* was in fashion; Enrico gets closer to the truth via a nude photo shoot as he tries to uncover the tale of sexual intrigue lying behind *Cosa avete fatto a Solange?*; *La dama rossa uccide sette volte / The Red Queen Kills Seven Times* (Emilio Miraglia, 1972) uses a fashion house setting to represent contemporaneity, in stark contrast to an old (and potentially haunted) castle; Jennifer works as a model in *Perché quelle strane gocce di sangue sul corpo di Jennifer?*; and the plot of *La morte accarezza a mezzanotte / Death Walks at Midnight* (Luciano Ercoli, 1972) revolves around a fashion model who lives in an ultra-modern luxury apartment and takes a mind-altering drug that causes her to hallucinate a gruesome murder.

Nude per l'assassino / Strip Nude for Your Killer (Andrea Bianchi, 1975) inherits the above *filone* thread of framing the fashion industry as a manifestation of modern licentiousness or dehumanising consumerism. The lustful sex-pest protagonist Carlo (a photographer for an international fashion magazine) pursues Lucia by taking unsolicited pictures of her in her bikini, persuades her to strip off for more photos, and has sex with her in a sauna, before describing her to the modelling agency as 'first class merchandise'. Such an odious characterisation could be read as a condemnation of this exploitative milieu, were it not for this film's extended scenes of sex and female nudity, which mean that it acts simultaneously as symptom and critique of the modern world's supposedly voracious desire for carnal titillation (Edwige Fenech's appearance here as a fashion photographer, for example, does not exempt her from a seemingly contractual obligation to remove her clothes).

In its apparently contradictory moral position, *Nude per l'assassino* is in fact a good illustration of both Koven's central thesis that this *filone* betrays 'ambivalence' toward modernity (Koven 2006: 45–59), and Dyer's argument that, in the *giallo*, 'modernity' constitutes a bewildering mixture of cosmopolitanism, hedonism and loose sexual morals. Dyer explains that 'the films both indulge in these, and their many opportunities for erotic or sinister display, and present them as decadent and corrupt' (Dyer 2015: 183). The latter perspective is realised through the fact that:

> The victims in most of these films have not only damaged the family, as the killer sees it, but are most often by definition enemies of the family, that is of proper reproduction. Straying wives and independent women, notably those in the professions of display (fashion, modelling, pornography, prostitution), and frolicking, undisciplined teenage girls all undermine patriarchal authority and threaten to create an alternative world not based on marriage and the family. (Dyer 2015: 189)

Accordingly, the serial killer's victims in *Nude per l'assassino* include a gynaecologist who performed a botched abortion, a homosexual fashion photographer, three promiscuous bisexual women (two models – Lucia and Doris – and Gisella, the owner of the model agency), and Gisella's impotent virgin husband.

As the above quotation from Dyer suggests, one of the most unmissable aspects of the *giallo* is its repeated representation of gender roles that subvert normative family-oriented structures. I have already made reference to a number of examples in which independent, unattached women enjoy the freedoms of globalised modernity, in *La ragazza che sapeva troppo*, *Paranoia*, *Perché quelle strane gocce di sangue sul corpo di Jennifer?* and *Il tuo vizio è una stanza chiusa e solo io ne ho la chiave*. It is therefore notable that issues surrounding the place of women in society, feminine liberation and contemporaneous feminist movements are repeated topics in the diegesis of many *gialli*. In *Il rosso segno della follia*, John rationalises his killing of women wearing bridal dresses when his interior monologue says: 'a woman should live only until her wedding night, love once and then die', while in *La morte accarezza a mezzanotte*, Stefano hassles Valentina to have a child with him, but she says that she has no desire to settle down. When she subsequently makes tea for him and two children who are staying with them, he compliments her on being a 'perfect housewife'. We are told that Dick and Ingrid in *Un posto ideale per uccidere* met when she was protesting with a feminist activist group, while *Profondo rosso* gives Marcus (David Hemmings) an entire scene to belittle such movements. When Gianna says 'a woman has to be independent to be equal to a man', Marcus responds with: 'Oh God, let's not start with sexual equality. It's all rubbish, not true at all. Men are different from women. Women are delicate and fragile.' The *giallo*'s ambivalent and contradictory position on such debates then becomes apparent once more, as Gianna challenges Marcus to an arm wrestle to prove him wrong, and beats him, but he continues: 'Statistics prove that you can't work seriously with liberated women.' As he then moodily prepares to leave without her, she abruptly capitulates to the patriarchal norm whereby a woman's worth is judged in relation to masculine ideals, pleading: 'Tell me the truth. Do you find me so unattractive? . . . Is it my smell? What?'

Bini explicitly ties the *giallo*'s representations of gender and sexuality to shifts in sexual mores, the arrival of the pill, the divorce law and the rise of radical feminist movements (such as the *Movimento Liberazione delle Donne*, the *Fronte Italiano Liberazione Femminile* and *Rivolta Femminile*) in Italy at the dawn of the 1970s. He goes on to argue that the preponderance of female killers in Argento's films in particular betrays a deep-seated anxiety on the part of Italian audiences around perceived dangers associated with the increasing independence of women in society (Bini 2011: 65–8). Jacqueline Reich has argued, meanwhile, that Argento's equally frequent depictions of women being mutilated demonstrate a projection of patriarchal anxiety onto the female (and specifically maternal) body (Reich 2001: 92). As is so often the case when considering the *giallo*, such an auteurist focus on Argento (or Bava) tends to overlook the ways in which these themes play out in the broader *filone*. *Cosa avete fatto a Solange?*, for example, tells the tale of a teenage girl who, having once been part of a sexually promiscuous clique, had a traumatic back-street abortion which drove her into 'infantile regression'. Her father has since been hunting down the girls who led her astray, and killing them by stabbing knives into their vaginas while dressed as a priest.

Certainly, we can read patriarchal phobia of female emancipation into such a framing of abortion as a traumatic invasion of the body. This apparent invasion then inspires (Catholic-coded) revenge through what the killer perceives to be an equivalently invasive assault on female genitalia (and the traumatic consequences of abortion are also at the centre of *Nude per l'assassino*). Such a reading would, however, be to ascribe a moral coherence to *Cosa avete fatto a Solange?* (and, indeed, to the *giallo* more broadly) that is not necessarily there. The central protagonist Enrico – a married Italian teacher working in London, who has been sleeping with one of his students – gradually pieces the mystery behind the killings together. The group of girls, he discovers, were 'only sixteen, and surrounded by secret boyfriends, petty jealousies, orgies and lesbian games . . . I wouldn't be surprised if they were doing the drug scene too.'

Enrico's line encapsulates the muddled, incoherent selection of ingredients that go into the *giallo*'s collective construction of a licentious 'modern' world. Promiscuity, abortion, drug abuse, homosexuality, sadomasochism, countercultural delinquency, prostitution, bourgeois decadence, consumerism and globalised cosmopolitanism are all conflated to become part of what Dyer dubs this *filone*'s 'fresco of corruption' (Dyer 2015: 189). Without doubt, certain aspects of this mode of representation are (from my subjective position in the year 2018) problematic relics of reactionary 1970s outlooks. Most notably, homosexuality is repeatedly and unquestioningly associated with predatory behaviour or sexual perversion: for example, in the characterisations of the antique shop owner in *L'uccello dalle piume di cristallo*, the killer in *Giornata nera per l'ariete / The Fifth Cord* (Luigi Bazzoni, 1971) or the fashion photographer in *Perché quelle strane gocce di sangue sul corpo di Jennifer?* (who says that he objects to the Islamic notion of paradise because 'that would be prohibited to minors under twenty one, and what fun would that be?'). However, such outmoded assumptions are more appropriately considered as part of the *giallo*'s cacophony of licentious modernity, precisely because they are assumptions, born of prejudice rather than any carefully thought-through moral stance. Having taken on the overarching thematic task of creating recognisably 'modern' settings, the filmmakers' choices are revealing for how they repeatedly coalesce around the same topics. Such is the modus operandi of *filone* cinema.

As I have previously argued in relation to both the vigilante and the mafia *filoni*, the assumptions that build this world are constructed as much through seemingly inconsequential asides and scene-setting comments as they are through overt symbolism. For example, in *Lo strano vizio della signora Wardh*, when Jennifer confides in her friend Carol that she is worried her husband will find out about her infidelity, Carol tells her not to worry because 'così è il mondo' ('it's the way of the world'). Her implication that promiscuity is a tacitly accepted component of modern life is starkly realised in the first ten minutes of Sergio Martino's later film *Il tuo vizio è una stanza chiusa e solo io ne ho la chiave*, which establishes this world through a series of signifiers for the rapidly shifting mores of contemporary society. After the opening credits have played over a shot of a couple cavorting under bed sheets, we find Oliviero (Luigi Pistilli) hosting a debauched party in his mansion. He first humiliates his wife Irina by forcing her to drink a cocktail of everybody's drinks, and then sexually assaults his maid in front of the guests. As these young hippies then break into song, one of the female guests starts dancing and stripping off her clothes. Once everybody has left, Irina dresses in Oliviero's late mother's clothes to sexually arouse him, and he hits her before raping her, as the portrait of his mother looks on. The film does not pass any clear moral judgement on this catalogue of debauchery (Irina, not Oliviero, turns out to be the film's killer). Rather, it serves to establish a resolutely 'modern' backdrop, whose taken-as-read licentious components remind the viewer of the pace of change in contemporary society. As a scene-setting device, it serves an equivalent (though more titillating) purpose to the policeman's passing comment to Oliviero that 'European integration's not bad, don't you think Mr Ruvigny? . . . Here we are in a tranquil Veneto town, drinking German beer and Scottish whisky.'

The 'modernity' that accumulates through repetition in the *giallo* is thus one that simplistically conflates loosening moral standards, shifting mores around sexual politics, the atomisation of urban living, increasing consumerism and a marked internationalisation of Italian (and broader European) society. This *filone* therefore acts as a document of a culture taking stock of rapid transformations, by immersing many of its films in settings that symbolise or represent those very changes. Not all *gialli*, however, are set in the midst of such cosmopolitanism or bourgeois decadence. Some are instead united by their setting in a parochial rural Italian underbelly. These provide a contrapuntal, rather than a direct, examination of modernity.

The Rural *Giallo*

Mario Bava's *Reazione a catena* (1971) takes thematic oppositions that would become common in the *giallo filone*, but removes them from their usual urban locations. The remote rural setting of 'the bay' provides a starkly alien milieu, in which a series of outsiders arrive, only to become embroiled in a local family blood feud. The most conspicuous interlopers are a group of four free-spirited young hippies hailing from various parts of Europe, who arrive to indulge in promiscuous fun. As one of them swims naked in the bay, the dead body of the murdered Countess's husband floats to the surface and brushes past her. A viewer would be forgiven for interpreting this as a symbol for the dark, violent urges of the hinterland rising to the surface to confront an unwelcome representative of licentious modernity. Sure enough, all four youths (two of whom are having sex as they are killed) are subsequently hacked or stabbed to death.

Clearly, the contrast between cosmopolitanism and parochialism is indeed being evoked in the above sub-plot, but the denouement reveals that these killings are not – as they might at first appear – a manifestation of violent resistance to the onset of modernity. In fact, the youths were killed by Simon: the son of the Countess and the person who also killed the Countess's husband Filippo (after Filippo had himself killed the

Countess). Far from embodying a provincial resistance to the encroachment of the modern world, Simon is in cahoots with a real-estate agent named Frank Ventura, to whom he intends to sell the land he will inherit, so that it can be developed into holiday homes. The young hippies were merely unfortunate witnesses who had to be disposed of for Frank and Simon's plan to succeed. In *Reazione a catena*, therefore, victims are not selected because they represent the changes wrought on society by the onset of modern lifestyles. Rather, people are more likely to be killed because they are standing in the way of such an encroachment. Before she was murdered, the Countess had rejected Frank's offer to buy the land and build 'exclusive modern villas', telling him: 'your arguments are not enough to convert me to modernism'. Paolo, a local entomologist, tells Filippo's daughter Renata (who arrives to claim the land for herself) that he always resisted her father's earlier attempts to sacrifice the area's natural beauty for tourism, the accoutrements of automotive transport and the general influx of a debased modern world: 'His idea to transform the bay into a fashionable resort was doomed to fail from the start . . . I only hope you don't intend reopening any nightclubs, gas stations, and all the other devilries installed by your father.' Paolo and his wife are duly murdered by Renata and her husband Albert.

This somewhat convoluted collection of brutal killings is therefore centred around the social tensions associated with rapid economic development. The rural underbelly is framed as an atavistic relic of a savagery that is supposed to be consigned to the past, when Paolo tells Simon that 'man is not an insect . . . We have thousands of years of civilisation behind us', but Simon retorts: 'I don't know about that. I wasn't there.' Frank Ventura – with his licentious lifestyle and his plans for the financial exploitation of the bay – is a conspicuous representative of capitalist modernity intruding on this archaic world and trying to sweep aside those who stand in his way. Having said this, I do not seek to claim this film as an underappreciated work of political commitment. *Reazione a catena* is more interesting on an industrial level, for how it spawned a strand of films that similarly utilised rural backwater settings to focus on tensions surrounding the rapid onset of modernity and schismatic outlooks on the recent past.

Each of these films utilises tropes common throughout the larger *giallo filone* – investigations piecing together fragments of past trauma, tensions between the global and the local, contemporaneity and nostalgia, modernity and tradition – as entry points into the dark history of a remote rural community. These films have been identified as manifestations of 'modernity's shattering of the idyllic isolation rural villages had experienced . . . as a result of outside interference and [being] exposed to the outside world' (Koven 2006: 57–8), with their settings being analysed as 'a dialectical binary of the late-modern city' (Kannas 2013). Both Koven and Kannas thus identify these films' pertinence for discourses surrounding the economic and cultural changes wrought on Italian society since the Second World War. I would go further still and suggest that, in the rural *giallo*, the larger *filone*'s common tension between cosmopolitanism and parochialism provides a form of time travel, in which a representative of modernity discovers a point of contact with the local past, which inescapably haunts or shapes the 1970s present. Each also demands that this 'time traveller' figure delves into the past to solve a mystery; but in each, as so often in the *giallo*, the 'facts' of the past are shown to be unstable, so that 'history' becomes a construct of competing memories, be they individual or cultural. In each film, therefore, the living past and the unreliability of its facts are presented as objects of intense scrutiny.

La casa dalle finestre che ridono is emblematic of this strand. This is due not only to its setting in a parochial, rural Italian locale, but also to the fact that its thematic construction overtly focuses on this setting by examining the tourist veneer of Italy's heritage industry. As the traveller figure Stefano is welcomed into the remote village by Mayor Solmi, it is made clear to him that the image of quaint antiquity must be restored in order for the local economy to recover through tourism. Indeed, this is why Stefano has been called for in the first place: to help maintain the tourist façade by repairing the fresco in an old rural church. The viewer is then presented with various symbols for this peeling veneer, which barely covers up the traumas of the past: most overtly, in the very painting Stefano is there to restore, which acts as a palimpsest as its historical layers and their disturbing meanings are uncovered through the course of the film. Furthermore, the traumas of the Second World War surface time and again as a past that lurks just beneath the community's present difficulties, haunting the collective memory of this village. The local river can no longer support wildlife because it remains littered with war surplus. The hotel landlady's lie that she is expecting a busload of tourists is exposed when the cleaner tells Stefano 'our last tourists were those German bastards in the 1940s'. Even the church itself acts as a historical palimpsest, since we are told that it was rebuilt after the SS used it as a hideout. The village in Avati's film (in reality Lido degli Scacchi in Emilia-Romagna) is therefore presented as more than just a stereotypically parochial backwater. Alongside this mode of representation runs a constant theme pertaining to the open wounds of the past, and how they continue to flow through the present.

The film is most illustrative of this argument when its plot proceeds to frame the past as an ever-shifting entity whose meanings demand deduction through the examination of collective or individual memories. A pivotal scene comes just after Stefano has found bones buried outside an abandoned building (giving him and the viewer clear evidence of historical murders), and then discovers the dead body of his accomplice Francesca hanging from a hook inside the same building. When he hurriedly returns to the scene with the local *Carabinieri* to show them the evidence, both the bones and Francesca's body have mysteriously disappeared. Time and again in this film, such pieces of evidence for the crimes of the past vanish, leaving only their memories (for both Stefano and the viewer). As well as the disappearance of the bones, a taped voice is inexplicably wiped and the restored painting is sabotaged. Just like Sam in *L'uccello dalle piume di cristallo* and Marcus in *Profondo rosso*, Stefano is therefore left to construct his story from his memory, and the meanings he attaches to these memories are more important than the bare facts, which are shown to be unreliable. Indeed, throughout *La casa dalle finestre che ridono*, the narrative of history does not merely consist of the facts of the past, but instead relies on what we make of those facts (Stefano's quest to piece the mystery together from the fragments he has at his disposal forms the entire narrative thrust) and which ones we can see. As the *Carabinieri* depart from the suddenly empty mass grave, the camera reveals to the viewer alone that a jawbone had in fact been left behind, but was missed during the search. Tantalising traces of the past do therefore remain, if only the characters can find them.

The commentary on the selective construction of history in the above scene (and in the film more broadly) is not particularly sophisticated, and does not necessarily require a more detailed textual deconstruction than that which I have just provided. It should, however, be situated in its cultural–political contexts and appraised for what its particular mode of address can tell us within larger discourses of its era. Firstly, and as already stated, *La casa dalle finestre che ridono* was not alone in sending a representative of contemporary Italy into a primitive rural backwater, or in using this setting as a means to examine the traumas of the past. Indeed, its industrial status as a product of the *filone* system (characterised by formulaic repetition alongside incremental innovation) is palpable when we compare its opening sequence to the almost identical equivalent in *Solamente nero*, made two years later. In both, an urbane young Italian art historian named Stefano and played by Lino Capolicchio arrives from a modern city into a remote, superstitious locale by boat, having just met a female visitor who will later become his accomplice in the investigation of historical murders. In both films, a painting then plays a key role in the unravelling of the plot (another echo of *L'uccello dalle piume di cristallo* and *Profondo rosso*), and in both, the denouement reveals a perverted priesthood to be the source of the psychosis. Koven identifies the similarities between these two films as an indication of the *giallo*'s iterative ambivalence towards the encroachment of modernity: the two Stefanos acting as harbingers who are resisted by the local community (Koven 2006: 57–8).

Entwined within this commentary on the onset of modernity is the contrapuntal framing of a residual Italy from a bygone era, whose antiquated mores cause tensions upon the arrival of the cosmopolitan protagonist. Each of the rural *gialli* under consideration here invests in and explores notions of a packaged 'picture book' Italy, whether by overtly focusing on the tourist trade (as in *La casa dalle finestre che ridono*), or by using locations with relevance to a tourist outlook. Baschiera's and Di Chiara's analysis of *I corpi presentano tracce di violenza carnale*, for example, examines the film's initial setting in Perugia – a provincial city containing a popular university for foreigners – as an apt space to frame a tension between local and touristic perspectives (Baschiera and Di Chiara 2010: 116). The locations of both *Solamente nero* (the Venetian islands) and *Non si sevizia un paperino* (the mountains of the southern interior), meanwhile, possess particular historical redolence of an Italy constructed by the Baedeker guidebook and the *Illustrazione Italiana* magazine.[6]

Such framings of Italy through an overt focus on location to explore the backwardness of rural or provincial communities can be informed by a consideration of the 'heritage film': a genre that is intimately tied to discourses of remembrance around national and local histories. Rosalind Galt takes issue with approaches that view such films as ahistorical myth, celebratory nostalgia or anodyne spectacle. She argues instead that *Nuovo Cinema Paradiso / Cinema Paradiso* (Giuseppe Tornatore, 1988), *Mediterraneo* (Gabriele Salvatores, 1991) and *Il postino / The Postman* (Michael Radford, 1994) possess political significance, not for their few direct references to the ideological schisms of their setting in the immediate post-war years, but through their very mode of address within the conventions of romantic melodrama. Galt's analysis diagnoses an exchange between the films' setting (in a moment of possibility and hope just before the foundation of Italy's First Republic) and the political moment of their production (when that same, now corrupted, republic was on the verge of implosion and demise): an exchange whose temporal specificity demanded the 'projection of politics onto romance' (Galt 2006: 38).

It goes without saying that the representations of provincial Italy to be found in the rural *giallo* are of a different tenor to those of the heritage films analysed by Galt: psychotic, nightmarish visions of occult superstition, which would be hard to shoehorn into the category 'romantic'. Furthermore, these *gialli* are physically set in the 1970s present rather than in the past, rendering their status as 'historical' films ambiguous. Galt's argument nevertheless points to an illuminating methodological context for appraising the mode of popular address through which the rural *giallo* invests in representations of Italy's antiquated underbelly:

> That all three [heritage] films should be made within a few years of one another, and that they should all deploy narratives of romantic loss to imagine the postwar years, is symptomatic not so much of the continuing influence of the postwar period in Italian culture but of a more precise shift in the relationship between this particular history and the films' present. (Galt 2006: 39)

Galt thus identifies this rapidly replicated popular format as a gauge for the ever-shifting dialogue between the historical period being evoked on screen and the significance of that period for the present moment. Related scholarly approaches have also thrown light on other cultural contexts. Julia Leyda, for example, has identified a strategy of temporal displacement in 'black Westerns' of the 1930s that targeted inner-city African American audiences by employing 'strategic anachronisms': 'the result is a western that creates a dual present. The fictional characters appear to be in the classic western setting, the nineteenth century, but the anachronistic dialogue, the titles, and the costumes place the film firmly in the 1930s' (Leyda 2002: 62, 63).

Both Galt and Leyda analyse how such films create a dialogue between the moment of the films' production and their physical settings in the historical past. Though rural *gialli* do not fall into this category, they can be said to create a similar kind of 'dual present' in which their protagonists appear peculiarly anachronistic in their surroundings, through the use of 'heritage' settings that overtly conjure the past. They thus demand that we consider the significance of this past for the concerns of the films' own cultural–political moment. Unlike the heritage film and the black Western, the rural *giallo* does not evoke a specific historical period. Rather, it presents a generically 'backward' world which is assumed to exist in the collective memory of many Italians, but which is swiftly being consigned to history by the encroachment of modern lifestyles. By definition, a 'mystery' narrative format (which, as we have seen, is a more accurate implication of the word '*giallo*' in an Italian cultural context than are oft-assumed 'horror' paradigms (Hunter 2009: 104–106)) demands that a film's plot burrows into past events. When allied to settings that pertain to Italy's 'heritage' antiquity, this provides an apt outlet for a preoccupation with local history at a moment of national crisis, when reflections on the past and its implications for contemporary identity were pressing.

Non si sevizia un paperino provides the most vivid illustration of this point. Shot mostly in the mountains of Puglia and Basilicata, this film is set in not only a distinctively Italian locale, but specifically a southern Italian locale. Accordingly, it invests heavily in traditions of representation that have surrounded the southern regions of the Italian peninsula for centuries. As we have seen in some detail in Chapter 3, the *Mezzogiorno* has long been framed as an archaic frontier land, serving simultaneously as a mirror for Italian national identity and a window into Italy's primitive or feudal past. Since the *Risorgimento*, the south has thereby offered an arena for deliberation around contemporary neuroses of the nation state: what John Dickie terms 'the testing-ground of Italy's modernity, the measure of its claims to civility, and the focus of national solidarity' (Dickie 1999: 56). Fulci's film inherits and recycles the local significance of the setting for a murder mystery around a series of child killings, and in so doing provides a stage for a culture clash between a dark, benighted underbelly and the onset of cosmopolitan modernity.

The film's overt focus on the primordiality of its fictional southern village of Accendura has been widely analysed in scholarly literature.[7] The opening pan shot (Figures 4.3 and 4.4) in particular has received attention for the way in which, in the words of Cosimo Urbano, it 'immediately establishes the film's basic and unresolvable conflict: a modernity fuelled by economic development traversing an ancient, almost archaic, rural community, disrupting age-old rhythms' (Urbano 2007: 74). A long shot of the mountainous landscape of the southern interior straight away pans to the concrete scar of an *autostrada* ploughing through the middle of the rugged natural beauty, providing a clear symbol for this culture clash in twentieth century Italy.[8] This very conflict is then represented through the narrative and the *mise en scène*, setting up a series of thematic and symbolic contrasts in the opening ten minutes. The intrusion into the quiet village of the liberated, licentious Milanese woman Patrizia (Barbara Bouchet),

Figures 4.3 and 4.4 The opening pan shot of *Non si sevizia un paperino* (Lucio Fulci, 1972) juxtaposes the modern *autostrada* with its primordial surroundings.

for example, provides a counterpoint to the ostracism of the feared witch Maciara (Florinda Bolkan). When Patrizia's strikingly modernist house is first seen, it is framed perching awkwardly above the ancient whitewashed village, and the editing accentuates the juxtaposition by cutting straight to the architectural hub of Italian rural community life, the *campanile* (bell tower). A subsequent scene of gaudily dressed women driving along the *autostrada* and loudly discussing their consumerist lives up north is followed by one of a mysterious, candle-lit voodoo ceremony. Fulci himself stated that his film's original setting was going to be Turin – a northern industrial metropolis that had seen a large influx of southern migrant workers during and after the Economic Miracle of the 1950s – where he claimed to have seen voodoo ceremonies taking place amongst factory workers (Palmerini and Mistretta 1996: 59). The anachronistic incongruity of what were perceived to be southern cultural mores in contemporary Italy was, therefore, the driving theme behind this film's production from the start.

Fulci's 'south' therefore inherits that region's long-established role of holding up a mirror to contemporary Italy as a means by which to scrutinise the condition of the modern state. This point is made explicit when the dying, bloodied Maciara, having been savagely beaten by the townsfolk, crawls agonisingly to the edge of the *autostrada*. Her final moments are spliced with images of comfortably well-off tourist families speeding past on their holidays in the picturesque south, oblivious to her suffering and, by extension, to the violence of Italy's underbelly literally lying just inches away from their consumerist dream. Stephen Thrower identifies this scene as a key moment of social criticism in the film: 'a devastating vision of the social isolation of these quiet, superficially picturesque backwaters' (Thrower 1999: 88). As Maciara at last expires, the scene cuts straight to police officers covering her dead body, and a detective provides an explanation (as if it were needed) for the obvious symbolism: 'we construct gleaming highways, but we're a long way from modernising'.

Side-by-side with this transparent critique of modernity lies another of the south's traditional cultural functions: that of a window into the past through an exploration of the nation's primal state. This is most manifest in the resolutely archaic *mise en scène*, which frequently arrests the viewer and the 'outsider' figures alike, to situate us in a perceptual time warp: as when Patrizia and Martelli (Tomas Milian) stop their car on a mountain road, and the passer-by they ask about a missing child is riding a donkey. The focus on a past that is fast disappearing is also woven into the film's thematic construction. The denouement reveals that (as in *La casa dalle finestre che ridono* and *Solamente nero*) the killer is the village priest. As he falls to his death, Don Alberto's motivations for the child murders are explained in a voice-over. Nostalgic flashbacks of his victims' youthful vigour are spliced with shots of the priest's violent demise, as we learn that his intention all along was to prevent the children from falling into sin by freezing them in their innocence. As a plot device, this merely repeats what Koven dubs the *giallo*'s 'pop-culture psychology', whereby the *filone* repeatedly lends itself to 'pat psychoanalytical explanations' for killers' psychoses (Koven 2014: 206). The decision to ally this thematic focus on preserving the past in aspic and resisting the progress of time with an overtly emphasised setting in a stereotypical rural south, however, is significant. It places Fulci's film within a continuum of cultural representations of the region that are always already implicit commentaries on the past. As Bondanella has pointed out, Accendura is a premodern relic, reminiscent of the anachronistic village described in Carlo Levi's 1945 memoir *Cristo si è fermato a Eboli / Christ Stopped at Eboli* (Bondanella 2009: 393).

Taken together, the rural *gialli* analysed here therefore confront the wider *filone*'s cosmopolitan protagonists with the remnants of societies that have been swept aside and consigned to the past by contemporary Italy's embrace of modernity. Dyer identifies an explicit line of influence on the *giallo* from the case of Leonarda Cianciulli, a notorious serial killer ('la Saponificatrice di Correggio' / 'the soap-maker of Correggio') who was imprisoned in 1946 for murdering three women and making jam, cakes, soap and candles from their bodies. For Dyer, the *giallo* demonstrates Cianciulli's enduring resonance into the 1970s since, beyond the specific monstrosity of her crimes, her case infuses this *filone*'s thematic oppositions. Her southern origins, allied to her explanation that a fortune teller had foreseen her children's deaths unless she committed human sacrifice, bring together 'central dynamics of contemporaneous Italian culture, situated on the cusp of rural and urban, ancient and modern, and, not least in terms of Italian regional sensitivities and prejudices, North and South' (Dyer 2015: 184). The rural *giallo* in particular dramatises the tensions between these worlds: one denoting an affluent future, the other a benighted past.

I corpi presentano tracce di violenza carnale is an appropriate film with which to draw this chapter to a close, since it is emblematic of many of the strands discussed so far. The film's use of location divides it into two parts: the first, in the medieval university city of Perugia, follows the pattern of many *gialli* set in urban centres; the second, shot in the small rural town of Tagliacozzo in Abruzzo, isolates representatives of globalised modernity in a remote backwater with a typically 'rural *giallo*' thematic structure.

The plot follows a group of young international students, who attend parties with drug-taking hippies and in their sexual behaviour enact the *giallo*'s usual conflation of promiscuity, homosexuality and prostitution. When a detective addresses their class in an appeal for information, his brief, dismissive reference to the tendency of students to 'protest and riot' in an attempt to 'dismantle the state' implicitly places recent youth protest movements alongside such licentiousness in the melting pot that comprises a generic 'modernity'. The city centre of Perugia – as both a site of medieval tourist attractions and a hub for cosmopolitan student lifestyles – is an appropriate setting for a typically '*giallo*' contrast between Italy's rich historical heritage and its globalised contemporaneity. A street vendor emphasises the impact of tourists and students on the city's social cohesion, when he says that he does not know who any of his customers are because 'this place is like a sea port. Strange faces every day, all sorts of colours, all sorts of races.' When four of the female students decide to escape Perugia and take a break in a remote rural town, the cultural contrast between cosmopolitan modernity and parochial backwardness is accentuated, and placed centre-stage. As Ursula, a young black woman, sits waiting for her friends, the town's menfolk stand transfixed, as their lustful reaction shots are spliced with close-ups of her scantily clad body. By positioning her as an exotic oddity, the film communicates the clear implication that ethnic diversity is still an unfamiliar concept in such provincial locales.

In Chapter 1, I explored John Foot's notion of Italy's 'divided memory', and the resurfacing of wartime traumas from a 'shared silence' (Foot 2009: 168). By the early 1970s, such memories were going hand-in-hand with a broader sense of taking stock of the social and economic transformations that had occurred in the intervening years. When we consider this context of an era in which both the details and the significance of historical events were highly politicised subjects of dispute, the *giallo*'s various preoccupations – with the rapid pace of change in modern society, with the piecing together of fragmented memories, with repressed traumas, with the unreliability of supposed facts and with settings evoking soon-to-be-historical, antiquated lifestyles – can be seen to be part of Italy's 'rich and complicated kaleidoscope of debates over the past' (Foot 2009: 206). Though these films are almost all physically set in contemporary 1970s Italy, they demonstrate that an engagement with local history and its ongoing significance for the present does not necessarily have to come through direct (or even purposeful) references. We can instead diagnose a preoccupation with the past that is inherited and recycled from the surrounding source material, and that takes on a particular significance in its own cultural moment. Any act of contemplating a national or local past is an inherently politicised one, and this was certainly the case in 1970s Italy. Through such modes of representation, these films display one available register within what Isaiah Berlin called this historical moment's 'room for manoeuvre' (Ignatieff 2000: 206),[9] and one cultural option open to Italian audiences at the time for the contemplation of their contemporary condition.

The extent to which the *giallo* can be said to constitute such a culturally specific 'national' (Italian) discourse should not, however, be taken at face value. The majority of *gialli* were international co-productions (most commonly with France, Spain or West Germany), and were therefore often attempting to exploit multiple markets simultaneously. Moreover, though *I corpi presentano tracce di violenza carnale* was not a co-production (it was produced by the Roman company Compagnia Cinematografica Champion alone), it would go on to enjoy greater success in anglophone export markets (under the considerably more succinct title *Torso*) than it did in Italy itself (Baschiera and Di Chiara 2010: 119). Focusing on the liminality of place and identity, Baschiera and Di Chiara argue that the constant tension between the local and the global that runs throughout this *filone*, and especially *I corpi presentano tracce di violenza carnale*, cuts it adrift from any clear 'national' moorings. The 'Italian-ness' of the settings is here read as the construction of an exotic tourist gaze on behalf of international audiences:

> *Torso*, like other *gialli* and horror films set in the Italian province, copes in a different way [from Mario Bava's 'touristic . . . uncanny space' (Baschiera and Di Chiara 2010: 114)] with the transnational productive nature of the genre itself. Instead of hiding the national character . . . it represents particular local places charged with artistic values, and renders them perfectly understandable and known for every audience thanks to their touristic features. (Baschiera and Di Chiara 2010: 118–19)

Thus, the provincial underbelly of Italy operates as an object of picture-postcard fascination across national and cultural boundaries, performing a generic 'Italian-ness' for audiences all over the world by enacting themes of 'dislocation, migration, transnational identity, and tourism' (Baschiera and Di Chiara 2010: 119).

This book has so far investigated various strands of Italian crime *filoni* and considered how they register, recycle or exploit tensions surrounding memories of the recent past and the pace of change in Italian society. In each case, this has been argued to be a process of iterative accumulation across groups of films, rather than individual films working separately from one another. Each strand has thus been seen to reveal collective assumptions being made by *filone* filmmakers about their audiences' shared cultural memories or levels of prior knowledge. Each case has also included a consideration of international influences (most often from the USA) that have come to bear upon the production of these films, thus allowing us to interpret them as symptoms of socio-economic change as much as commentaries on it. In Chapter 1, however, I argued that a narrow focus on the moment of films' production and initial domestic release is ultimately insufficient, if we wish fully to place them in their historical contexts. A broader focus on what Barbara Klinger calls 'diachronic' reception patterns – the changing meanings of films across time and space (Klinger 1997: 111) – is still therefore required in this volume. The final chapter will attempt to fulfil this requirement. Given the global appeal of 1970s Italian crime cinema since the films' initial releases, and the attendant diversity of meanings that have been attached to these *filoni*, to what extent can we (or should we) situate such films solely as documents of the specific historical, cultural and industrial concerns of 1970s Italy, as this book has so far sought to do?

Notes

1. As is usually the case with *filone* cinema, exact numbers are impossible to quantify due to the porosity of the boundaries between various trends. Richard Dyer's estimate that around 200 *gialli* were made in the 1960s and 1970s (Dyer 2015: 204) is as good as any.
2. Xavier Mendik (2014) has labelled such films the '*Mezzogiorno giallo*'. I opt for 'rural *giallo*', to avoid conflating Italy's rural spaces with specific discourses surrounding the nation's southern regions, since these films (with the notable exception of *Non si sevizia un paperino*) are in fact mostly set and shot in the north of the country.
3. This is not to say that these two *filoni* adopt identical explanations for such acts of violence. As we have seen, the plots of *poliziotteschi* such as *La polizia ringrazia* / *Execution Squad* (Stefano Vanzina, 1972) and *Milano trema – la polizia vuole giustizia* / *The Violent Professionals* (Sergio Martino, 1973) are engaged firmly with the socio-political moment, leading towards the exposure of official cover-ups lurking behind politically motivated acts of violent crime. In contrast, the best-known *gialli*, such as *L'uccello dalle piume di cristallo* and *Perché quelle strane gocce di sangue sul corpo di Jennifer?*, as well as the 'rural *gialli*' examined later on in this chapter, tend to offer psychological explanations of individual psychosis.
4. This Latin phrase is taken from Cicero's *First Catilinarian*: a speech to the Roman Senate on 8 November 63 BC, in which the famed orator lamented the corruption of contemporary Rome. Translating literally as 'Oh the times! Oh

the customs!', the phrase has become a common exclamatory mantra of exasperation at the era in which one lives (see Beard 2015: 41).
5. It is worth noting here that two other *gialli* set in London – *Gli occhi freddi della paura* / *Cold Eyes of Fear* (Enzo G. Castellari, 1971) and *Cosa avete fatto a Solange?* / *What Have You Done to Solange?* (Massimo Dallamano, 1972) – both feature groups of youths engaged in either free love and drugs, or violence against the state. Clearly, such generational rebellion was seen as a constituent part of being one of the world's most sought-after 'modern' cities.
6. The *Illustrazione Italiana* was one of a number of Milanese magazines that emerged in the second half of the nineteenth century, which coincided with increasing northern urbanisation and catered for an attendant fascination with 'exotic' areas of the world, including the south of Italy. For a detailed analysis of this particular publication's modes of representing the south, see Dickie 1999: 85–111.
7. The significance of this film's southern setting is for example central to Mendik's identification of Italy's 'rural repressed', which reveals hidden depths within the national psyche (Mendik 2014: 398–400).
8. As Chapter 3 has demonstrated, the image of a new road sitting conspicuously amidst the landscape of the south also immediately evokes other, mafia-related, stereotypes of the *Mezzogiorno*.
9. The debate between Isaiah Berlin and E. H. Carr that provoked this line of argument has already been alluded to in this book's introduction.

CHAPTER 5

Enter . . . If You Dare! The Cross-cultural Reception of Crime *Filoni*

At the bottom of the local film listings page in Wilmington, Delaware's *The Morning News* on Monday 24 July 1972, one banner advert stands out. Potential cinemagoers are confronted with 'the first motion picture to require a <u>face-to-face</u> warning! diabolical! fiendish! Savage . . . you may not walk away from this one! . . . Every ticket holder MUST pass through THE FINAL WARNING STATION. We MUST warn you <u>face-to-face</u>!' (Figure 5.1). The film in question is *Reazione a catena* (Mario Bava, 1971), here marketed under its US theatrical release title *Twitch of the Death Nerve*, playing at the ABC Ciné Mart theatre. Upon seeing this ballyhoo nestled between more sedate adverts for such prestige cinematic fare as *Fiddler on the Roof* (Norman Jewison, 1971), *The Godfather* (Francis Ford Coppola, 1972) and *The War Between Men and Women* (Melville Shavelson, 1972), and for ragtime musician Max Morath's performance at the University of Delaware's Mitchell Hall, one might suppose that Bava's film was received by the Wilmington public as a wildly transgressive shock to the system. Yet, further up the very same page, a one-line review of the film abruptly punctures this notion: 'Melodramatic schlock that doesn't live up to its sensational advertising' (Anon 1972b: 14).

This small snapshot of one film's marketing in an overseas distribution context points to a number of issues that have so far been merely alluded to in this book, but which require further investigation. Various competing readings of the film here become available through such extra-filmic factors as cross-cultural retitling, promotional taglines, the supposed authority of the film reviewer, the proximity of a given film to other films (physically, on the page) and its simultaneous distance from those same films (culturally, in terms of high / low distinctions of taste), as well as the carnivalesque (and presumably imaginary) 'final warning station' through which the prospective cinemagoer must pass. In particular, the striking dissonance between the lurid tone of the advert and the reviewer's sober dismissal of that same advert's sensationalism emphasises the extent to

Figure 5.1 Banner ad for *Reazione a catena* (Mario Bava, 1971) in *The Morning News* (Wilmington, Delaware), 24 July 1972.

which such promotional materials do not necessarily direct or dictate a viewer's experience of a film. Rather, they exemplify Barbara Klinger's argument when she describes these materials as cinematic 'digressions', which fragment a film by producing 'multiple avenues of access' to it (Klinger 1989: 10). Faced with such a contradiction, the consumer may choose to accept, reject or negotiate with any of the various readings on offer.

The above discussion may appear to be anomalous in a book whose focus has so far been on the contents of various Italian crime *filoni* and the historical–political contexts that surrounded their production and domestic releases, but such a consideration of promotional materials and their surrounding discourses is required, to fill a gap that remains in my analysis. Chapters 2, 3 and 4 have all arrived at the conclusion that the significance of these films ultimately lies in their status as overlapping sets of rapidly produced 'serial' repetitions, rather than as individual or self-contained works. Yet such a claim cannot be deduced simply by interpreting the contents of the films themselves, since the proximity of their distribution in a given market is as decisive to this status being conferred, as is the rapidity of their production. A highly concentrated release pattern of closely related films (such as that outlined in Chapter 3, in the case of the mafia *filone*'s Italian distribution) is materially different to a scenario in which a select few of those same films are released sporadically, over a longer period, dubbed into English, and in a different order. This latter pattern – which is precisely how the various *filone* strands discussed in this book arrived into the North American market – is in turn likely to produce divergent promotional strategies and surrounding discourses.

In the introduction to this book, I advocated an approach that would seek to 'appraise the cultural options open to Italian audiences at the time to "think historically"'. Such an undertaking has long been a defining goal of cinematic 'reception studies' which, broadly speaking, analyse various extra-filmic elements in an attempt to gauge how the viewing experience is guided by historically constituted factors lying outside the contents of the films themselves. For Janet Staiger, a historically grounded attempt to gauge audience response should seek to assess 'the range of strategies available in particular social formations' (Staiger 1992: 80–1), while Klinger aims to provide 'a sense of what the historical prospects were for viewing at a given time by illuminating the meanings made available within that moment' (Klinger 1997: 114). My previous three chapters' assessment of historical, cultural and political surroundings has been one important factor in aiming to meet this goal. This chapter will seek to enrich this contextual tapestry further, by assessing reviews, release patterns and promotional materials that accompanied the various crime *filoni* as they entered the Italian marketplace. My purpose here is to assess how these films were being packaged to the film-going public, and in what ways their 'digressions' were providing 'multiple avenues of access' to them (Klinger 1989: 10).

As indicated above, however, a narrow focus on the Italian context alone is not sufficient, since the significance of these films' concentrated release patterns in the Italian market can best be judged when compared to their presence in a different context. This chapter will therefore also assess how equivalent extra-filmic factors (reviews, adverts, distribution patterns and double-bill pairings) surrounded these *filoni* in the US market. I will thus additionally seek to answer the question: when the 'serial' distribution patterns that defined the viewing experience of *filone* cinema in its place of origin were removed, how did this affect the interpretive strategies being offered up in surrounding discourses?

In order to assess these factors, I have made a list of sixty-eight films that have been central to my analyses in Chapters 2, 3 and 4 of this book. I have then conducted a wide-ranging search of Italian and US newspaper film listings to ascertain these films' release patterns and marketing strategies in these two countries (see Appendix A). Having established these factors, I have consulted a total of 131 film reviews in regional newspapers (sixty-nine reviews from the USA; sixty-two from Italy), and conducted discourse analyses to identify patterns of critical reception that accompanied the films' releases into these two markets. I do not pretend that this in any way grants me access to the thoughts or responses of actual audience members. Rather, through a combination of these various primary materials, I seek to assess what Martin Barker has termed 'discursive preparations for the act of viewing'. For Barker, this combination of different ancillary materials is crucial, in order to establish how 'all the circulating prior information, talk, images and debates generate and shape expectations which will influence how we watch a movie' (Barker 2004). By charting various critical trends, contradictions and interpretive options on display across these two national contexts, this chapter will thus provide another layer to my argument that 1970s Italian crime *filoni* act as historical documents: not only of their immediate political contexts, of their surrounding culture's preoccupations with past events, and of their industrial conditions of rapid production, but also of a dialogue across differing reception contexts and cultural mores.

Italian Critical Reception

As discussed in Chapter 2, *Roma violenta / Violent City* (Marino Girolami, 1975) was one of a group of films released in 1975 and 1976 that depicted clandestine vigilante gangs fighting back against rampant crime in contemporary Italy. Aurora Santuari's review of the film in the Roman newspaper *Paese Sera* did not pull its punches:

> L'ideologia di pura marca fascista che circola per tutto il film non è nemmeno mascherata, come altre volte nel filone 'poliziotto' . . . Inoltre c'è una vera e propria istigazione alla violenza privata con l'esaltazione delle squadre di 'vigilantes' presentate come unica difesa del cittadino . . . Il publico non è certo tutto così supinamente suggestionabile e così completamente acritico come quella maggioranza rumorosa che gridava 'ammazzalo, ammazzalo' ogni volta che Maurizio Merli il metteva

> pesantemente le mani sul capro espiatorio . . . La criminalità è un argomento serio che non si può lasciare alle dissennate elucubrazioni del regista Franco Martinelli.
>
> The fascist ideology that circulates throughout the film is not even hidden, as is so often the case in the *poliziotto filone* . . . There is also an explicit instigation of private violence with the glorification of 'vigilante' gangs presented as the citizen's only defence . . . The public are not all so passively suggestible and completely uncritical as the noisy majority who shouted 'kill him, kill him' every time Maurizio Merli [who plays the film's protagonist] catches and beats the scapegoat . . . Crime is too serious a subject to be left to the foolish analysis of director Franco Martinelli [pseudonym of Marino Girolami]. (Santuari 1975: 15)

On one level, this response of course arises from the contents of this particular film, whose vigilante gang carries clear associations with the far right. Yet when we place this film in its broader cinematic context (as the reviewer does), this is also indicative of notable trends in the Italian reception of the *poliziottesco* and vigilante *filoni*.

My sample of Italian newspaper reviews includes twenty-three that address films that I have categorised under *poliziottesco* or 'vigilante' labels in Chapter 2 of this book. Of these twenty-three reviews, seventeen criticise the films for a careless, irresponsible, objectionable or naïve approach to contemporary Italy's political upheavals (see Appendix B). Accusations of reactionary political stances are one of the most common kinds of criticism, with at least one of the adjectives *'reazionario'*[1] (reactionary), *'fascista'*[2] (fascist), *'populista'*[3] (populist) *'autoritario'*[4] (authoritarian) or *'qualunquista'*[5] being used to describe the films in seven of the reviews. Furthermore, four of the reviews use the words *'impegno'* or *'denuncia'* to contrast the films unfavourably with the more 'serious' category of political investigation known as *cinema d'impegno* ('committed cinema') or *cinema di denuncia* ('cinema of denunciation').[6]

It should come as no surprise to find *filone* cinema being discussed in such terms in the Italian press of the 1970s. In his study of the cross-cultural (Italy–UK) critical reception patterns that surrounded the career of Dario Argento, Russ Hunter emphasises the importance for such a methodology of considering the political polarisation of 1970s Italy, and its impact on those working in the creative arts. This meant that 'for intellectuals in Italy during this period, one was either for or against the *Carabinieri* . . . or for or against one of the left (or right) wing terrorist organisations' (Hunter 2009: 239). If these considerations are important for assessing a relatively apolitical filmmaker such as Argento (who, as Hunter explains, was himself accused in the leftist press of propagating a fascistic ideology (Hunter 2009: 248)), it is to be expected that such controversies would also be attached to films that were explicitly intervening in political debates around violent crime. In an attempt to chart a cross section of opinion, I have consulted six newspapers spanning a range of political outlooks in the 1970s to gather my sample. *L'Unità* and *Paese Sera* positioned themselves on the political left; *Il Messaggero* identified as centrist; *La Stampa* and *Corriere della Sera* represented the interests of the northern bourgeoisie and oscillated between centre-left and centre-right positions; and *Il Tempo* was on the political right. While all of these publications criticised the political contents of the *poliziottesco* or vigilante *filoni*, a relatively obvious snapshot of this divisive milieu can be ascertained by observing in Appendix B that it was largely the three consistently leftist or centrist newspapers that condemned the films as reactionary.

The closing sentence of Santuari's review of *Roma violenta* – 'crime is too serious a subject to be left to ... foolish analysis' – gives a clear sense that an over-simplified *filone* film is not the appropriate place to address the political issues surrounding contemporary violence, implicitly pointing to *cinema d'impegno* / *cinema di denuncia* as a more suitable (and more 'serious') conduit. As mentioned above, a number of reviews more overtly judge their films by these standards, and similarly find *filone* cinema wanting. *Città violenta* (Sergio Sollima, 1970) displays only a 'vago impegno di "denuncia"' / 'vague commitment to "[cinema di] denuncia"' (Pestelli 1970: 7); *La polizia accusa: il servizio segreto uccide* (Sergio Martino, 1975) is 'un altro film di pseudo denuncia' / 'another pseudo-denuncia film' (Porro 1975: 15); and *La città sconvolta: caccia spietata ai rapitori* (Fernando Di Leo, 1975) 'poteva essere un film denuncia ... Ma il risultato è un ulteriore variante del più corrivo genere avventuroso' / 'could be a film of denunciation ... But the result is another variant of the superficial adventure genre' (Casazza 1975: 7).

Nor is such critique restricted to the *poliziottesco* or vigilante films, since an identical and repeated trend is also to be found in reviews of the mafia *filone*. We are told that *L'onorata famiglia – Uccidere è cosa nostra* (Tonino Ricci, 1973) 'ha però scarso valore sul piano della denuncia sociale' / 'has little value in terms of social denunciation' (Vice 1973b: 12), while it is made clear that the director of *Camorra* (Pasquale Squitieri, 1972) missed his opportunity to learn from one of the maestros of *cinema d'impegno*:

Squitieri ha collaborato con Rosi e da quella scuola ha preso il gusto dello sfondo violento e popolare; ma non quello della denuncia motivata e stringente.

Squitieri worked with [Francesco] Rosi and from that schooling he took the taste for violent and popular settings; but not for the motivated and persuasive denunciation. (Reggiani 1972: 7)

The assumption that pervades such criticisms is that the *cinema d'impegno* of such directors as Francesco Rosi is the benchmark, which *filone* films containing political subject matter should be trying to reach. When they are perceived to have got close to this standard, they are damned with faint praise, as when *Il boss* (Fernando Di Leo, 1973) is seen to contain 'un accenno, sia pur convenzionale, di polemica socio-politica' / 'a hint, albeit a conventional one, of socio-political polemic' (Biraghi 1973d: 8). The notion that these films might embody a mode of political address that operates according to a different set of rules – predicated upon ritual performance and simplified assumptions in a cycle of repetition and renewal – is not considered. Again, these reviews should be placed within the highly politicised nature of cultural discourse in 1970s Italy, in which such words as *'convenzionale'* / 'conventional' or *'genere'* / 'genre' would often be used as euphemisms for reactionary political outlooks, whether or not a film's plot has endorsed neofascist vigilante squads.

If the political backdrop renders the above reception patterns unsurprising, the industrial conditions of the *filone* production model make another, related trend almost inevitable. Critical opprobrium towards escapist 'genre' cinema was often to be found in close proximity to a lament at the ubiquity of American cultural formats on the Italian market. The inherently opportunistic nature of *filoni*, which tended to capitalise on box-office successes through a process of rapid replication, meant that cycles with clear points of origin in Hollywood filmmaking were particularly prone to such disapproval. For example, of the eleven reviews in my sample that address vigilante films, five either draw parallels with the Western genre or with *Death Wish* (Michael Winner, 1974).[7] This pattern is more pronounced still around the mafia *filone*, where twelve out of twenty-one reviews discuss their films within the framework of the Hollywood gangster genre, either by comparing the Italian locations to 1930s Chicago or by pointing out similarities to *The Godfather* (see Appendix C).

This returns me to one of this chapter's central points: that the timing of a film's release in relation to other films is decisive in shaping its reception patterns. As has been explored in Chapter 3, the mafia *filone* in particular was characterised by a marked concentration of releases in a short period of time, in close proximity to the release of a related American film. As a result, most of the reviews' references to *The Godfather* do not simply point out that the film in question resembles Coppola's blockbuster. Rather, they place the film within this pattern of proliferation in the Italian market (see Appendix C). *La Stampa*'s review of *La mano lunga del padrino* (Nardo Bonomi, 1972) (which was released the month before *The Godfather* arrived in Italy) begins by anticipating the deluge to come:

> Prima del capostipite, arrivano gli epigoni. Sfruttando la macchina pubblicitaria messa in moto per il film sul 'Padrino' . . . i nostri distributori stanno già immettendo sul mercato i suoi succedanei, per un filone ritenuto evidentemente redditizio.
>
> Before the progenitor, the imitators arrive. Taking advantage of *The Godfather*'s advertising machine . . . our distributors are already introducing its substitutes onto the market, for a *filone* clearly considered to be profitable. (G.C. 1972: 8)

Subsequently, *Camorra* was seen to be 'nel quadro del Padrino e dei suoi accoliti' / 'in the framework of *The Godfather* and its acolytes' (Reggiani 1972: 7); *Il boss* was 'nel filone nato da "Il padrino"' / 'in the *filone* born of *The Godfather*' (Biraghi 1973d: 8); *L'amico del padrino* (Frank Agrama, 1972) was 'realizzato per sfruttare . . . la voga della "padrinite"' / 'made to exploit . . . the vogue of "*Godfather*-itis"' (Valdata 1973b: 7); and *Il consigliori* (Alberto De Martino, 1973) moved its *L'Unità* reviewer to observe that 'prosperano le appendici cinematografiche al *Padrino*' / 'cinematic appendages to *The Godfather* are thriving' (D.G. 1973: 7).

Such an identification of rapid replication on the part of critics is unremarkable when confined to the mafia *filone*, whose sudden proliferation was obvious to anybody paying attention to the Italian film market at the time. Indeed, all of my analyses so far in this chapter have been taking one *filone* category at a time, and have not uncovered anything about attitudes to popular cinema in 1970s Italy that are not already known about. The reviews I have collected, however, become considerably more interesting if we disregard perceived boundary lines between these *filone* categories and behold the full data set as one entity consisting of sixty-two articles, and spanning a period from March 1970 to August 1978 (see Appendix D). What becomes apparent upon doing this is that, while particular cycles attracted specific kinds of discourse that were largely dependent on their films' settings or narrative contents, discussions of the repetitive, 'serial' nature of *filone* cinema per se are a constant across the entire period, appearing in thirty-eight (just over 61 per cent) of the sixty-two reviews, with a frequency of at least 40 per cent in every year sampled (see Appendix E). The sample thus provides an evolving chronicle of the discourses of seriality that accompanied this kind of cinema-going as the films were being released.

Certainly, many critics did not view *filoni* as distinct cycles, but rather as a continuous output of rapidly produced, interchangeable ephemera. *Il giustiziere sfida la città* (Umberto Lenzi, 1975), for example, was described as the 'ennesimo poliziesco all'italiana forgiato sulla falsariga di un "western-spaghetti"' / 'umpteenth Italian-style police film made along the lines of a Spaghetti Western' (Leo 1975c: 14), while *Perché quelle strane gocce di sangue sul corpo di Jennifer?* (Giuliano Carnimeo, 1972) led one critic to comment that its director had 'passato dal western . . . al thriller d'ugual confezione' / 'passed from the Western . . . to a thriller of the same pattern' (Valdata 1972b: 7).[8] Such comments validate Christopher Wagstaff's argument that all *filoni* should be seen as component parts of a larger pattern of seriality:

> It can sometimes be hard to tell from the credits of a film and its synopsis whether a particular film is a spaghetti western or . . . another formula such as bandit, gangster, Mafia, thriller or political suspense. A still, particularly if someone in the shot is wearing a hat, usually clears up the mystery. (Wagstaff 1992: 252)

This book has so far categorised crime *filoni* by the kinds of criminality on show, since my purpose has been to chart specific lines of influence that led to the proliferation of political conspiracy, vigilante, organised crime and serial killer narratives at this particular point in Italian history. Many critics at the time, however, used the various *filone* labels more or less interchangeably. For example, we find both the gangster film *Milano calibro 9* (Fernando di Leo, 1972) and the vigilante / mafia film *No alla violenza* (Tano Cimarosa, 1977) described using the term *'giallo'* (Biraghi 1972b: 12; Palazzi 1977: 19), while *Milano rovente* (Umberto Lenzi, 1973), *L'uomo della strada fa giustizia* (Umberto Lenzi, 1975), *La città sconvolta: caccia spietata ai rapitori* (Fernando di Leo, 1975) and *Roma, l'altra faccia della violenza* (Marino Girolami, 1976) – none of which use the police force as their primary focus – are all categorised as *'poliziesco'* (Vice 1973c: 21; Leo 1975a: 14; Leo 1975b: 10; Valdata 1976: 12).

It is not my intention here to split hairs, since *'giallo'* and *'poliziesco'* are both fluid terms in Italian cinematic terminology, loosely equating to 'mystery' and 'crime' narratives respectively. Rather, I want to emphasise that the specific thematic or narrative details of individual films or cycles were less often the concern of critical discourse than were the modes of production, distribution and consumption that traversed and united all *filone* cinema. At times, this equated to little more than disdain for the supposedly feckless masses who were paying to see such rubbish, and who – in a refrain as old as cinema itself – were assumed to be uncritically manipulated into assuming a mob mentality. We have already observed a *Paese Sera* critic lamenting one cinema's 'maggioranza rumorosa che gridava "ammazzalo, ammazzalo"' / 'noisy majority who shouted "kill him, kill him'" (Santuari 1975: 15), and this sentiment was echoed (about a different film) in *La Stampa* the following month:

> la platea non va tanto per il sottile e presa nel furbo meccanismo para-populista finisce con l'applaudire il privato massacro del vendicatore solitario.

> the audience does not really go for subtlety and, taken in by the clever para-populist machinery, ends up applauding the lone avenger's private massacre. (Casazza 1975: 7)[9]

Occasionally, such opprobrium, though appearing to be little more than snobbishness, reveals a degree of insight into the mode of cinema-going being discussed. One film, for example, is seen to be typical of 'la moda fruttuosa a certo cinema di consumo di serie C' / 'the profitable trend at a certain kind of C-grade consumer cinema' (Vice 1971a: 6), while others are judged to be 'adatto ai lettori di fumettoni cinematografici' / 'suitable for readers of cinematic comic books' (Vice 1971d: 9) and full of the 'eccessi di . . . situazioni da *feuilleton*' / 'excesses of *feuilleton* [a French word for a serialised fictional story in a newspaper, and more recently for a television soap opera] situations' (Pestelli 1974: 7). The implication that *filoni* were chiefly playing at *terza visione* ('serie C') cinemas is inaccurate (since most of these films opened at *prima visione*, first-run theatres), but in other respects, these three quotations encapsulate many of the hallmarks of *filone* cinema: produced with the express intention of exploiting lucrative trends, in a pattern of rapid replication with incremental variation, to keep audiences coming back for more until a particular formula became stale. The comparisons with comic books and *feuilletons* are particularly apt, to denote a form of cinema-going that Wagstaff has described as 'a nightly appointment [to] receive a series of discrete gratifications that were part of a longer-term sequence' (Wagstaff 1992: 254).

In Appendix F, I have isolated the thirty-eight reviews that discuss or allude to the notion of serial repetition from Appendix D, and subdivided these to identify the frequency and distribution of the three most common categories of such discourse: the economics of filmmaking (identified by the use of such words as '*commerciale*' / 'commercial' or '*consumismo*' / 'consumerism', and the use of such metaphors as the production line to denote the rapidity of production); distribution patterns (identified by discussions of how cycles are proliferating in cinemas); and weariness (identified by comments stating that a pattern of proliferation is running out of steam or becoming boring). The resulting graph shows a revealing pattern. The logic of the *filone* system – rapid and opportunistic replication until such time as a cycle dries up – might reasonably cause one to expect comments about the profit imperative of such films to at first be the most frequent kind, observing the emergent phenomenon and its implications for the film industry. We might then expect discussions of how *filone* films are proliferating to become just as frequent, as the sheer volume of releases hits the market. Finally, it is to be expected that a saturation point would cause weariness and boredom with a stale formula. This is indeed the exact process we can observe in the graph in Appendix F, but it is notable that this does not take place numerous times, in a cyclical *filone*-by-*filone* pattern (we might, for example, have expected critics to tire of the mafia *filone* by the start of 1974, after twenty-four such films had been released in the space of nineteen months). Instead, we can see that this process plays out just once, and more slowly, over the entire eight-year period being sampled. This suggests once again that the various 'crime' *filoni* were being received together as one large cycle, rather than as a succession of smaller cycles. Weariness and exasperation at these films' repetitiveness does not register as the dominant trend until near the end of the timescale.

Charting dominant trends across my sample of reviews has therefore provided an indication that the concentrated release patterns of *filone* cinema had a decisive influence on how these films were received in surrounding cultural discourse. These films were seldom being viewed as standalone works of art. Far more often, their relationship to external influences (especially from Hollywood) and to each other was the immediately pertinent frame of reference. There is, however, a note of caution to be sounded at this juncture. Martin Barker explains:

> There is a problem in the sheer privileging of reviews over other kinds of ancillary materials, a privileging which associates with the greater attention this leads to, towards 'serious' over popular films. It is troublesome because, of course, it is popular cinema which is most seriously engrossed in the phenomenon of publicity, gossip, and other ancillary materials. (Barker 2004)

It is indeed noticeable that, while my sample of reviews has produced some interesting commentary on the films' historical circumstances, the vast majority of these pieces have been dismissive or contemptuous of their subject matter (only two of the columns in Appendix D indicate enthusiasm for the films, and these are the two columns with the lowest frequencies). The comparisons with *cinema d'impegno* discussed earlier are particularly illustrative of Barker's point that film critics are predisposed to hold 'serious' films up as the assumed standard. As Derek Malcolm points out, however, 'most of the public doesn't read reviews' (cited in Barker 2004). In order to build a picture of how these films were being packaged and framed for the cinema-going public, I therefore additionally need to take account of the publicity campaigns that accompanied them.

Cross-cultural Marketing

The banner ad placed in the *Corriere della Sera* on 5 June 1974 to publicise the mafia *filone* film *Quelli che contano* (Andrea Bianchi, 1974) is entirely typical of its idiom. Nestled next to an advert for *The Graduate* (Mike Nichols, 1968), it promises the potential cinemagoer a fresh, air-conditioned experience at the Tonale cinema in central Milan, where they will encounter 'Henry Silva: un killer duro, spietato, violento. Barbara Bouchet: bella conturbante e femmina più che mai' / 'Henry Silva: a tough, ruthless, violent killer. Barbara Bouchet: more beautiful, seductive and feminine than ever.' Beneath this tagline, a bare-chested Henry Silva stands with gun in hand, as an almost-naked Barbara Bouchet takes cover behind him (see Figure 5.2). The visual implication that Silva's role is one of a protector for Bouchet's is spurious (since Tony in fact assaults and rapes Margie in the film), but the tagline has already signalled that the advert's emphasis is less on the contents of this individual film than on both actors' familiar and repeated personae from numerous earlier *filone* films. Given the release patterns already analysed in this book, such a publicity strategy is to be expected.

This advert becomes instantly more intriguing when we compare it to the same film's publicity in the USA just over three years later. Jackson, Mississippi's *Clarion-Ledger* of 19 August 1977 lists the films showing at the Showtown East twin drive-ins that evening (see Figure 5.3): *Naughty Schoolgirls* (tagline: 'five swinging seniors who want to graduate with a bang!'); *Teenage HitchHikers* ('ride us – for the time of your life!'); *Teenage Tramp* ('don't pass her up . . . she's looking for more than a ride! Old enough. Ripe enough!'); *Cry of a Prostitute* ('for a lousy twenty-five bucks some people think they can do anything!'); and *Love Object*. *Cry of a Prostitute* was the English-language release title for *Quelli che contano*, shifting the emphasis from Tony's role in the mafia ('quelli che contano' literally translates as 'those who count': a euphemism for 'men of honour') onto Margie's status as an ex-prostitute (while omitting any mention of her role as a mob moll). This shift in the film's genre identity explains its listing among lurid sexploitation titles (instead of prestige productions in the same vein as *The Graduate*), and carries over into other extra-filmic framing devices. The social space of the cinema on offer, for example, is a low-cost out-of-town drive-in on the interstate highway, advertising

Figures 5.2 and 5.3 Banner ads for *Quelli che contano* (Andrea Bianchi, 1974), in *Corriere della Sera*, 5 June 1974, p. 13, and the *Clarion-Ledger* (Jackson, Mississippi), 19 August 1977, p. 47.

double- and triple-bills for '$2 a carload', rather than a city-centre theatre showing single features and boasting of such luxuries as air-conditioning. The images used in the advert are also different: firstly, Bouchet's bloodied face forms a striking backdrop, hinting at sexual violence in keeping with the suggestive tagline; secondly, the publicity still that was used in Italy has been doctored, to remove the gun from Silva's hand. Instead, he stands with his arms down by his sides, instantly changing his appearance from an implacable man of action to a melancholic lover.

The above example epitomises dominant trends in the publicity surrounding Italian crime films in these two markets. In Italy, such adverts frequently exploited the allure of repetition, either by foregrounding the serial star personae of a film's cast, or by relating the film to previous successes in the same *filone*. This latter trend is enacted in a particularly blatant manner in the Italian banner ad for *La polizia ha le mani legate* (Luciano Ercoli, 1975), which implies that the film is part of a coordinated annual series of instalments by listing *La polizia ringrazia* (Stefano Vanzina, 1972), *La polizia sta a guardare* (Roberto Infascelli, 1973) and *La polizia chiede aiuto* (Massimo Dallamano, 1974) under their respective years, before inserting its own tagline under 1975: 'l'ordine è in pericolo, la violenza incombe, ma . . . la polizia ha le mani legate' / 'order is in danger, violence looms, but . . . the police have their hands tied' (see Figure 5.4).[10] The advert's image – of grasping hands helplessly bound together – is also closely reminiscent of the earlier publicity for *La polizia ringrazia*, which depicts handcuffed arms reaching for a gun (Figure 5.5).

The most frequent trend in the Italian adverts surrounded the exploitation of serial star appeal, when a film featured actors who were familiar to Italian audiences from previous iterations of a given *filone*. This is enacted in a particularly striking manner in the marketing for *Anna, quel particolare piacere* (Giuliano Carnimeo, 1973), which seeks to capitalise on the recognisability of its four main cast members:

> Edwige Fenech: sexy e dolce come mai / Corrado Pani: la sua più grande interpretazione: cattivo, subdolo, vile e sfruttatore / Richard Conte: il grande attore che oramai tutti conoscono nella parte di un BOSS senza scrupoli / J Richardson: l'uomo che ogni donna sogna.
>
> Edwige Fenech: sexy and sweet as ever / Corrado Pani: his greatest performance: bad, sneaky, vile and exploitative / Richard Conte: the great actor who everyone knows by now in the part of a BOSS without scruples / J Richardson: the man that every woman dreams of. (*Corriere della Sera*, 2 January 1974, p. 11)

Fenech's established star persona is also exploited as the main draw in the publicity for *Nude per l'assassino* (Andrea Bianchi, 1975), which

Figure 5.4 Banner ad for *La polizia ha le mani legate* (Luciano Ercoli, 1975), in *La Stampa*, 4 April 1975, p. 8.

Figure 5.5 Italian publicity poster for *La polizia ringrazia* (Stefano Vanzina, 1972).

announces 'Edwige Fenech sempre più sexy' / 'Edwige Fenech more and more sexy' (*La Stampa*, 22 October 1976, p. 6). In other cases, a *filone* star's serial image alone is seen to be a sufficient sales pitch, as when Franco Nero's name and face are used to market *Giornata nera per l'ariete* (Luigi Bazzoni, 1971) with no explanatory text (*La Stampa*, 7 September 1971, p. 6), or when the faces of Henry Silva and Richard Conte dominate the banner ad for *Il boss* (Fernando di Leo, 1973) (*Corriere della Sera*, 3 February 1973, p. 13), or when Conte's image suffices to sell *L'onorata famiglia – Uccidere è cosa nostra* (Tonino Ricci, 1973) (*Corriere della Sera*, 14 August 1973, p. 9).

The reference to Richard Conte in the above example from *Anna, quel particolare piacere* also points to another trend in these films' marketing strategies. His status as 'the great actor who everyone knows by now in the part of a BOSS without scruples' is of course recognisable, not only from Italian *filone* cinema, but also from US cinema: specifically, in this case, *The Godfather*. Indeed, many of these films' adverts make more overt references to US precedents. On occasion, this refers to Hollywood genre conventions, as when the tagline for *La città sconvolta: caccia spietata ai rapitori* evokes the Western through the use of the word 'frontiera': 'Nella città terrorizzata del crimine, l'ultima frontiera è . . . un uomo col mitra in pugno e tanta rabbia in corpo' / 'In a city terrorized by crime, the last frontier is . . . a man with a machine gun in his fist and rage in his body' (*La Stampa*, 13 September 1975, p. 7). *Il grande racket* (Enzo G. Castellari, 1976) goes a step further, explicitly stating that contemporary Italy is suffering from the same urban malaise as the USA (and therefore presumably requiring a similar solution to that proffered by *Dirty Harry* and *Death Wish*):

> un film aggressivo . . . bruciante . . . crudele! ROMA, MILANO, TORINO sono ormai come NEW YORK, CHICAGO, LOS ANGELES città sconvolte da una dilagante delinquenza
>
> an aggressive . . . scorching . . . cruel film! Rome, Milan, Turin are now like New York, Chicago, Los Angeles: cities devastated by rampant criminality. (*La Stampa*, 2 September 1976, p. 13)

Unsurprisingly, given the opportunistic nature of many *filone* films in response to specific US box-office successes, *The Godfather* is a frame of reference in a number of adverts. *L'amico del padrino*'s publicity in the Italian press, for example, positions it as if it is a canonical companion piece or sequel, filling in gaps in the plot of Coppola's film: 'mentre il Padrino operava in America, gli "AMICI" sparsi nel mondo morivano e uccidevano per Lui' / 'while the Godfather worked in America, the "FRIENDS" scattered around the world died and killed for him' (*Corriere della Sera*, 3 February 1973, p. 13). The Italian advert for *Il consigliori* exploits its Hollywood precedent in a more business-minded manner, by highlighting the likely audience figures around the corner for this kind of film:

> Un 'referendum' lanciato nel mondo dalla stampa Americana ha stabilito in 180.000.000 di spettatori l'indice di attesa per questo film – indice di gradimento pari a quello stabilito a suo tempo per 'il padrino'
>
> A 'referendum' launched by the American press has established that 180,000,000 spectators are waiting to see this film – a satisfaction rating equal to that previously established for *The Godfather*. (*La Stampa*, 6 September 1973, p. 6)

Figure 5.6 Banner ad for *Il consigliori* (Alberto De Martino, 1973), in the *Santa Cruz Sentinel*, 10 September 1975, p. 8.

Figure 5.7 Banner ad for *Città violenta* (Sergio Sollima, 1970), in the *Star Tribune* (Minneapolis), 13 April 1973, p. 17.

Such shameless use of these reference points to make a fast buck was certainly not restricted to the Italian market. If anything, these films' publicity materials in the US market were more brazen still in this respect. *Il consigliori*'s 1975 release in the USA was accompanied by an ad campaign that not only mentioned *The Godfather*, but did so using the same font as the previous film's posters (Figure 5.6), in an attempt to give the impression that this was an official tie-in. Moreover, the fact that the poster only deploys this font to present film titles and the words 'The Family' is surely intended to lead a cinemagoer to think that it might also be a sequel to *Città violenta / The Family*, which had used this very same font-based marketing ploy two years previously (Figure 5.7).

The Godfather's prominent position in this opportunistically intertextual marketing network can also be seen in US adverts for *La mala ordina / The Italian Connection* (tagline: 'The Godfather wants revenge!', in *The Indianapolis Star*, 5 October 1973, p. 28) and *I padroni della città / Mister Scarface* ('It's *The Godfather* thing . . . sharper than *The Sting* . . . A wilder ride than *Bonnie and Clyde*', in the *Hattiesburg American*, 13 November 1977, p. 33). In each of these cases, the connections made are predictable, given the mafia / outlaw narratives of the films. The advert for *Città violenta* referred to above (Figure 5.7), however, shows how the transition across the Atlantic resulted in a process of rebranding for some of these films. As we have seen, Sollima's film does not feature the mafia as its central focus, but its backdrop of organised crime was a beneficial aspect to foreground for its release into the US market the year after *The Godfather*. Conversely, the mafia-related contents of *Quelli che contano* were seen to be less profitable in the USA than a 'sexploitation' rebranding by 1977.

Transitions to the US market did not always result in such obvious repackaging. Especially in the case of the serial killer / slasher films now known as *gialli*, the journey across the Atlantic often resulted in a shift in emphasis rather than a wholesale rebranding. For example, *Una lucertola con la pelle di donna / A Lizard in a Woman's Skin* (Lucio Fulci, 1971) was announced in the Italian marketing as 'Il più agghiacciante film di tutti i tempi' / 'The most chilling film of all time', in an otherwise sober advert featuring the film's title and an illustration of a lizard's silhouette (*La Stampa*, 13 May 1971, p. 6). The same film's US release was announced as 'an erotic nightmare that keeps you on the edge of an abyss of terror!', with an accompanying montage of a nude Florinda Bolkan (one of the film's female stars) with acts of sex and violence taking place in the background. In a similar vein, the Italian marketing for *I corpi presentano tracce di violenza carnale / Torso* (Sergio Martino, 1973) was relatively restrained, with the announcement 'é sconsigliata la visione di questo film alle persone facilmente impressionabili' / 'this film is not recommended for people who are easily impressionable' being accompanied by a picture of a man assaulting a woman (*Corriere della Sera*, 15 January 1973, p. 6). The publicity for this film in the US market adopted a markedly more lurid tone, investing in the kind of advisory address to its audience as seen previously in the example from *Reazione a catena / Twitch of the Death Nerve* with which this chapter opened:

> WE DARE YOU to keep your eyes open during every terror-saturated scene of 'Torso' / Enter . . . if you dare the bizarre world of the psychosexual mind / One day she met a man who loved beautiful girls . . . but not all in one piece'. (Figure 5.8)

In both of the above cases, the more titillating aspects of the films are given greater emphasis in the US market. Yet this observation alone does not tell us very much about the exhibition contexts into which the films were entering in the USA. A better impression of these factors can be ascertained by looking at the evolution of one marketing campaign over time. *Torso* was first released onto the US market in April 1973, but the above marketing campaign was launched for its re-release in January 1975. It then played as a single feature in downtown cinemas across the country until around May 1975, when it entered the drive-in and neighbourhood markets, playing in double- and triple-bills. Figure 5.9 (from November 1975) contains the same text and almost the same image as Figure 5.8 (from February 1975), but with some notable differences. Firstly, the picture has been altered to reveal the young woman's cleavage; secondly, the film is playing in a double-bill alongside the West German sexploitation film *Mädchen mit Gewalt / Cry Rape* (Roger Fritz, 1970). *Torso*'s widespread presence in double-bills ran uninterrupted until June 1976, and included pairings with other sexploitation films such as *Ginger* (Don Schain, 1971) and *The Abductors* (Don Schain, 1972), as well as thrillers such as *Open Season* (Peter Collinson, 1974) and horror films including *The Texas Chain Saw Massacre* (Tobe Hooper, 1974). The film (along with its familiar image and taglines) then reappeared in December 1977, its pairing with *The Texas Chain Saw Massacre* now being heralded as 'two horror classics of all time!!!' (see Figure 5.10).[11]

This evolution of *Torso*'s US publicity materials provides a glimpse of how contexts of viewing, driven by distribution patterns and release strategies, exert a decisive influence on the tone and content of a film's packaging and framing for the cinema-going public. A closer look at Figure 5.8 appears to reveal that the young woman's blouse had been drawn on by hand for *Torso*'s downtown theatrical run, perhaps providing some insight into the moral squeamishness of first-run cinema chains when it came to exposed flesh. Such prudishness would clearly have been out of place on the drive-in circuit, where sexually suggestive advertising was de rigueur. Finally, *Torso*'s longevity on that circuit meant that it could eventually be labelled a 'horror classic'. Once again, we need to look beyond the contents of the individual film, if we are to appreciate its cultural significance. In the Italian market, the concentration and volume of similar *filone* releases meant that they were frequently packaged as parts of larger (and culturally familiar) trends. In the US market, these films' far more sporadic release patterns and occasional successes in drive-in or grindhouse circuits meant that a different emphasis in their interpretive strategies was sometimes required. It is to this context that I shall now turn, to investigate how these Italian crime films were received by critics in the USA.

US Critical Reception

The above examination of *Torso*'s US distribution patterns gives an indication of how and why a number of Italian crime films – *gialli* in

Figures 5.8, 5.9 and 5.10 Banner ads for *I corpi presentano tracce di violenza carnale* (Sergio Martino, 1973), in *The Indianapolis Star*, 6 February 1975, p. 26, the *Asheville Citizen-Times* (North Carolina), 8 November 1975, p. 6, and the *San Antonio Express*, 2 December 1977, p. 116.

particular – have since become lionised as transgressive 'cult' classics in anglophone markets. Their investment in scenes of brutal violence and their often sexually suggestive framings of female stars made them an easy fit for sexploitation and horror double bills, with suitably titillating publicity campaigns. Accordingly, it is indicative of scholarly trends in this area that the *giallo* provides a key case study for Ian Olney's study of 'Euro horror cinema', in which they are included in a category of cinema that was

> shown in the United States at rural drive-ins and at urban grindhouse theaters . . . Gorier, sexier, and just plain stranger than most British and American horror films of the time, they were embraced by hardcore genre fans and denounced by critics as the worst kind of cinematic trash. (Olney 2013: xi)

The US banner ad for *L'uccello dalle piume di cristallo* / *The Bird with the Crystal Plumage* (Dario Argento, 1970) – which, as we have seen, is commonly seen to be one of the *giallo*'s founding texts – partially lends itself to such a reading. A montage mostly consisting of terrified or murdered women surrounds an image of a hand holding a polished carving knife. Quotes from critics comparing the film favourably to the terrifying suspense of Alfred Hitchcock accompany taglines daring audiences to face their fears:

> If you think you are being followed home from this movie, keep telling yourself that it's all in your mind . . . COLD AND CALCULATING! A phantom figure wearing black leather stalks pretty girls . . . a sound track composed of heavy passionate breathing . . . *It is only a question of how bloody the killing will be!* (Figure 5.11; emphasis in original)

It goes without saying that the quotes from critics included in this advert were carefully selected from a wider range of reviews, many of which (as Olney suggests) were not quite so enthusiastic. The tone of the publicity campaign and Olney's description of 'gorier, sexier, and just plain stranger' films might reasonably lead us to expect this particular film's less enthusiastic reviewers to aim their opprobrium at its lurid adult themes. Yet a close look at the bottom of Figure 5.11 reveals that *The Bird with the Crystal Plumage* was given a 'GP' rating. This was the renaming of the previous 'M' rating (soon to be renamed again to 'PG') – which did not prohibit any age group from viewing, but instead suggested parental discretion – and may seem out of place given the advert's promise of gory violence, unsettling horror and the stalking of 'pretty girls'. A review from the month after this advert ran, however, suggests that this film was not exactly being seen as a scandalous aberration:

Figure 5.11 Banner ad for *L'uccello dalle piume di cristallo* (Dario Argento, 1970), in *The Philadelphia Enquirer*, 16 September 1970, p. 27.

> The movie carries a rather ineffective GP rating. Ineffective because at least this performance was attended almost entirely by kids with nary a parent in sight. Which is why we recommend to the thriller fans that they see an evening show. There won't be so many screamers to contend with. (Heinrich 1970: 11)

Indeed, *The Bird with the Crystal Plumage* was far from the only *giallo* whose sensationalistic ballyhoo belied a distribution context that seemed markedly blasé about such films' contents. When *Cosa avete fatto a Solange?* (Massimo Dallamano, 1972) was released as *Terror in the Woods*, in a double bill with the horror film *Tender Flesh* (Laurence Harvey, 1974), the programme's banner ad warned audiences: 'If you have a weak stomach, don't see this movie' (in the *Star-Gazette* (Elmira, New York), 15 August 1976, p. 18.). Yet, that same summer, *Terror in the Woods*'s pairing with the zombie film *Non si deve profanare il sonno dei morti / Don't Open the Window* (Jorge Grau, 1974) advertised 'children under 12 free' (*The Portsmouth Herald* (New Hampshire), 9 June, 1976, p. 10).

Furthermore, if *gialli* were indeed being received as the shocking oddities their taglines and marketing imagery aimed to convey, some advertisers and schedulers were clearly not convinced. As we have seen, *Reazione a catena / Twitch of the Death Nerve* (Mario Bava, 1971) and *I corpi presentano tracce di violenza carnale / Torso* (Sergio Martino, 1973) were both accompanied into the US market by sensationalised publicity campaigns in the form of dire warnings to audiences about the horrors lurking within. It therefore seems incongruous to find *Twitch of the Death Nerve* advertised alongside Disney children's cartoon *Dumbo* (Samuel Armstrong et al., 1941) (Figure 5.12), and *Torso* playing in matinee and evening screenings alongside two more Disney films: *Winnie the Pooh and Tigger Too* (John Lounsbery, 1974) and *The Island at the Top of the World* (Robert Stevenson, 1974) (Figure 5.13).

It is not my intention to claim that these juxtapositions are in any way out of the ordinary or outlandish. Indeed, Figure 5.12 is indicative of the 1970s US drive-in circuit's business model: a melting pot of disparate kinds of cinematic output, ranging from the adult-oriented to the decidedly innocuous. Richard Nowell's study of Crown International Pictures' distribution strategy identifies this milieu as one that embraced, rather than eschewed, the profit-driven accessibility more often associated with the putative 'mainstream':

> Stakeholders conceptualized exploitation cinema in ways that accommodated calculatedly anodyne fare ... Rather than accentuating profanity, sexuality, or violence, as is commonly assumed, numerous companies operating in this sector are likely to

CROSS-CULTURAL RECEPTION 171

Figure 5.12 Banner ads for *Reazione a catena* (Mario Bava, 1971) and *Dumbo* (Samuel Armstrong et al., 1941) in *The Palm Beach Post*, 9 December 1972, p. 21.

Figure 5.13 Banner ads for *I corpi presentano tracce di violenza carnale* (Sergio Martino, 1973), *Winnie the Pooh and Tigger Too* (John Lounsbery, 1974) and *The Island at the Top of the World* (Robert Stevenson, 1974) in *The Republic* (Columbus, Indiana), 7 February 1975, p. 2.

have also tailored and framed at least some of their output in ways which distanced it – and, by extension, themselves – from the tawdrier aspects of exploitation. (Nowell 2016: 110, 122)

Italian *filone* films were simply incorporated as one profitable part of this larger context. Moreover, there is little evidence to suggest that they were even seen to be at the 'tawdrier', transgressive end of this spectrum, as subsequent critical and scholarly myths would have us believe. When *Profondo rosso / Deep Red* (Dario Argento, 1975) entered the US drive-in circuit in 1976, one review described it as 'almost unusual enough to be interesting', before querying its 'R' rating: 'No sex or nudity, so the rating must be based on the violence, although comparable blood-letting occurs in many PG movies' (Hammen 1976: 19).

Clearly, therefore, we should not assume that the sensationalised tone of these films' publicity materials in the US market is necessarily a reliable indicator of how they were being received and viewed. Rather, we need to take account of the competing reading protocols that provided 'multiple avenues of access' to them (Klinger 1989: 10). The dissonance between the lurid marketing and such an anodyne reception was providing the consumer with a range of available pre-constituted interpretive strategies. Olney is broadly correct when he claims that critical dismissal surrounded such films in the US market, but to imply that this was purely because they were 'gorier, sexier, and just plain stranger than most British and American horror films of the time' (Olney 2013: xi) is an oversimplification.

This is not to say that the violent contents of these films escaped critical opprobrium. Appendix G lists repeated trends across my sample of sixty-nine reviews of this book's key films in US newspapers. Of these, forty-five (just over 65 per cent) contain at least one of the words 'violence', 'gore', 'gory', 'gruesome', 'bloody', 'blood', 'bloodletting', 'bodies', 'brutal', 'slaughter', 'sadism' or 'vicious'. Yet such a quantitative approach only tells us that these films were discussed in relation to the existence of cinematic violence. A closer look at the contextual factors that frame these words reveals that a number of the reviews were not accusing these films of anomalous or aberrational gruesomeness. On the contrary, they were often seen to be entirely typical (and on occasion tedious) signs of the times. *Città violenta*, for example, was seen to be 'like most of the rash of gangster films being put out these days' (Heinlein 1973: 21), containing 'not excessive violence by today's standards' (Anderson 1973a: 34), while *Crazy Joe* (Carlo Lizzani, 1974) was condemned as both a 'brainless hodgepodge of sado-masochistic violence [that will] probably clean up at the box office. Which, I suppose, says something about where we're at with movies these days' (Baltake 1974: 18) and 'nothing more than commercial fodder for the violence market' (Guarino 1974: 30). We have already seen that one critic found *Profondo rosso* entirely anodyne ('almost unusual enough to be interesting' (Hammen 1976: 19)), while another saw it as merely 'another psychological suspenser steeped in blood, gore, violence, and gross detail' (Cafone 1976: 12).

This chapter opened with an indication that the sensational marketing of *Reazione a catena* was not taken entirely seriously. Indeed, far from being received as more extreme, shocking or transgressive than contemporary

US horror films (as the quotation from Olney suggests it might be), Bava's film was seen by one reviewer as having a considerably more mainstream appeal than the directorial debut of future genre legend Wes Craven (*The Last House on the Left*, 1972):

> It has the merit, at least, of being made by professionals, and therefore, it comes as a relief to those of us who had to sit through such amateur attempts as 'Last House on the Left' and 'Mark of the Devil' . . . a step or two above the psycho-sicko-sado garbage with which its cheap exploitation campaign associates it. (Anderson 1972b: 26)

Such scepticism around the reliability of these films' publicity materials was another repeated trend in the critical reception. For example, upon noting the comparisons with Hitchcock in the banner ad for *L'uccello dalle piume di cristallo* (see Figure 5.11), one reviewer commented: 'If I were Alfred, I would sue!' (Sparks 1970: 18). The opportunism of attaching a film to a major box-office success (which, as we have seen, was a common feature of the marketing for *filone* films) was a repeated target for critical ire. *La mala ordina*'s retitling as *The Italian Connection* did not fool one reviewer, who observed: 'Apparently, with such a title, the producers hoped somebody would mistake the picture for a sequel to "The French Connection" or even "The Chinese Connection"' (Thompson 1973: 48). *Città violenta*'s equally blatant rebranding as *The Family* (see Figure 5.7) was seen to be just as transparent. Its Pittsburgh release in December 1973 moved two reviewers from different local newspapers to concur, one day after another: 'There was no need to latch onto "The Godfather" in promotional gimmicks. Except for its violence and gangster story line, it really isn't comparable in any way' (Cloud 1973: 30); 'Adding to the confusion is the misleading title and an advertising campaign linking the film to "The Godfather"' (Anderson 1973a: 34).

These refusals to acquiesce to such marketing ploys should come as no surprise. Film critics are of course a constituent part of the complex network of discourses and financial exchanges that form the film industry, and understanding how that industry operates is part of their job. Accordingly, a notable (if not dominant) trend in my sample shows critics discussing the status of these films as exploitation products tailored to a certain market. If we merge the second and third columns of Appendix G's reception patterns, we see that twenty-two out of the sixty-nine reviews in my sample (just under 32 per cent) either criticised a film's marketing for being misleading (as discussed above) or placed these films within the realms of low-budget 'schlock' (Anon 1972b: 14), 'trash' (Dietrich 1973: 17; Baltake 1974: 18), 'commercial fodder' (Guarino 1974: 30), 'bargain basement' (Hammen 1976: 19) and 'potboiler' fare (Blank 1975: 15; Johnson 1975: 26), or did both. We might interpret these descriptions as part of a hard-nosed approach to the business of cinematic distribution, accurately identifying these films as little more than money-spinning commodities. Again, Nowell's study of the 1970s drive-in circuit provides crucial contextual insight:

> Exploitation was thought of as unequivocally commercial in motivation; unashamedly derivative and unchallenging in execution; and unapologetically tailored for venues, viewers, and modes of engagement boasting little cultural or subcultural capital . . . Industry-insiders and industry-watchers . . . largely conceived of exploitation films as inexpensive, undemanding potboilers handled mainly by independent companies, and primarily screened at rundown rural, urban, or drive-in theaters to animated audiences devoid of discerning college-educated adults. (Nowell 2016: 110)

The reviews in my sample illustrate such perceptions of an unapologetically low-budget and lowbrow cinematic milieu. Moreover, while the above comments might be interpreted as relatively detached observations of a marketplace, many others did not hold back in their disdain for the films and their audiences. At least one of the words 'incompetent', 'incoherent', 'erratic', 'inept', 'stupid', 'messy', 'silly', 'absurd', 'rubbish', 'ludicrous', 'mediocre', 'dumb', 'slovenly', 'crummy', 'mindless', 'brainless', 'unthinking', 'clumsy', 'garbage' or 'blundering' appears in twenty-three (just over 33 per cent) of the sixty-nine reviews (see Appendix G). Critical attitudes towards the kind of person who would choose to watch such films were at times equally unequivocal. *Reazione a catena* was, in the judgement of one critic, 'made to quench the blood thirsts of those who love to gawk at gore. "Hey neat!" was a gleeful cry from one in the audience during a particularly heinous slash of death. It deserved retching, not raving' (Gerds 1972: 11); *La mala ordina* was 'made to pander to those whose interest in mindless violence is insatiable' (Dietrich 1973: 17); while *I padroni della città* 'starts off in slow motion – a pace that accords with the audience mentality at which it is directed' (Ryan 1977a: 32).

Such comments are testament to the problem outlined by Barker of privileging reviews over other ancillary materials when trying to ascertain the nature of a film's reception patterns, since critics tend to favour 'serious' over more 'popular' films (Barker 2004). The stark discrepancies between the publicity materials and the reviews can thus be seen to be culturally constituted, as professional commentators (whose writing most movie-goers do not read) place the films and their audiences within the broader, critically scorned cinematic milieus of the out-of-town drive-in and the inner-city grindhouse. Once again, we can see that Italian crime films were in many ways not seen to be scandalous or shocking, but instead were incorporated within familiar frames of reference.

The US reception patterns so far appraised appear to corroborate David Church's claims that the urban grindhouse's status as a site of subcultural rebelliousness and transgressive notoriety 'is more probably rooted in retrospective fantasies than in fans' personal experiences' (Church 2015a: 19). Church argues that the decisions of film distributors who 'assembled lurid publicity materials, strategized where and how to exhibit films [and] retitled or recut prints' have proven to be a decisive factor in fostering this myth (Church 2015a: 11). Moreover, and analogously with the contemporaneous drive-in circuit discussed by Nowell above, the culturally maligned status of the grindhouse distribution context frequently manifested itself in value judgements about its audiences, who had long been discussed in the industry press as an undifferentiated (and uneducated) mass. The supposed shock-value of the films that were playing in such contexts is thus intimately linked to class- and race-based biases in surrounding socio-political discourses of urban decay (Church 2015a: 86). The Italian films discussed in this chapter were being received as part of this larger picture, not as an anomaly lying outside it.

This is not say that these Italian films were seen to be entirely ordinary. Rather, the criticisms they received within this wider discursive milieu of lowbrow 'trash' took particular forms. The most frequent of these forms (indeed, a comfortable majority) were predicated upon their foreignness. Appendix G shows that forty-nine (just over 71 per cent) of the sixty-nine sampled reviews contain the words 'Italian' or 'Italy', while twenty-eight (just over 40 per cent) use the words 'dubbing', 'dubbed' or 'postsynchronization'. Taken together, these two columns account for fifty-two (over 75 per cent) of the sample. Again, these bare statistics do not in and of themselves explain the contents of the reviews, beyond pointing to factual observations that the films were both Italian and dubbed. A closer look reveals particular trends of incorporating these words into primarily pejorative phrases surrounding foreignness. One such trend invests in culinary metaphors, so that *L'uccello dalle piume di cristallo* 'has so many holes, it looks like Swiss, if not Italian-German, cheese' (Cedrone 1970: 13) and *La mala ordina* is 'one of those brainless "international" goulashes' (Baltake 1973: 26), while *Crazy Joe* is 'littered with bodies and pasta and by its conclusion all that blood and tomato paste run together' (Smiljanich 1974: 58) and 'spaghetti . . . equal to the kind you'd expect to be served in a greasy spoon out of a can' (Block 1974: 15). Christopher Frayling explains that the phrase 'spaghetti western' (though since appropriated as a term of endearment among fans) arose 'as a pejorative in America in the 1960s and 1970s, meaning "not at all like the real thing"' (Frayling 1998: x). The 'real thing' being referred to by Frayling is of course the Hollywood Western, with the culinary language he identifies denoting the pollution of this supposedly pure format by a foreign import. This sense of impurity carries over into the reviews quoted above (which were contemporaneous with those being cited by Frayling), as if these films' foreignness had left a strange and sour taste in the mouth, infecting the propriety of the cinematic space itself.

Such perceptions of oddness are articulated in their clearest terms when the films' English-language dubbing is the subject of critique. On occasion, the reviews convey a sense that the very experience of movie-going has been rendered uncanny, as when *La mala ordina* is said to feature 'sub-standard dubbing which makes the poor actors sounds as if they're talking through a nearby radio' (Baltake 1973: 26), or when *Città violenta* appears to have violated an unspoken rule: 'Perversely, "The Family" is an Italian production . . . which means that the stars' English dialog sounds post-synched and that the supporting actors are mostly dubbed' (Thomas 1973b: 112). In other cases, the alienating effect of the dubbing is an object of ridicule: '[Jack] Palance . . . appears to be enjoying a private joke in his part as a Roman mobster. Perhaps he sensed what a public joke the movie [*I padroni della città*] would emerge as in its dubbed manifestation' (Ryan 1977b: 30). On the rare occasion that the dubbing is deemed to be of a high quality, this fact is held up as a surprising exception to the rule, worthy of comment in itself ('believe it or not, the film's dubbing is downright first-rate' (Baltake 1975b: 44)), but still a source of strangeness: 'The dubbing is technically far better than usual [in *Una lucertola con la pelle di donna*], but it's funny to see upper-class English accents coming out of so many patent non-Britishers' (Thomas 1971: 88).

The above comments point to a multi-layered sense of alienation engendered by the dubbing process. Charlotte Bosseaux argues that dubbing, by foregrounding the fact that the cinematic voice is disembodied, adds another layer to the already uncanny experience of film spectatorship. If, following Tom Gunning (2003) and Laura Mulvey (in van den Oever 2010), cinema has historically and inherently de-familiarised the 'everyday' through the illusion of movement, then dubbing goes a step further:

> Dubbing creates an intellectual uncertainty in viewers, who may find themselves wondering whose voice they are actually hearing . . . [the audience] is accepting of the new situation while suspending disbelief over the fact that someone (noticeably) foreign is speaking perfectly in the target audience's language. (Bosseaux 2015: 80)

Bosseaux's words closely accord with the sense of bewilderment expressed in the above review of *Una lucertola con la pelle di donna*, perhaps going some way towards explaining the broader critical distaste for these films' discomfiting oddness.

Such a psychological effect is also reliant on cultural context, and the associations that are attached to different distribution practices in particular markets. Bondanella writes the following of *filone* cinema's international distribution:

> American audiences familiar with the so-called art films of the most respected Italian directors generally prefer subtitles . . . but Hollywood studios distributing popular genre films such as the peplum or the spaghetti western feared losing their audiences to subtitles, and so generally had these films dubbed. (Bondanella 2009: 162)

In other words, Italian crime *filoni* were scorned twice over, not only by arriving into a culturally maligned distribution milieu, but also by being attached to a mode of translation that carried further connotations of laughable cheapness. Contrast this to the place of dubbing in Italian cinema, where the practice had been ubiquitous since the Fascist regime had banned foreign languages from film in 1930 (Gili 1981: 34). As a result, post-synchronisation rather than location sound was the accepted production practice throughout the Italian film industry long after the regime fell. Antonella Sisto argues that this cultural familiarity with dubbing since the dawn of the talkies resulted in Italy's peculiar national practice of accepting and normalising 'the vocal colonization of the acting body' (Sisto 2017: 398).

We can therefore see once again how the distribution contexts of these films were decisive in shaping their reception. Various factors – the culturally alien mode of audio-visual delivery, the sporadic release patterns, the exhibition space of the drive-in and the grindhouse, and the sensationalised marketing campaigns – combined to render Italian crime *filoni* a peculiar experience for a North American viewer. It has become apparent that these films were not necessarily as shocking or scandalous to a US audience as their lurid banner ads (and subsequent 'cult' discourses) would have us believe, since in many ways they were seen to be typical (and at times tedious) 'exploitation' fare. Rather, they were seen to be cultural oddities, whose intermittent appearance in the US market was the subject of amusement, disdain and bewilderment. In Appendix G, it has not been possible to chart a broad pattern of seriality across the reception patterns of these various *filone* strands, as it was in Appendices D, E and F. The obvious explanation for this is that only twenty-eight of the case-study films were released in the USA, and that these releases were spread over the same period of time as were all sixty-eight films in Italy (see Appendix A). As a result of this (and of many of the films not being deemed worthy of reviews in US newspapers), my sample of sixty-nine US reviews spans only twelve films, compared to the fifty films covered by the sixty-two Italian reviews.

The lack of 'serial' repetition as a noticeable factor in the marketing materials or the critical reception in the US context is therefore in stark contrast to the Italian market, where repetitiveness and intertextuality were at once a lucrative selling point and (eventually) a target of weariness from the critics. This contrast has highlighted the centrality of this distribution pattern to the films' significance in the Italian context. On top of the contents of the films themselves and the rapidity of their production, we can now add the frequency of their release patterns, the tenor of their critical reception and the tone of their marketing campaigns as evidence for my attempt to appraise the cultural options open to Italian audiences at the time. It now remains to consider what the implications of such seriality are for how we continue to think about the *filone* phenomenon and its place in film history.

Notes

1. Savioli 1973: 9; Ferraù 1976: 17.
2. Santuari 1975: 15.
3. Casazza 1975: 7.
4. Biraghi 1973a: 10.
5. 'Qualunquismo' roughly translates as 'political apathy', but carries a more specific association with the right-wing political party *Fronte dell'Uomo Qualunque* ('the Common Man's Front'), which emerged in the immediate post-war era when it attracted over a million votes in the June 1946 elections (Ginsborg 1990: 99–100). This word (or one of its derivatives) is used in the following reviews: Biraghi 1973a: 10; Leo 1975a: 14; Leo 1975c: 14.
6. Pestelli 1970: 7; Savioli 1973: 9; Casazza 1975: 7; Porro 1975: 15.
7. M.C. 1974: 7; Biraghi 1974a: 16; Leo 1975a: 14; Casazza 1975: 7; Leo 1975c: 14.
8. Giuliano Carnimeo had directed ten Westerns between 1966 and 1972, prior to the release of *Perché quelle strane gocce di sangue sul corpo di Jennifer?*, and would go on to make three more.
9. It is worth noting here that this particular quotation could easily describe any number of *filoni* featuring a '*vendicatore solitario*' / 'lone avenger', again validating Wagstaff's argument that these cycles' synopses are often interchangeable.
10. *La polizia ringrazia* and *La polizia sta a guardare* do possess a direct link, in that Roberto Infascelli produced the former and directed the latter. The similarly 'serial' marketing for *La polizia sta a guardare*, which opens with

the words '1972 *La polizia ringrazia* / 1973 *La polizia sta a guardare*' (in *La Stampa*, 29 November 1973, p. 10) therefore carries a more legitimate implication of coordinated seriality.
11. This distribution history has been compiled by consulting the cinema listings pages of local newspapers from across the USA over the period in question: *Pittsburgh Post-Gazette*, *The Philadelphia Inquirer*, *Philadelphia Daily News*, *The Indianapolis Star*, *The Indianapolis News*, *The Republic* (Columbus, Indiana), *Chicago Tribune*, *Standard-Speaker* (Hazleton, Pennsylvania), *The Akron Beacon Journal* (Akron, Ohio), *The Monroe News-Star* (Monroe, Louisiana), *Daily World* (Opelousas, Louisiana), *Enterprise Journal* (McComb, Mississippi), *The Delta Democrat-Times* (Greenville, Mississippi), *The News Item* (Shamokin, Pennsylvania), *Iowa City Press-Citizen*, *The Marion Star* (Marion, Ohio), *Des Moines Tribune*, *The Newark Advocate* (Newark, Ohio), *Los Angeles Times*, *The Salina Journal* (Salina, Kansas), *Independent Press-Telegram* (Long Beach, California), *The Burlington Free Press* (Burlington, Vermont), *The La Crosse Tribune* (La Crosse, Wisconsin), *The Missoulian* (Missoula, Montana), *The Sheboygan Press* (Sheboygan, Wisconsin), *Asheville Citizen-Times* (Asheville, North Carolina), *Lubbock Avalanche-Journal* (Lubbock, Texas), *Garden City Telegram* (Garden City, Kansas), *Biddeford-Saco Journal* (Biddeford, Maine), *San Antonio Express* and *The Miami News*.

Conclusion

Throughout this book, the notion of a '*filone*' has time and again arisen as a central consideration. This mode of categorising films has been framed in these pages as serving several related purposes. I have argued on a number of occasions that the *filone*'s industrial conditions of rapid production schedules allowed swift responsiveness to political events, cinematic trends and attendant economic opportunities. This immediacy has in turn been seen to necessitate a simplified construction of believable backdrops within the filmic worlds themselves, whose hasty composition betrays taken-as-read assumptions on the part of the filmmakers about audiences' levels of prior knowledge. The repetitive accumulation of these backdrops, through large numbers of closely related films being released within concentrated periods of time, has thereby been analysed as the defining feature of these films' often muddled negotiation with both the intrigues of their contemporary moment and the weight of the recent past. Finally, the centrality of these very distribution patterns to the identification of any such significance has been demonstrated, with a noticeably different reception emerging when these films encountered more sporadic release patterns and a less culturally familiar context.

It remains to consider the meaning, significance and usefulness of the very word '*filone*' itself since, on the surface, there is an inherent contradiction in the organisation of this book. Chapters 2, 3 and 4 have each set out to identify and delineate the characteristics of various smaller cinematic strands or subsets that have often been subsumed within the large and reductive *filone* headings of *poliziottesco* and *giallo*. At the same time, this book has programmatically grouped all of these strands together under the even larger and even more all-encompassing category of 'Italian crime film', and then identified a particular unifying thematic thread (a degree of preoccupation with the past) existing within that larger category, but recurring across *filone* boundaries. In Chapter 5, I have then argued that the various strands I have identified are indeed productively analysed as component parts of one large pattern of repetition over a prolonged period. A reader might reasonably now be wondering whether I am claiming that received *filone* categories are too broad or too narrow.

The answer depends on which aspects of cinema we are looking at and what we are seeking to discover when we ascribe meaning to the term '*filone*'. My synchronic analyses of the industrial conditions, political contexts and commercial imperatives surrounding the films' production and initial domestic release patterns have shown that these films can be productively divided into smaller thematic categories (for example, conspiracy *poliziottesco*, vigilante, mafia, 'wartime trauma' *giallo* and rural *giallo*) in order to trace specific cultural antecedents and differing modes of engagement with the past. Simultaneously, a notable degree of cross-pollination between these strands has become apparent in these same analyses. This is most obvious when we observe how the production personnel crossed from strand to strand,[1] but is also manifest in the Italian reception patterns, which broadly eschewed clear divisions within *filone* cinema, instead perceiving one continuous stream of interchangeable ephemera.

My diachronic analysis of US reception patterns, on the other hand, has shown how different distribution and exhibition contexts, along with more sensationalised marketing strategies, framed these films as oddities rather than familiar repetitions. Additional diachronic analysis into how their 'cult' status was subsequently nurtured through VHS, Betamax, DVD, Blu-ray and online streaming markets would further delineate how the categories '*giallo*' and '*poliziottesco*' took on particular retrospective significance among fan communities, but this endeavour is beyond the scope of this volume.[2] I have instead tried to offer different interpretations of these films' position in cinematic and cultural history. The majority of my analysis has surrounded the films' initial circumstances of production, exhibition and reception, and is therefore open to Klinger's accusation of being 'stuck in synchrony' (Klinger 1997: 111). By also considering transnational routes of influence and cross-cultural reception patterns, I hope to have at least provided a sense of the 'flux of meaning brought on by changing social and historical horizons over time' (Klinger 1997: 111).

This said, my chief focus has deliberately been on charting how the repetitive nature of these films was embedded in their immediate moment, and it is here that the concept of a *filone* has been most useful. Angela Dalle Vacche describes *filoni* as 'well-planned investments of the industry into a regulated, but also stimulating, oscillation between repetition and difference, convention and invention' (Dalle Vacche 1992: 55). We have seen that this process was manifested on a textual level (in the iterative construction of the films' story worlds) and an industrial / economic level (in the rapid production of films according to the profitable formula *du jour*), but also on the levels of distribution, reception and consumption (due to the concentrated release patterns in Italian cinemas, often in the wake of a particular box-office success that indicated a route to the next profitable formula). If we are to even get close to appreciating the experience of viewing these films in Italy at this historical moment, we therefore need to reflect on the implications of the fundamentally cyclical or 'serial' nature of this mode of cinematic output.

At various points in this volume, studies into the notion of 'seriality' have provided useful reference points to conceptualise these films, not as standalone entities or self-contained texts, but instead as pluralities. These have been seen to exist in a state of perpetual and innate intertextuality, through which meanings accumulate across various iterations (Klein and Palmer 2016; Kelleter 2017). As has been explained in Chapter 2, however, it is relatively rare for *filone* films to deploy actual 'serialised' narratives (that is, a set of regular episodes comprising a single storyline or existing in a unified story world). The broader field of 'seriality studies' is therefore an illuminating model for understanding how such texts exist in relation to other texts, but needs to be adapted to the specific contexts of the Italian *filone*.

Robbie Edmonstone analyses structural, visual and thematic patterns across a wide and seemingly diverse collection of Italian *filoni* from the 1960s and 1970s, including peplums, Westerns, *gialli*, *poliziotteschi*, gothic horror films, and numerous other smaller strands including 'mondo' travelogues, cannibal films, spy films, fantasy films and post-apocalyptic science-fiction dramas. One of his conclusions is particularly revealing:

> The films' patterns of violence, spectacle and narrative are remarkably similar: similar enough, in fact, to suggest that they are far more usefully analysed as a cohesive body of films, subdivided into cycles that are largely distinguished by their configurations of *mise-en-scène* and formulaic narratives. (Edmonstone 2008: 40)

This analysis is in keeping with Wagstaff's claim that plot synopses and personnel tended to be interchangeable across many *filoni*, and that 'a still, particularly if someone in the shot is wearing a hat, usually clears up the mystery [of which *filone* we are viewing]' (Wagstaff 1992: 252). These arguments maintain that the various *filoni* are so similar to one another in terms of narrative structure, character types and the thrills on offer to an audience that they are primarily differentiated only by their costumes and settings. This usefully serves to distinguish a Western from a peplum, or a fantasy film from a spy film, but does little to delineate the various strands that have been analysed in this book that frequently share costumes and settings. Perhaps 'crime film' is indeed the most appropriate all-encompassing *filone* category for these films after all.

If we approach these films from an industrial rather than a textual perspective, however, Edmonstone's use of the word 'cycle' hints at a productive method of charting this book's various *filone* strands. Richard Nowell's study of US 'teen slasher' films made between 1974 and 1981 offers a model for analysing film cycles as 'series of chronologically distinct phases of activity [that] illuminate the ways in which industrial developments, market shifts, and changing commercial imperatives underwrite production and distribution' (Nowell 2011: 5). Using a metaphor of frontier settlement, Nowell argues that a cycle is preceded by either a 'pioneer' production (a highly innovative, high-risk film) or, more commonly, a 'speculator' production (a less innovative film that invests in an existing but dormant format). The first phase of a new cycle proper comes in the form of a 'trailblazer hit': a commercial success that begins life as either a 'pioneer' or a 'speculator' production, and stands apart from contemporaneous hits, thus pointing the way to a future profit route. After this come the 'cash-ins', which respond opportunistically to the success of a 'trailblazer' by closely and rapidly modelling themselves on it (and from this point onwards, a cycle will begin to attract the opprobrium of critics, due to the transparency with which the formula is being repeated). These 'cash-ins' are themselves divided into two distinct phases: higher-risk 'prospector' cash-ins (those that appear soon after the 'trailblazer', before the formula's profitability has been fully proven) and lower-risk 'carpetbagger' cash-ins (a proliferation of films that follow in the wake of successful 'prospector' cash-ins). A cycle is complete when 'carpetbaggers' saturate the market, so that returns become harder to come by, resulting in a drop in production levels (Nowell 2011: 46–52).

Nowell's careful delineation of these phases is useful when considering the internal dynamics of *filone* cinema. At numerous points in this book, we have seen that any given strand did not simply comprise a single homogeneous glut imitating one film, but instead tended to replicate elements from a number of films, often merging references to international box-office successes with references to recent Italian films. David Church emphasises this point when considering the network of transnational influences on the films of Lucio Fulci: 'Some *filoni* capitalized on popular Anglo-American imports, some emerged after an Italian-made hit reinforced an Anglo-American one, and others were primarily imitative of homegrown Italian hits' (Church 2015b: 5). Accordingly, Nowell emphasises that some cycles can have multiple points of origin, particularly when they start abortively with a 'pioneer' film that does not manage to spawn a period of proliferation. In this case, the rapid escalation in production will only arrive once a later 'speculator' film has distilled the formula (Nowell 2011: 47).

The various cinematic strands discussed in this book correlate with Nowell's categories to differing degrees. The most obviously proliferating cycle I have looked at has been the collection of mafia films that followed the Italian release of *The Godfather* (Francis Ford Coppola, 1972) (analysed in Chapter 3). Table C.1 charts my attempt to map this strand onto the above model, and one departure from Nowell's definitions is immediately apparent. This cycle's 'trailblazer' did not begin life as either a 'pioneer' or a 'speculator' in the Italian context, but was instead an imported game-changer, which was in effect parachuted into the process of cycle creation (some home-grown 'pioneer' films can be identified, since elements from them would go on to become incorporated within the cycle, but these were not themselves the catalyst for the period of proliferation). Once this foreign 'trailblazer' has arrived, the cycle closely accords with the model, with seven 'prospector' productions arriving in the immediate wake of the 'trailblazer' (as previously discussed, the fact that three of these actually reached theatres a few weeks before *The Godfather* had even arrived on the market is testament to their producers' astute opportunism). These are then followed by sixteen 'carpetbagger' cash-ins, which saturate the market over the course of a year, thus completing the cycle and causing production levels of the strand thereafter to drop to a base level.

Table C.2 shows the same process applied to the vigilante *filone* analysed in Chapter 2, and again we can see correlation with a degree of variation. Early 'pioneer' productions can be seen to provide some indication that a 'vigilante' cycle might be in the offing, but neither film sparked a process of proliferation. The 'speculator' production (a well-timed investment in the existing format, which then becomes a 'trailblazer') eventually arrives in the form of *Il cittadino si ribella* / *Street Law* (Enzo G. Castellari, 1974). From this point onwards, there are two alternative models for charting this *filone*'s development. Model 1 positions *Death Wish* (Michael Winner, 1974) as a co-'trailblazer' with *Il cittadino si ribella*, the cumulative impact of both films' arrival onto the Italian market within a short space of time pointing the way to future profits. However, this model assumes that the American import acted as a primary catalyst, rather than a secondary one. An alternative interpretation of how the *filone* system operated can be seen in Model 2, in which (as has been discussed in Chapter 1) Enzo G. Castellari is given credit for anticipating the impending arrival of *Death Wish* (which had already been released in the USA in July 1974) and

Table C.1 The mafia *filone* mapped onto Richard Nowell's 'film cycle' model.

Pioneer	Speculator	Trailblazer	Prospector cash-in	Carpetbagger cash-in
Il giorno della civetta (February 1968)	n/a	*The Godfather* (Italian release September 1972)	*I familiari delle vittime non saranno avvertiti* (August 1972)	*Il boss* (February 1973)
Milano calibro 9 (February 1972)			*La mano lunga del padrino* (August 1972)	*Gli amici degli amici hanno saputo* (February 1973)
			Camorra (August 1972)	*Milano rovente* (February 1973)
			La mala ordina (September 1972)	*Baciamo le mani* (February 1973)
			Torino nera (September 1972)	*La padrina* (March 1973)
			Afyon oppio (December 1972)	*La mano nera* (March 1973)
			L'amico del padrino (December 1972)	*L'onorata famiglia – Uccidere è cosa nostra* (March 1973)
				La legge della Camorra (July 1973)
				Il consigliori (August 1973)
				Servo suo (September 1973)
				Tony Arzenta (September 1973)
				Anna, quel particolare piacere (November 1973)
				Quelli che contano (January 1974)
				I guappi (February 1974)
				Crazy Joe (February 1974)
				Il poliziotto è marcio (Mar 1974)

Table C.2 The vigilante *filone* mapped onto Richard Nowell's 'film cycle' model.

	Pioneer	Speculator	Trailblazer	Prospector cash-in	Carpetbagger cash-in
Model 1	*Città violenta* (September 1970) *Revolver* (September 1973)	*Il cittadino si ribella* (September 1974)	*Il cittadino si ribella* (September 1974) and *Death Wish* (Italian release October 1974)	*L'uomo della strada fa giustizia* (May 1975) *La città sconvolta: caccia spietata ai rapitori* (August 1975) *Roma violenta* (August 1975) *Il giustiziere sfida la città* (August 1975)	*Vai gorilla* (November 1975) *Roma l'altra faccia della violenza* (July 1976) *Torino violenta* (October 1977) *No alla violenza* (October 1977)
Model 2	*Città violenta* (September 1970) *Revolver* (September 1973)	*Il cittadino si ribella* (September 1974)	*Il cittadino si ribella* (September 1974)	*Death Wish* (Italian release October 1974)	*L'uomo della strada fa giustizia* (May 1975) *La città sconvolta: caccia spietata ai rapitori* (August 1975) *Roma violenta* (August 1975) *Il giustiziere sfida la città* (August 1975) *Vai gorilla* (November 1975)

Table C.3 The 'conspiracy' *poliziottesco* mapped onto Richard Nowell's 'film cycle' model.

Pioneer	Speculator	Trailblazer	Prospector cash-in	Carpetbagger cash-in
Indagine su un cittadino al di sopra di ogni sospetto (February 1970)	*La polizia ringrazia* (February 1972)	*Dirty Harry* (Italian release January 1972)	*Milano trema – la polizia vuole giustizia* (August 1973)	n/a
Confessione di un commissario di polizia al procuratore della repubblica (March 1971)		and *La polizia ringrazia* (February 1972)	*La polizia sta a guardare* (November 1973)	

getting in there first.³ By this model, the release of *Il cittadino si ribella* just before the arrival of *Death Wish* shifts the role of the US film in the Italian market so that it behaves just like a 'prospector' cash-in (a production that confirms the profitable potential of the 'trailblazer' and thus emboldens the 'carpetbaggers' to replicate the formula in quick succession the following year).

The other strands analysed in this book do not fit this model of film cycle development so neatly, either because they never ultimately entered a period of proliferation, or because they became so dominant over a prolonged period of time that they did not display the short-lived explosion of activity followed by a saturation point that characterises a 'cycle'. The 'conspiracy' *poliziottesco*, for example, shows the early signs of becoming a cycle (see Table C.3), with early 'pioneer' productions anticipating potential future profits without themselves spawning a mass of imitations. *La polizia ringrazia / Execution Squad* (Stefano Vanzina, 1972) then fits the 'speculator' mould by testing the market, and becomes a co-'trailblazer' in close proximity to the release of *Dirty Harry* (Don Siegel, 1971). The proliferation that followed these 'trailblazers', however, was the vast and enduring *poliziottesco filone* (whose productions numbered in their hundreds over the following decade), rather than an exact replication of the 'conspiracy' formula. This precise formula instead produced a couple of films the following year, and a few more thereafter, but never progressed into the 'carpetbagger' phase of proliferation and saturation.

The 'rural *giallo*' also does not fit this definition of a 'cycle' since, though *Reazione a catena / A Bay of Blood* (Mario Bava, September 1971) could be said to constitute a 'pioneer' and a 'trailblazer', the next such film was *Non si sevizia un paperino / Don't Torture a Duckling* (Lucio Fulci, September 1972) a whole year later, and releases thereafter were sporadic, with *I corpi presentano tracce di violenza carnale / Torso* (Sergio Martino) coming out in January 1973, *La casa dalle finestre che ridono / The House of the Laughing Windows* (Pupi Avati) in August 1976, and *Solamente nero / Bloodstained Shadow* (Antonio Bido) in July 1978. Similarly, my identification and analysis of wartime trauma in the *giallo* does not resemble a 'cycle' since it consists of only four films, which are spaced sporadically over an eight-year period: *Nelle pieghe della carne / In the Folds of the Flesh* (Sergio Bergonzelli, May 1970), *Ragazza tutta nuda assassinata nel parco / Naked Girl Killed in the Park* (Alfonso Brescia, May 1972), *Il gatto dagli occhi di giada / Watch Me When I Kill* (Antonio Bido, August 1977) and *Pensione paura / Hotel Fear* (Francesco Barilli, February 1978). These two groups of films are closer to what Nowell calls 'fads': recognisable elements such as settings or themes that recur but do not lead to any large-scale replication (Nowell 2011: 44–5). Conversely, *gialli* that are set in contemporary urban centres became so numerous over such a prolonged period that Nowell directly refers to these as an example of a 'staple': a regular, sustained and continuously profitable category (Nowell 2011: 45, 69). Such a 'staple' is akin to the Spaghetti Western or the larger *poliziottesco*, since these each incorporate their own fads and cycles that ebb and flow over a prolonged period.

The category 'crime film' could therefore be framed in much the same way: a large set of interlocking strands, consisting of some full-blown cycles and some abortive cycles, over a number of years. The patterns of critical reception identified in Chapter 5 certainly suggest that these films were all being seen as a single trend amongst many industry commentators in contemporary Italy. However, rather than worry too much about which labels we should be using, or whether we should be drawing *filone* boundary lines at all, or whether these strands constitute full-blown 'cycles' or not, I would like to focus on what the varying levels of correlation to Nowell's model tell us about the surrounding industrial system. All *filoni* were part of a large-scale process that was focused squarely on the regular production of 'pioneers' and 'speculators' in the hope of spawning new cycles, and then of 'cash-ins' once a cycle had shown its profitable potential, often making opportunistic use of American films along the way to fill a variety of vacant roles in that process. If we comprehend a *filone* as simply the latest speculation in this volatile market, we can see how a variety of outcomes were inevitable. Some trends (such as Spaghetti Westerns, *poliziotteschi* and 'urban' *gialli*) came to dominate entire sectors of the industry over a number of years; others began life as small-scale speculative gambles to test the water, and of these, some would spawn cycles, while others would not.

Peter Stanfield makes a further case for the centrality of commercial imperatives when conceptualising film cycles. He argues that, since cycles are intimately tied to the moments of their production, distribution, exhibition and reception, the study of repetition and innovation across those cycles produces a history of film understood through its relationship to the 'topical'. Analysing the common practice of rushing films out to capitalise on (often fleeting) popular interest in a given topic or issue therefore 'allows for a verifiable account of continuities and shifts in film production and the manner in which that production is linked to the public sphere' (Stanfield 2013: 223). Stanfield conceptualises the word 'cycle' through a dual focus on related definitions taken from cultural and economic history. The former definition, following Franco Moretti's theory of literary cycles (Moretti 2005: 49), delineates three time frames: the 'event' (a short-lived moment), the *longue durée* (an overarching, long-term historical structure) and the 'cycle' (a middle ground of regularly repeated patterns, which comprise contiguous 'events' and are in turn constrained by the larger forces of the *longue durée*). The latter definition, following W. C. Mitchell's business cycle theory, seeks to forecast patterns in a volatile economic system by dividing developments in the marketplace into 'fluctuations' (localised, short-lived activity), 'trends' (long-term underlying forces) and 'cycles' (recurring patterns of departure from an overarching trend). Such cycles are each simultaneously unique to their time and place and a repetition of previous cycles, allowing an insight into the process by which business conditions repeat themselves, but with an element of difference in each iteration (Stanfield 2013: 221–3). Both of the above definitions of a 'cycle' seek to comprehend the relationships between individual units, whose patterns are characterised simultaneously by reiteration and incremental variation.

This approach allows us further to understand *filone* filmmaking as a product emanating from a marketplace whose dual *raison d'être* was firstly to create speculations in an attempt to predict where the next profitable cycle might lie, and secondly to exploit the short-lived favourable market conditions of successful cycles. These endeavours were informed by previous patterns, but each attempt at cycle creation was slightly different from the last, as it sought (sometimes successfully, sometimes not) to adapt past successes to shifts in popular taste. This perpetual attempt to capitalise on topicality in turn necessitated the efficient construction of recognisable manifestations of contemporaneity. As Stanfield explains, one determinant of film cycles' oscillation between repetition and difference is their need to maintain a dialogue with contemporary culture and tastes, which often results in 'the incorporation of everyday objects into a film's mise-en-scène' (Stanfield 2013: 224). Accordingly, we have seen in these pages several examples in which repetitions in the construction of story worlds betray taken-as-read assumptions on the part of filmmakers, which reveal themselves in the accumulation of seemingly inconsequential asides or scene-setting details. Together, the inevitability of historically constituted corruption, the impact of rapid socio-economic change and the lingering vestiges of wartime conflict are all united as key components of a contemporaneity that is assumed to be instantly recognisable to Italian audiences of the 1970s.

Christopher Wagstaff is therefore correct to say that 'the production sector, rather than relaying valuable social discourses, was simply tailoring a product to a protected and subsidized market' (Wagstaff 2013: 39). I too have no interest in reductive reflectionism, in claims of direct correlations between the contents of films and their socio-political contexts, or even in a 'symptomatic' analysis that seeks unproblematically to read unconscious, hidden biases from beneath the surface of particular films. Rather, my argument has sought to understand how material conditions and cultural precedents that surrounded *filone* cinema facilitated the accumulation of particular decisions in the processes of production, distribution, exhibition and reception. Identifying and understanding these decisions in turn allows us to comprehend one particular mode in which the contemporary moment's place in a historical continuum was being presented to the cinema-going public.

From this economic perspective, studying *filoni* as hit-and-miss attempts to foment cycles offers a means of understanding them as oscillations around longer-term trends. The Italian critical response that tended to frame all contemporary-set 'crime films' as one continuous whole shows that this was itself seen to be one such trend, comprising a number of attempted cycles. My delineation throughout this book of *filone* subsets, strands, cycles or fads of varying sizes on the one hand, and of thematic traits that traversed and united these categories on the other, allows us to comprehend an organic network of responses to commercial imperatives. These evolved and adapted to surrounding circumstances (such as political events, terrorist activities, suspicions of official cover-ups or the release of a successful Hollywood film) while all the time cohering around a larger generic trend, and existing within an industrial framework of subsidised, low-risk and low-cost production opportunities.

At the start of this book, I framed my arguments through recourse to historical debates concerning the options open to human beings in a given moment. Isaiah Berlin rejected determinist notions of the inevitability of overarching historical patterns beyond human control, insisting that individuals retained a capacity for choice within those larger structures. As his biographer Michael Ignatieff explains, for Berlin:

> The function of historical understanding was to identify the precise range within which historical actors enjoyed room for manoeuvre, to understand how and why they used their freedom, and to evaluate their actions by the standard of what real alternatives were possible to them at the time. (Ignatieff 2000: 206)

This perspective offers a way of conceptualising *filone* cinema, as one small register of the broader cultural–historical continuum of the Italian nation. By placing such cinematic output within its industrial, political and cultural contexts, as I have sought to do in these pages, we can begin to understand how filmmakers working within this milieu were part of a larger structure of economic, intertextual and cross-cultural relationships. Their short-term decisions to make particular types of film oscillated around the evolving demands of the market and a longer-term, overarching business model.

I have tried to investigate numerous ways in which Italian crime films can be seen as 'historical documents', which thereby illuminate how we approach such popular cinematic forms. They have been appraised as documents of immediate political events, documents of a preoccupation with the past that was seen to be characteristic of their time and place, and documents of their industrial conditions of production, distribution, exhibition and reception. These various cycles, trends and strands constitute units of culture that take on different meanings in different contexts. My intention has been to throw light on one particular register of historical address available to audiences in 1970s Italy.

Notes

1. Appendix A, for example, shows us that Umberto Lenzi directed six of this book's key films: three urban *gialli*, one mafia film and two vigilante films. Sergio Martino directed five: two conspiracy *poliziotteschi*, two urban *gialli* and one rural *giallo*. Enzo G. Castellari directed three: one vigilante film, one conspiracy *poliziottesco* and one urban *giallo*.
2. The remediation of *gialli* and their integration into broader 'horror' discourses have been analysed by numerous scholars. See especially Guins (2005), Church (2015b) and Baschiera (2017).
3. This line of argument may seem contradictory, since I have not considered *I familiari delle vittime non saranno avvertiti*, *La mano lunga del padrino* or

Camorra as potential 'trailblazers' for the mafia *filone* in Table C.1, even though they also opportunistically appeared in the month before their related US film. As has been argued in Chapter 2, however, *Il cittadino si ribella* was a clear precedent for the 'vigilante' strand due to its setting in an Italian locale and responsiveness to Italian news stories, while the mafia films mentioned here were more obviously capitalising on the impending arrival of *The Godfather*. The very fact that this point is open to interpretation and debate further illustrates the complex nature of the transatlantic relationships that led to multiple points of origin within certain cycles.

Appendices

Appendix A: Italian and US cinematic release dates of key films

Italian cinematic release title	US cinematic release title	Director	Italian cinematic release date	US cinematic release date
Sei donne per l'assassino	Blood and Black Lace	Bava	April 1964	April 1965
L'uccello dalle piume di cristallo	The Bird with the Crystal Plumage	Argento	February 1970	September 1970
Paranoia		Lenzi	February 1970	–
Nelle pieghe della carne		Bergonzelli	May 1970	–
Il rosso segno della follia	A Hatchet for the Honeymoon	Bava	June 1970	February 1972
Città violenta	The Family	Sollima	September 1970	March 1973
Una lucertola con la pelle di donna	A Lizard in a Woman's Skin	Fulci	February 1971	September 1971
Lo strano vizio della signora Wardh	The Next Victim	Martino	February 1971	December 1971
Gli occhi freddi della paura		Castellari	April 1971	–
Giornata nera per l'ariete		Bazzoni	August 1971	–
Un posto ideale per uccidere	Dirty Pictures	Lenzi	August 1971	December 1974
Reazione a catena	Twitch of the Death Nerve	Bava	September 1971	May 1972
Milano calibro 9		Di Leo	February 1972	–
La polizia ringrazia		Vanzina	February 1972	–
Cosa avete fatto a Solange?	Terror in the Woods	Dallamano	March 1972	April 1974
Ragazza tutta nuda assassinata nel parco		Brescia	May 1972	–
La mano lunga del padrino	The Long Arm of the Godfather	Bonomi	August 1972	January 1977
Perché quelle strane gocce di sangue sul corpo di Jennifer?		Carnimeo	August 1972	–
I familiari delle vittime non saranno avvertiti	Crime Boss	De Martino	August 1972	January 1975
Il tuo vizio è una stanza chiusa e solo io ne ho la chiave		Martino	August 1972	–
Camorra		Squitieri	August 1972	–
La mala ordina	The Italian Connection	Di Leo	September 1972	November 1973
Non si sevizia un paperino		Fulci	September 1972	–

(Continued)

Appendix A: continued

Italian cinematic release title	US cinematic release title	Director	Italian cinematic release date	US cinematic release date
Torino nera		Lizzani	September 1972	–
La morte accarezza a mezzanotte		Ercoli	November 1972	–
L'amico del padrino		Agrama	December 1972	–
Afyon oppio	The Sicilian Connection	Baldi	December 1972	January 1977
I corpi presentano tracce di violenza carnale	Torso	Martino	January 1973	April 1973
Il boss		Di Leo	February 1973	–
Milano rovente		Lenzi	February 1973	–
Gli amici degli amici hanno saputo		Marcolin	February 1973	–
Baciamo le mani		Schiraldi	February 1973	–
La mano nera		Racioppi	March 1973	–
L'onorata famiglia – Uccidere è cosa nostra		Ricci	March 1973	–
La padrina		Vari	March 1973	–
La legge della Camorra		Fidani	July 1973	–
Il consigliori	Counselor at Crime	De Martino	August 1973	April 1975
Milano trema – la polizia vuole giustizia	The Violent Professionals	Martino	August 1973	February 1975
Serco suo		Scavolini	September 1973	–
Revolver	Blood in the Streets	Sollima	September 1973	November 1975
Tony Arzenta	No Way Out	Tessari	September 1973	October 1975
Anna, quel particolare piacere		Carnimeo	November 1973	–
La polizia sta a guardare		Infascelli	November 1973	–
Quelli che contano	Cry of a Prostitute	Bianchi	January 1974	May 1977
I guappi		Squitieri	February 1974	–
Crazy Joe	Crazy Joe	Lizzani	February 1974	February 1974
Il poliziotto è marcio		Di Leo	March 1974	–
Il cittadino si ribella	Anonymous Avenger	Castellari	September 1974	February 1976
Gatti rossi in un labirinto di vetro	Eyeball	Lenzi	January 1975	July 1978
Profondo rosso	Deep Red	Argento	March 1975	June 1976

Title	English Title	Director	Date
La polizia ha le mani legate	Killer Cop	Ercoli	March 1975
Ricatto alla mala	Summertime Killer	Isasi	April 1975
La polizia accusa: il servizio segreto uccide		Martino	April 1975
L'uomo della strada fa giustizia		Lenzi	May 1975
Nude per l'assassino		Bianchi	August 1975
La città sconvolta: caccia spietata ai rapitori	Kidnap Syndicate	Di Leo	August 1975
Roma violenta	Violent City	Girolami	August 1975
Il giustiziere sfida la città		Lenzi	August 1975
Poliziotti violenti		Tarantini	June 1976
Roma, l'altra faccia della violenza		Girolami	July 1976
La casa dalle finestre che ridono		Avati	August 1976
Il grande racket		Castellari	August 1976
I padroni della città	Mister Scarface	Di Leo	December 1976
Il gatto dagli occhi di giada		Bido	August 1977
Torino violenta		Ausino	October 1977
No alla violenza		Cimarosa	October 1977
Pensione paura		Barilli	February 1978
Solamente nero		Bido	July 1978

			October 1976
			July 1975
			September 1976
			December 1975
			September 1977

Appendix B: Political judgements of 'poliziottesco' or 'vigilante' films in Italian newspaper reviews

Film title	Review date	Newspaper	Unfavourable comparison with 'impegno' or 'denuncia'	Film failing to address political complexities	Reactionary political outlook identified	Source
Città violenta	1 October 1970	La Stampa	x			Pestelli 1970: 7
La polizia ringrazia	12 April 1972	Il Messaggero		x		Biraghi 1972a: 8
La polizia ringrazia	14 April 1972	La Stampa				Pestelli 1972b: 7
Milano trema – la polizia vuole giustizia	26 August 1973	La Stampa				Valdata 1973a: 7
Milano trema – la polizia vuole giustizia	1 September 1973	Il Messaggero				Vice 1973a: 13
La polizia sta a guardare	24 November 1973	L'Unità	x		x	Savioli 1973: 9
La polizia sta a guardare	24 November 1973	Il Tempo		x		Rondi 1973: 8
La polizia sta a guardare	24 November 1973	Il Messaggero			x	Biraghi 1973a: 10
Revolver	26 May 1974	Paese Sera		x		Santuari 1974: 15
Il cittadino si ribella	20 September 1974	La Stampa				M.C. 1974: 7
Il cittadino si ribella	22 September 1974	Il Messaggero		x	x	Biraghi 1974a: 16
La polizia ha le mani legate	29 March 1975	L'Unità		x		Anon 1975: 9
La polizia accusa: il servizio segreto uccide	15 April 1975	Corriere della Sera	x			Porro 1975: 15
L'uomo della strada fa giustizia	1 June 1975	Il Messaggero			x	Leo 1975a: 14
Roma violenta	22 August 1975	Paese Sera		x	x	Santuari 1975: 15
La città sconvolta: caccia spietata ai rapitori	5 September 1975	La Stampa	x		x	Casazza 1975: 7
La città sconvolta: caccia spietata ai rapitori	6 September 1975	Il Messaggero		x		Leo 1975b: 10

Il giustiziere sfida la città	19 September 1975	Il Messaggero	x	Leo 1975c: 14
Poliziotti violenti	11 June 1976	Paese Sera	x	Ferraù 1976: 17
Poliziotti violenti	12 June 1976	Il Messaggero		Pepoli 1976: 12
Roma, l'altra faccia della violenza	19 August 1976	La Stampa		Valdata 1976: 12
Il grande racket	23 August 1976	Il Messaggero	x	Cer 1976: 7
No alla violenza	13 November 1977	Corriere della Sera	x	Palazzi 1977: 19

Appendix C: Dominant patterns in Italian newspaper reviews of the mafia *filone*

Film title	Review date	Newspaper	Mentions of 'Chicago'	Mentions of '*Il padrino*' (*The Godfather*)	Mentions of the mafia *filone*'s proliferation	Source
Milano calibro 9	11 March 1972	*Il Messaggero*	x			Biraghi 1972b: 12
I familiari delle vittime non saranno avvertiti	20 August 1972	*La Stampa*				Valdata 1972a: 8
La mano lunga del padrino	20 August 1972	*L'Unità*		x		Vice 1972c: 9
La mano lunga del padrino	3 September 1972	*La Stampa*		x	x	G.C. 1972: 8
Camorra	15 September 1972	*La Stampa*		x	x	Reggiani 1972: 7
Torino nera	6 October 1972	*La Stampa*				Pestelli 1972a: 7
Afyon oppio	23 December 1972	*Il Messaggero*				Vice 1972a: 15
Afyon oppio	24 December 1972	*Corriere della Sera*				Autera 1972: 17
Il boss	10 February 1973	*Il Messaggero*		x	x	Biraghi 1973d: 8
L'amico del padrino	25 February 1973	*La Stampa*		x	x	Valdata 1973b: 7
Il boss	2 March 1973	*La Stampa*		x	x	Casazza 1973: 7
Baciamo le mani	23 March 1973	*Il Messaggero*		x		Biraghi 1973c: 12
La mano nera	12 April 1973	*Il Messaggero*				Vice 1973e: 13
La mano nera	13 April 1973	*La Stampa*				Pestelli 1973: 7
Gli amici degli amici hanno saputo	14 April 1973	*L'Unità*				Vice 1973d: 9
Milano rovente	20 May 1973	*Il Messaggero*	x			Vice 1973c: 21
L'onorata famiglia – Uccidere è cosa nostra	6 July 1973	*Il Messaggero*		x	x	Vice 1973b: 12
Il consigliori	31 August 1973	*L'Unità*		x		D.G. 1973: 7
Tony Arzenta	15 September 1973	*Il Messaggero*				Biraghi 1973b: 13
Crazy Joe	9 February 1974	*Il Messaggero*		x	x	Biraghi 1974b: 12
I guappi	1 March 1974	*La Stampa*				Pestelli 1974: 7

Appendix D: Critical reception patterns around key films in Italian newspaper reviews

Film title	Review date	Imitation of Hollywood models	Genre cliches, recycling old patterns	Incoherence, ineptitude, absurdity	Politically insightful	Politically naïve or reactionary	Violence – excessive, brutal etc.	Commentary on Italy's shifting identity	Serial repetition	Source
L'uccello dalle piume di cristallo	1 March 1970	x								Savioli 1970: 9
Città violenta	1 October 1970		x			x				Pestelli 1970: 7
Lo strano vizio della signora Wardh	12 February 1971			x						Vice 1971e: 7
Una lucertola con la pelle di donna	19 February 1971								x	Vice 1971d: 9
Gli occhi freddi della paura	17 April 1971			x		x				Vice 1971c: 8
Gli occhi freddi della paura	20 May 1971			x		x	x		x	Vice 1971b: 7
Nelle pieghe della carne	3 July 1971			x					x	Vice 1971a: 6
Milano calibro 9	11 March 1972	x	x						x	Biraghi 1972b: 12
La polizia ringrazia	12 April 1972					x				Biraghi 1972a: 8
La polizia ringrazia	14 April 1972				x					Pestelli 1972b: 7
Cosa avete fatto a Solange?	26 April 1972			x						Vice 1972d: 7
Perché quelle strane gocce di sangue sul corpo di Jennifer?	18 August 1972			x					x	Valdata 1972b: 7

(Continued)

Appendix D: continued

Film title	Review date	Imitation of Hollywood models	Genre cliches, recycling old patterns	Incoherence, ineptitude, absurdity	Politically insightful	Politically naïve or reactionary	Violence – excessive, brutal etc.	Commentary on Italy's shifting identity	Serial repetition	Source
I familiari delle vittime non saranno avvertiti	20 August 1972		x							Valdata 1972a: 8
Il tuo vizio è una stanza chiusa e solo io ne ho la chiave	20 August 1972								x	P.Per. 1972b: 7
La mano lunga del padrino	20 August 1972	x	x							Vice 1972c: 9
La mano lunga del padrino	3 September 1972	x		x						G.C. 1972: 8
Camorra	15 September 1972	x	x			x	x			Reggiani 1972: 7
Non si sevizia un paperino	30 September 1972					x	x		x	Vice 1972b: 11
Torino nera	6 October 1972							x		Pestelli 1972a: 7
La morte accarezza a mezzanotte	22 December 1972						x		x	P.Per. 1972a: 7
Afyon oppio	23 December 1972				x					Vice 1972a: 15
Afyon oppio	24 December 1972		x	x						Autera 1972: 17
I corpi presentano tracce di violenza carnale	26 January 1973			x						P.Per. 1973: 7
Il boss	10 February 1973	x			x	x			x	Biraghi 1973d: 8
L'amico del padrino	25 February 1973	x							x	Valdata 1973b: 7
Il boss	2 March 1973	x				x	x		x	Casazza 1973: 7
Baciamo le mani	23 March 1973	x						x	x	Biraghi 1973c: 12
La mano nera	12 April 1973		x				x			Vice 1973c: 13

Title	Date								Reference
La mano nera	13 April 1973		x						Pestelli 1973: 7
Gli amici degli amici hanno saputo	14 April 1973		x	x			x		Vice 1973d: 9
Milano rovente	20 May 1973	x	x						Vice 1973c: 21
L'onorata famiglia – Uccidere è cosa nostra	6 July 1973	x	x		x				Vice 1973b: 12
Milano trema – la polizia vuole giustizia	26 August 1973		x						Valdata 1973a: 7
Il consigliori	31 August 1973	x							D.G. 1973: 7
Milano trema – la polizia vuole giustizia	1 September 1973			x					Vice 1973a: 13
Tony Arzenta	15 September 1973				x				Biraghi 1973b: 13
La polizia sta a guardare	24 November 1973				x	x			Biraghi 1973a: 10
La polizia sta a guardare	24 November 1973				x	x			Rondi 1973: 8
La polizia sta a guardare	24 November 1973				x			x	Savioli 1973: 9
Crazy Joe	9 February 1974	x			x			x	Biraghi 1974b: 12
I guappi	1 March 1974				x	x	x	x	Pestelli 1974: 7
Revolver	26 May 1974				x		x		Santuari 1974: 15
Il cittadino si ribella	20 September 1974	x	x		x		x		M.C. 1974: 7
Il cittadino si ribella	22 September 1974	x	x		x		x		Biraghi 1974a: 16
Gatti rossi in un labirinto di vetro	25 January 1975			x			x		D.G. 1975: 9
La polizia ha le mani legate	29 March 1975			x	x		x		Anon 1975: 9
La polizia accusa: il servizio segreto uccide	15 April 1975			x	x		x		Porro 1975: 15

(*Continued*)

Appendix D: continued

Film title	Review date	Imitation of Hollywood models	Genre cliches, recycling old patterns	Incoherence, ineptitude, absurdity	Politically insightful	Politically naive or reactionary	Violence – excessive, brutal etc.	Commentary on Italy's shifting identity	Serial repetition	Source
L'uomo della strada fa giustizia	1 June 1975	x				x			x	Leo 1975a: 14
Roma violenta	22 August 1975					x	x		x	Santuari 1975: 15
La città sconvolta: caccia spietata ai rapitori	5 September 1975	x	x			x			x	Casazza 1975: 7
La città sconvolta: caccia spietata ai rapitori	6 September 1975					x			x	Leo 1975b: 10
Il giustiziere sfida la città	19 September 1975	x	x			x	x		x	Leo 1975c: 14
Nude per l'assassino	22 October 1975						x			Valdata 1975: 7
Poliziotti violenti	11 June 1976					x			x	Ferraù 1976: 17
Poliziotti violenti	12 June 1976			x					x	Pepoli 1976: 12
Roma, l'altra faccia della violenza	19 August 1976								x	Valdata 1976: 12
La casa dalle finestre che ridono	21 August 1976						x			Pestelli 1976: 6
Il grande racket	23 August 1976					x	x		x	Cer 1976: 7
Il gatto dagli occhi di giada	26 August 1977	x		x					x	D.G. 1977: 7
No alla violenza	13 November 1977			x		x			x	Palazzi 1977: 19
Pensione paura	11 March 1978			x					x	Valdata 1978: 24
Solamente nero	17 August 1978						x		x	P.Per. 1978: 17
		19	16	19	7	25	17	5	38	

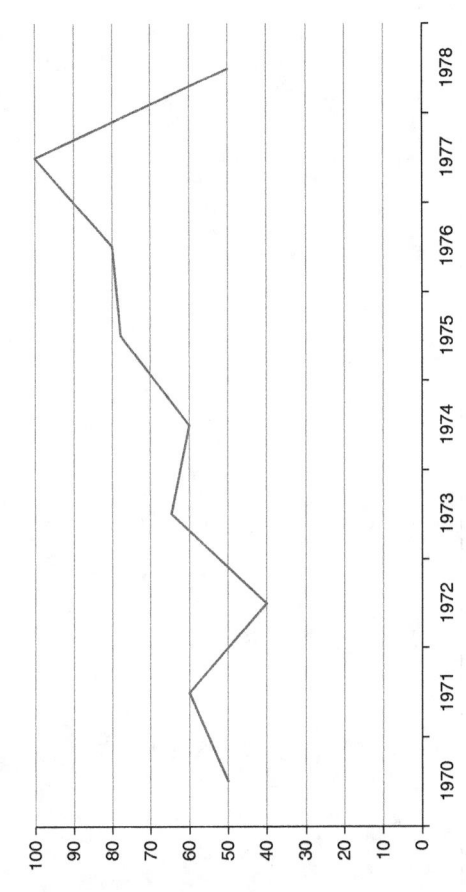
Appendix E: Percentage of Italian newspaper reviews discussing seriality by year

Appendix F: Critical reception patterns around key films in Italian newspaper reviews

Review date	Economics – 'commercial' / 'consumerism' / production line / rapidity of production	Distribution – proliferation	Weariness – cycles drying up	Source
1 October 1970	x			Pestelli 1970: 7
19 February 1971				Vice 1971d: 9
20 May 1971	x			Vice 1971b: 7
3 July 1971	x			Vice 1971a: 6
11 March 1972				Biraghi 1972b: 12
18 August 1972				Valdata 1972b: 7
20 August 1972			x	P.Per. 1972b: 7
3 September 1972	x			G.C. 1972: 8
15 September 1972		x		Reggiani 1972: 7
30 September 1972	x			Vice 1972b: 11
10 February 1973	x			Biraghi 1973d: 8
25 February 1973	x			Valdata 1973b: 7
2 March 1973	x			Casazza 1973: 7
23 March 1973	x			Biraghi 1973c: 12
13 April 1973		x		Pestelli 1973: 7
20 May 1973		x		Vice 1973c: 21
6 July 1973		x		Vice 1973b: 12
31 August 1973				D.G. 1973: 7
24 November 1973			x	Savioli 1973: 9
24 November 1973		x		Rondi 1973: 8
24 November 1973				Biraghi 1973a: 10
9 February 1974		x		Biraghi 1974b: 12
1 March 1974				Pestelli 1974: 7
20 September 1974	x			M.C. 1974: 7
25 January 1975	x			D.G. 1975: 9
15 April 1975			x	Porro 1975: 15

Date						Reference
1 June 1975				x		Leo 1975a: 14
22 August 1975						Santuari 1975: 15
5 September 1975						Casazza 1975: 7
6 September 1975				x		Leo 1975b: 10
19 September 1975				x		Leo 1975c: 14
11 June 1976				x		Ferraù 1976: 17
12 June 1976				x		Pepoli 1976: 12
19 August 1976				x		Valdata 1976: 12
23 August 1976				x		Cer 1976: 7
26 August 1977				x		D.G. 1977: 7
13 November 1977				x		Palazzi 1977: 19
17 August 1978						P.Per. 1978: 17

Frequency of 'Economics', 'Distribution' and 'Weariness' Discourses, 1970–8

Appendix G: Critical reception patterns around key films in US newspaper reviews

Italian film title	Review date	Publication	Violence' lexicon	Trashy, exploitation fare, potboiler, low budget etc.	Marketing criticised for being misleading	Incompetence' lexicon	Audiences (judgement cast on their intelligence)	Dubbing'/'dubbed'/ 'postsynchronization'	Italian', 'Italy' (these words appearing in the review)	Source
Sei donne per l'assassino	11 June 1965	*The Los Angeles Times*								Thomas 1965: 84
Sei donne per l'assassino	31 October 1965	*The Ogden Standard-Examiner*	x							Anon 1965: 45
Sei donne per l'assassino	11 November 1965	*The New York Times*	x					x	x	Weiler 1965: 58
L'uccello dalle piume di cristallo	23 July 1970	*The Journal News*						x	x	Drew 1970: 38
L'uccello dalle piume di cristallo	23 July 1970	*The New York Times*						x		Canby 1970
L'uccello dalle piume di cristallo	9 August 1970	*The Daily News-Journal*			x			x	x	Sparks 1970: 18
L'uccello dalle piume di cristallo	27 August 1970	*The Los Angeles Times*						x		Thomas 1970: 94
L'uccello dalle piume di cristallo	9 September 1970	*The Baytown Sun*								Anon 1970b: 8
L'uccello dalle piume di cristallo	14 September 1970	*The Evening Sun*			x	x		x	x	Cedrone 1970: 13
L'uccello dalle piume di cristallo	17 September 1970	*Philadelphia Daily News*							x	Baltake 1970: 48

Title	Date	Newspaper					Citation
L'uccello dalle piume di cristallo	27 September 1970	Star Tribune	x				Kern 1970: 53
L'uccello dalle piume di cristallo	12 October 1970	The Post-Standard			x		N.A. 1970: 17
L'uccello dalle piume di cristallo	20 October 1970	The Miami News	x				Heinrich 1970: 11
L'uccello dalle piume di cristallo	29 October 1970	Pittsburgh Post-Gazette		x	x		Anderson 1970: 30
L'uccello dalle piume di cristallo	1 November 1970	The Orlando Sentinel					Anon 1970a: 36
L'uccello dalle piume di cristallo	9 November 1970	Tampa Bay Times	x	x	x		Atkins 1970: 55
L'uccello dalle piume di cristallo	24 December 1970	The Seguin Gazette–Enterprise					Castillo 1970: 7
L'uccello dalle piume di cristallo	4 February 1971	The Courier-Journal	x	x	x		Mootz 1971: 32
Una lucertola con la pelle di donna	31 March 1971	The Miami News					Anon 1971: 25
Una lucertola con la pelle di donna	29 September 1971	The Los Angeles Times	x	x	x		Thomas 1971: 88
Una lucertola con la pelle di donna	5 February 1972	Fort Lauderdale News			x		Scott 1972: 59
Una lucertola con la pelle di donna	9 April 1972	Detroit Free Press					Ryan 1972: 70
Reazione a catena	24 July 1972	The Morning News	x	x			Anon 1972b: 14
Reazione a catena	6 October 1972	The Pittsburgh Press	x	x	x		Blank 1972: 19

(*Continued*)

Appendix G: continued

Italian film title	Review date	Publication	'Violence' lexicon	'Trashy, exploitation fare, potboiler, low budget etc.	Marketing criticised for being misleading	'Incompetence' lexicon	Audiences (judgement cast on their intelligence)	'Dubbing'/'dubbed'/ 'postsynchronization'	'Italian', 'Italy' (these words appearing in the review)	Source
Reazione a catena	6 October 1972	*Pittsburgh Post-Gazette*	x		x			x	x	Anderson 1972b: 26
Reazione a catena	8 October 1972	*The Pittsburgh Press*		x						Anon 1972a: 129
Reazione a catena	31 October 1972	*Pittsburgh Post-Gazette*	x						x	Anderson 1972a: 18
Reazione a catena	11 November 1972	*Green Bay Press-Gazette*	x				x	x	x	Gerds 1972: 11
Città violenta	16 March 1973	*The Los Angeles Times*						x	x	Thomas 1973b: 112
Città violenta	25 March 1973	*The Los Angeles Times*							x	Anon 1973c: 398
Città violenta	1 April 1973	*The Herald Banner*							x	Anon 1973b: 25
Città violenta	29 April 1973	*Star Tribune*	x	x						Anon 1973a: 67
I corpi presentano tracce di violenza carnale	30 April 1973	*Pittsburgh Post-Gazette*	x						x	Anderson 1973b: 23
Città violenta	7 June 1973	*Des Moines Tribune*	x							Heinlein 1973: 21

Film	Date	Newspaper							Reference
La mala ordina	20 October 1973	The Cincinnati Enquirer	x	x					McElfresh 1973: 12
La mala ordina	25 October 1973	The Pittsburgh Press	x				x		Stearns 1973: 23
La mala ordina	1 November 1973	The New York Times	x	x	x		x		Thompson 1973: 48
La mala ordina	8 November 1973	Philadelphia Daily News	x	x			x		Baltake 1973:26
La mala ordina	29 November 1973	The Courier-Journal	x	x	x		x		Dietrich 1973: 17
Città violenta	6 December 1973	The Pittsburgh Press	x	x		x			Cloud 1973: 30
Città violenta	7 December 1973	Pittsburgh Post-Gazette	x	x			x		Anderson 1973a: 34
La mala ordina	7 December 1973	The Los Angeles Times	x				x		Thomas 1973a: 111
Crazy Joe	16 February 1974	The Philadelphia Inquirer	x	x			x		Collins 1974: 5
Crazy Joe	16 February 1974	Asbury Park Press	x	x					Cafone 1974: 4
Crazy Joe	16 February 1974	The New York Times	x		x		x		Canby 1974: 36
Crazy Joe	18 February 1974	Philadelphia Daily News	x	x		x	x		Baltake 1974: 18
Crazy Joe	21 February 1974	The Miami News	x	x			x		Block 1974: 15
Crazy Joe	23 February 1974	Fort Lauderdale News	x	x					Guarino 1974: 30
Crazy Joe	25 February 1974	Courier-Post	x				x		Drew 1974: 30

(*Continued*)

Appendix G: continued

Italian film title	Review date	Publication	Violence' lexicon	Trashy, exploitation fare, potboiler, low budget etc.	Marketing criticised for being misleading	Incompetence' lexicon	Audiences (judgement cast on their intelligence)	Dubbing'/'dubbed'/ 'postsynchronization'	Italian', 'Italy' (these words appearing in the review)	Source
Crazy Joe	6 March 1974	The Los Angeles Times	x	x		x	x		x	Thomas 1974:78
Crazy Joe	8 March 1974	St. Louis Post-Dispatch	x						x	Avins 1974: 39
Crazy Joe	19 March 1974	Tampa Bay Times	x						x	Smijanich 1974: 58
Crazy Joe	22 March 1974	Pittsburgh Post-Gazette	x			x			x	Anderson 1974: 24
I corpi presentano tracce di violenza carnale	23 January 1975	Philadelphia Daily News	x	x				x	x	Baltake 1975b: 44
I corpi presentano tracce di violenza carnale	4 April 1975	The Pittsburgh Press	x	x		x			x	Blank 1975: 15
I corpi presentano tracce di violenza carnale	20 June 1975	The Los Angeles Times	x			x			x	Gross 1975: 84
Tony Arzenta	31 October 1975	Philadelphia Daily News	x				x		x	Baltake 1975a: 33
Tony Arzenta	31 October 1975	The Philadelphia Inquirer	x					x		Ryan 1975: 26

Film	Date	Newspaper								Citation
Tony Arzenta	5 November 1975	Hartford Courant	x	x		x			x	Johnson 1975: 26
I corpi presentano tracce di violenza carnale	14 December 1975	Sunday Gazette-Mail	x			x		x	x	Canby 1975: 116
Tony Arzenta	31 December 1975	Pittsburgh Post-Gazette	x						x	Anderson 1975: 6
Tony Arzenta	23 January 1976	The Los Angeles Times	x						x	Gross 1976: 79
Profondo rosso	11 June 1976	Asbury Park Press	x		x			x	x	Cafone 1976: 12
Profondo rosso	29 October 1976	The Courier-Journal	x	x					x	Hammen 1976: 19
Il consigliori	9 December 1976	Albuquerque Journal	x			x		x	x	Mittlestadt 1976: 28
Profondo rosso	13 May 1977	The Los Angeles Times	x		x			x	x	Gross 1977: 105
I padroni della città	22 September 1977	The Philadelphia Inquirer				x		x	x	Ryan 1977b: 30
I padroni della città	3 October 1977	The Salt Lake Tribune				x	x	x	x	Ryan 1977a: 32
I padroni della città	16 October 1977	The Philadelphia Inquirer				x		x	x	Anon 1977: 118
			45	13	10	23	8	28	49	

Bibliography

Alexander, Jeffrey C. (2004), 'Toward a theory of cultural trauma', in Alexander, Jeffrey C., Eyerman, Ron, Giesen, Bernard, Smelser, Neil J. and Sztompka, Piotr, *Cultural Trauma and Collective Identity*, Berkeley: University of California Press, pp. 1–30.

Allen-Hornblower, Emily (2016), *From Agent to Spectator: Witnessing the Aftermath in Ancient Greek Epic and Tragedy*, Berlin: De Gruyter.

Anderson, George (1975), '"Cuckoo's Nest" best movie of December', *Pittsburgh Post-Gazette*, 31 December, p. 6.

Anderson, George (1974), '"Crazy Joe" proves forgettable godson', *Pittsburgh Post-Gazette*, 22 March, p. 24.

Anderson, George (1973a), 'New film reviews', *Pittsburgh Post-Gazette*, 7 December, p. 34.

Anderson, George (1973b), '"And Now My Love" movie of the month', *Pittsburgh Post-Gazette*, 30 April, p. 23.

Anderson, George (1972a), 'Stage and screen', *Pittsburgh Post-Gazette*, 31 October, p. 18.

Anderson, George (1972b), '"Death Nerve" at Gateway', *Pittsburgh Post-Gazette*, 6 October, p. 26.

Anderson, George (1970), 'Mystery at Forum and Encore', *Pittsburgh Post-Gazette*, 29 October, p.30.

Anemone, Anthony (2008), 'About killers, freaks, and real men: the vigilante hero of Aleksei Balabanov's films', in Norris, Stephen M. and Torlone, Zara M. (eds), *Insiders and Outsiders in Russian Cinema*, Bloomington: Indiana University Press, pp. 127–41.

Anon (1977), 'Mister Scarface', *The Philadelphia Inquirer*, 16 October, p. 118.

Anon (1975), 'La polizia ha le mani legate', *L'Unità*, 29 March, p. 9.

Anon (1973a), 'Movie guide', *Star Tribune*, 29 April, p. 67.

Anon (1973b), 'Mystery film due at Texan', *The Herald Banner*, 1 April, p. 25.

Anon (1973c), 'The Family', *The Los Angeles Times*, 25 March, p. 398.

Anon (1972a), 'Current movies in brief', *The Pittsburgh Press*, 8 October, p. 129.

Anon (1972b), 'Films', *The Morning News*, 24 July, p. 14.

Anon (1971), 'Dogs tortured for film', *The Miami News*, 31 March, p. 25.

Anon (1970a), 'Four new films due this week', *The Orlando Sentinel*, 1 November, p. 36.

Anon (1970b), 'Mystery thriller now playing at Brunson', *The Baytown Sun*, 9 September, p. 8.
Anon (1969), 'Altre prove contro lo squartatore', *Corriere della Sera*, 28 July, p. 12.
Anon (1965), '30 models in chiller', *The Ogden Standard-Examiner*, 31 October, p. 45.
Antonello, Pierpaolo and O'Leary, Alan (2009), 'Introduction', in Antonello, Pierpaolo and O'Leary, Alan (eds), *Imagining Terrorism: The Rhetoric and Representation of Political Violence in Italy 1969–2009*, London: Maney, pp. 1–15.
Aristotle [*c.*335 BCE] (2008), *Poetics*, New York: Cosimo Classics.
Atkins, Eric (1970), 'Delightful fright', *St. Petersburg Times*, 9 November, p. 55.
Autera, Leonardo (1972), 'Afyon oppio', *Corriere della Sera*, 24 December, p. 17.
Avins, Mimi (1974), 'Crazy Joe', *St. Louis Post-Dispatch*, 8 March, p. 39.
Baltake, Joe (1975a), 'Hall of shame', *Philadelphia Daily News*, 31 October, p. 33.
Baltake, Joe (1975b), '"Torso": loose limbs fly', *Philadelphia Daily News*, 23 January, p. 44.
Baltake, Joe (1974), 'Sadism, violence and gore Fill "Crazy Joe"', *Philadelphia Daily News*, 18 February, p. 18.
Baltake, Joe (1973), '"Italian Connection" is a screaming lulu', *Philadelphia Daily News*, 8 November, p. 26.
Baltake, Joe (1970), '"Bird With Crystal Plumage" a chiller', *Philadelphia Daily News*, 17 September, p. 48.
Barker, Martin (2004), 'News, reviews, clues, interviews and other ancillary materials: a critique and research proposal', *Scope: an Online Journal of Film and Television Studies*. <https://www.nottingham.ac.uk/scope/documents/2004/february-2004/barker.pdf> (last accessed 5 April 2018).
Barry, Christopher (2004), 'Violent justice: Italian crime / cop films of the 1970s', in Mathijs, Ernest and Mendik, Xavier (eds), *Alternative Europe: Eurotrash and Exploitation Cinema Since 1945*, London: Wallflower, pp. 77–89.
Baschiera, Stefano (2017), 'Streaming Italian horror cinema in the United Kingdom: Lovefilm Instant', *Journal of Italian Cinema & Media Studies*, 5:2, pp. 245–60.
Baschiera, Stefano and Di Chiara, Francesco (2010), 'A postcard from the grindhouse: exotic landscapes and Italian holidays in Lucio Fulci's *Zombie* and Sergio Martino's *Torso*', in Weiner, Robert G. and Cline, John (eds), *Cinema Inferno: Celluloid Explosions from the Cultural Margins*, Plymouth: Scarecrow Press, pp. 101–23.
Baudrillard, Jean (1986), *America*, trans. Chris Turner, London: Verso.
Beard, Mary (2015), *SPQR: A History of Ancient Rome*, London: Profile Books.
Benjamin, Walter (1999), *Illuminations*, trans. Harry Zorn, London: Pimlico.
Bergfelder, Tim (2005), 'National, transnational or supranational cinema? Rethinking European film studies', *Media, Culture and Society*, 27:3, pp. 315–31.

Bini, Andrea (2011), 'Horror cinema: the emancipation of women and urban anxiety', in Brizio-Skov, Flavia (ed.), *Popular Italian Cinema: Culture and Politics in a Postwar Society*, London: I. B. Tauris, pp. 53–82.
Biraghi, Guglielmo (1974a), 'Il cittadino si ribella', *Il Messaggero*, 22 September, p. 16.
Biraghi, Guglielmo (1974b), 'Crazy Joe', *Il Messaggero*, 9 February, p. 12.
Biraghi, Guglielmo (1973a), 'La polizia sta a guardare', *Il Messaggero*, 24 November, p. 10.
Biraghi, Guglielmo (1973b), 'Tony Arzenta', *Il Messaggero*, 15 September, p. 13.
Biraghi, Guglielmo (1973c), 'Baciamo le mani', *Il Messaggero*, 23 March, p. 12.
Biraghi, Guglielmo (1973d), 'Il boss', *Il Messaggero*, 10 February, p. 8.
Biraghi, Guglielmo (1972a), 'La polizia ringrazia', *Il Messaggero*, 12 April, p. 8.
Biraghi, Guglielmo (1972b), 'Milano calibro 9', *Il Messaggero*, 11 March, p. 12.
Blank, Edward L. (1975), '"Torso" lean thriller', *The Pittsburgh Press*, 4 April, p. 15.
Blank, Edward L. (1972), 'Confusion reigns in Gateway's "Twitch of the Death Nerve"', *The Pittsburgh Press*, 6 October, p. 19.
Block, Alex Ben (1974), '"Crazy Joe" stale, plot-thin failure', *The Miami News*, 21 February, p. 15.
Bondanella, Peter (2009), *A History of Italian Cinema*, New York and London: Continuum.
Bondanella, Peter (2006), *Hollywood Italians: Dagos, Palookas, Romeos, Wise Guys, and Sopranos*, New York: Continuum.
Bordwell, David and Thompson, Kristin (2010), *Film Art: An Introduction*, New York: McGraw-Hill.
Bosseaux, Charlotte (2015), *Dubbing, Film and Performance: Uncanny Encounters*, Oxford: Peter Lang.
Brunetta, Gian Piero (2009), *The History of Italian Cinema*, Princeton and Oxford: Princeton University Press.
Bull, Anna Cento (2007), *Italian Neofascism: The Strategy of Tension and the Politics of Nonreconciliation*, Oxford: Berghahn Books.
Bull, Anna Cento (2005), 'Casting a long shadow: the legacy of *stragismo* for the Italian extreme right', *The Italianist*, 25:2, pp. 260–79.
Bull, Anna Cento and Cooke, Philip (2013), *Ending Terrorism in Italy*, London: Routledge.
Bull, Martin J. and Newell, James L. (2005), *Italian Politics: Adjustment Under Duress*, Cambridge: Polity.
Burgoyne, Robert (2013), 'Generational memory and affect in *Letters from Iwo Jima*', in Rosenstone, Robert A. and Parvulescu, Constantin (eds), *A Companion to Historical Film*, Oxford: Blackwell, pp. 349–64.
Burgoyne, Robert (2007), *The Hollywood Historical Film*, Oxford: Wiley-Blackwell.
Burke, Frank (ed.) (2017), *A Companion to Italian Cinema*, Oxford: Wiley-Blackwell.

Cafone, Frank (1974), 'On area screens: "Crazy Joe"', *Asbury Park Press*, 16 February, p. 4.
Cafone, Robert (1976), 'Deep Red', *Asbury Park Press*, 11 June, p. 12.
Canby, Vincent (1975), 'Torso', *Sunday Gazette-Mail*, 14 December, p. 116.
Canby, Vincent (1974), 'The Screen: "Crazy Joe"', *The New York Times*, 16 February, p. 36.
Canby, Vincent (1970), 'Argento's "Bird with Crystal Plumage"', *The New York Times*, 23 July.
Carr, E. H. [1961] (2001), *What is History?*, New York: Palgrave Macmillan.
Casazza, Sandro (1975), 'La città sconvolta: caccia spietata ai rapitori', *La Stampa*, 5 September, p. 7.
Casazza, Sandro (1973), 'Il boss', *La Stampa*, 2 March, p. 7.
Casillo, Robert (2011), 'Prelude to *The Godfather*: Martin Ritt's *The Brotherhood*', in Renga, Dana (ed.), *Mafia Movies: A Reader*, Toronto: University of Toronto Press, pp. 85–93.
Casillo, Robert (1991), 'Moments in Italian-American cinema: from *Little Caesar* to Coppola and Scorsese', in Tamburri, Anthony Julian, Giordano, Paolo, A. and Gardaphé, Fred L. (eds), *From the Margin: Writings in Italian Americana*, West Lafayette: Purdue University Press, pp. 374–96.
Castillo, Mary (1970), 'Bird with the Crystal Plumage', *The Seguin Gazette-Enterprise*, 24 December, p. 7.
Catanzaro, Raimondo (1991), 'Subjective experience and objective reality: an account of violence in the words of its protagonists', in Catanzaro, Raimondo (ed.), *The Red Brigades and Left-Wing Terrorism in Italy*, London: Pinter Publishers, pp. 174–203.
Cedrone, Low (1970), '"Plumage" is a mystery', *The Evening Sun*, 14 September, p. 13.
Cer (1976), 'Il grande racket', *Il Messaggero*, 23 August, p. 7.
Church, David (2015a), *Grindhouse Nostalgia: Memory, Home Video and Exploitation Film Fandom*, Edinburgh: Edinburgh University Press.
Church, David (2015b), 'One on top of the other: Lucio Fulci, transnational film industries, and the retrospective construction of the Italian horror canon', *Quarterly Review of Film and Video*, 32:1, pp. 1–20.
Cloud, Barbara (1973), 'Charles Bronson is orphan in "The Family" at Fiesta', *The Pittsburgh Press*, 6 December, p. 30.
Collins, William B. (1974), '"Crazy Joe" stock mafia action flick', *The Philadelphia Inquirer*, 16 February, p. 5.
Cortés, Carlos E. (1987), 'Italian-Americans in film: from immigrants to icons', *MELUS*, 14:3/4, pp. 107–26.
Coulthard, Lisa (2011), 'Violence makes victims of us all': pathos, vengeance and the politics of Clint Eastwood's *Mystic River*', *European Journal of American Culture*, 30:1, pp. 43–55.
Curti, Roberto (2013), *Italian Crime Filmography, 1968–1980*, London: McFarland.

Curti, Roberto (2006), *Italia Odia: il Cinema Poliziesco Italiano*, Turin: Lindau.
D.G. (1977), 'Il gatto dagli occhi di giada', *L'Unità*, 26 August, p. 7.
D.G. (1975), 'Gatti rossi in un labirinto di vetro', *L'Unità*, 25 January, p. 9.
D.G. (1973), 'Il consigliori', *L'Unità*, 31 August, p. 7.
Dalle Vacche, Angela (1992), *The Body in the Mirror: Shapes of History in Italian Cinema*, Princeton, New Jersey: Princeton University Press.
Della Porta, Donatella (1995), *Social Movements, Political Violence, and the State: A Comparative Analysis of Italy and Germany*, Cambridge: Cambridge University Press.
Dickie, John (2007), *Cosa Nostra: A History of the Sicilian Mafia*, London: Hodder.
Dickie, John (1999), *Darkest Italy: The Nation and Stereotypes of the Mezzogiorno 1860–1900*, London: Macmillan.
Dietrich, Jean (1973), 'Even chase scene's bad in "Italian Connection"', *The Courier-Journal*, 29 November, p. 17.
Domenico, Roy Palmer (1991), *Italian Fascists on Trial, 1943–1948*, Chapel Hill: University of North Carolina Press.
Downing, Lisa (2013), *The Subject of Murder: Gender, Exceptionality and the Modern Killer*, Chicago: University of Chicago Press.
Drew, Bernard (1974), 'It was bad idea to shoot "Crazy"', *Courier-Post*, 25 February, p. 30.
Drew, Bernard (1970), 'The question is: why the birds?', *The Journal News*, 23 July, p. 38.
Dunnage, Jonathan (2002), *Twentieth Century Italy: A Social History*, London: Longman.
Dyer, Richard (2015), *Lethal Repetition: Serial Killing in European Cinema*, London: British Film Institute.
Edmonstone, Robert J. (2008), *Beyond 'Brutality': Understanding the Italian Filone's Violent Excesses*, PhD thesis: University of Glasgow.
Eleftheriotis, Dimitris (2001), *Popular Cinemas of Europe: Studies of Texts, Contexts and Frameworks*, London: Continuum.
Ellwood, David (2005), 'The never-ending liberation', *Journal of Modern Italian Studies*, 10:4, pp. 385–95.
Erikson, Kai T. (1976), *Everything in its Path: Destruction of Community in the Buffalo Creek Flood*, New York: Simon and Schuster.
Faldini, Franca and Fofi, Goffredo (1979), *L'avventurosa storia del cinema italiano raccontata dai suoi protagonisti 1935–1959*, Milan: Mondadori.
Farrell, Kirby (1998), *Post-traumatic Culture: Injury and Interpretation in the Nineties*, Baltimore: Johns Hopkins University Press.
Ferraù, Alessandro (1976), 'Parà e commissario "giustizieri"', *Paese Sera*, 11 June, p. 17.
Ferro, Marc [1977] (1988), *Cinema and History*, trans. Naomi Greene, Detroit: Wayne State University Press.

Fisher, Austin (2013), 'A cult called Django: on the controversial tail of a transnational bandito', *Cine-Excess*, 1. <http://www.cine-excess.co.uk/a-cult-called-django.html> (last accessed 30 June 2018).
Fisher, Austin (2011), *Radical Frontiers in the Spaghetti Western: Politics, Violence and Popular Italian Cinema*, London: I. B. Tauris.
Foot, John (2009), *Italy's Divided Memory*, Basingstoke: Palgrave Macmillan.
Frayling, Christopher (1998), *Spaghetti Westerns: Cowboys and Europeans from Karl May to Sergio Leone*, London I. B. Tauris.
Frye, Northrop, Baker, Sheridan and Perkins, George (1985), *The Harper Handbook to Literature*, New York: Harper and Row.
G.C. (1972), 'La mano lunga del padrino', *La Stampa*, 3 September, p. 8.
Galt, Rosalind (2006), *The New European Cinema: Redrawing the Map*, New York: Columbia University Press.
Gardaphé, Fred L. (2006), *From Wiseguys to Wise Men: the Gangster and Italian American Masculinities*, London: Routledge.
Garofalo, Piero (2011), 'Damiano Damiani's *The Day of the Owl*: a western flirtation', in Renga, Dana (ed.), *Mafia Movies: A Reader*, Toronto: University of Toronto Press, pp. 252–60.
Gavin, Dominic (2014), 'The "betrayed resistance" in Valentino Orsini's *Corbari* (1970) and Bernardo Bertolucci's *1900* (1976)', *California Italian Studies*, 5:2, pp. 155–82.
Gerds, Warren (1972), '"Death Nerve" is a dog', *Green Bay Press-Gazette*, 11 November, p. 11.
Giesen, Bernhard (2004), 'The trauma of perpetrators: the Holocaust as the traumatic reference of German national identity', in Alexander, Jeffrey C., Eyerman, Ron, Giesen, Bernard, Smelser, Neil J. and Sztompka, Piotr, *Cultural Trauma and Collective Identity*, Berkeley: University of California Press, pp. 112–54.
Gili, Jean A. (1981), *Stato fascista e cinematografia: repressione e promozione*, Rome: Bulzoni.
Ginsborg, Paul (1990), *A History of Contemporary Italy, 1943–1980*, London: Penguin.
Glynn, Ruth (2013), *Women, Terrorism, and Trauma in Italian Culture*, New York: Palgrave Macmillan.
Glynn, Ruth (2006), 'Trauma on the line: terrorism and testimony in the *anni di piombo*', in Jansen, Monica and Jordão, Paola (eds), *The Value of Literature in and after the Seventies: The Case of Italy and Portugal*, Utrecht: Igitur Publishing, pp. 317–35.
Gonella, Guido (1945), 'Giustizia', *Il Popolo*, 30 April, p. 1.
Gordon, Robert, Hipkins, Danielle and Pickering-Iazzi, Robin (2013), 'Reflections', *The Italianist*, 33:2, pp. 225–8.
Grindhouse Cinema Database (2012), 'Poliziotteschi'. <http://www.grindhousedatabase.com/index.php/Category:Poliziotteschi> (last accessed 11 July 2018).

Gross, Linda (1977), 'A dark chiller from sunny Italy', *The Los Angeles Times*, 13 May, p. 105.
Gross, Linda (1976), 'Decline of a don in "No Way Out"', *The Los Angeles Times*, 23 January, p. 79.
Gross, Linda (1975), '"Torso" – a lazy suspense movie', *The Los Angeles Times*, 20 June, p. 84.
Guarino, Ann (1974), '"Crazy Joe" pushes violence', *Fort Lauderdale News*, 23 February, p. 30.
Guins, Raiford (2005), 'Blood and black gloves on shiny discs: new media, old tastes, and the remediation of Italian horror films in the United States', in Schneider, Steven Jay and Williams, Tony (eds), *Horror International*, Detroit: Wayne State University Press, pp. 15–32.
Gundle, Stephen (2000), *Between Hollywood and Moscow: The Italian Communists and the Challenge of Mass Culture, 1943–1991*, London: Duke University Press.
Gundle, Stephen (1996), 'Fame, fashion, and style: the Italian star system', in Forgacs, David and Lumley, Robert (eds), *Italian Cultural Studies: An Introduction*, Oxford: Oxford University Press, pp. 309–26.
Gunning, Tom (2003), 'Renewing old technologies: astonishment, second nature, and the uncanny in technology from the previous turn-of-the-century', in Thorburn, David and Jenkins, Henry (eds), *Rethinking Media Change: The Aesthetics of Transition*, London: MIT Press, pp. 39–60.
Hammen, Scott (1976), 'Fashion, violence fight to draw in "Deep Red"', *The Courier-Journal*, 29 October, p. 19.
Heinlein, Gary (1973), 'Superficial variations in "Family"', *Des Moines Tribune*, 7 June, p. 21.
Heinrich, Ken (1970), 'It'll tickle your brain and shock your psyche', *The Miami News*, 20 October, p. 11.
Herzel, Roger H. (1974), '"Anagnorisis" and "peripeteia" in comedy', *Educational Theatre Journal*, 26:4, pp. 495–505.
Higbee, Will and Hwee Lim, Song (2010), 'Concepts of transnational cinema: towards a critical transnationalism in film studies', *Transnational Cinemas*, 1:1, pp. 7–21.
Higson, Andrew (2006), 'The limiting imagination of national cinema', in Ezra, Elizabeth and Rowden, Terry (eds), *Transnational Cinema: The Film Reader*, Abingdon: Routledge, pp. 15–25.
Holdaway, Dom (2013a), 'The pleasure of political readings: participation and the anti-mafia film', *The Itanianist*, 33:2, pp. 40–6.
Holdaway, Dom (2013b), *A Return to Cinema d'Impegno? Cinematic Engagements with Organized Crime in Italy, 1950–2010*, PhD Thesis: University of Warwick.
Hughes-Warrington, Marnie (2007), *History Goes to the Movies: Studying History on Film*, London: Routledge.
Hunt, Leon (1992), 'A (sadistic) night at the opera: notes on the Italian horror film', *The Velvet Light Trap*, 30 (Fall), pp. 65–75.

Hunt, Lynn (2002), 'Against presentism', *Perspectives on History*, 40: 5. <https://www.historians.org/publications-and-directories/perspectives-on-history/may-2002/against-presentism> (last accessed 9 February 2017).

Hunter, Russ (2009), *A Reception Study of the Films of Dario Argento in the UK and Italy*, PhD Thesis: University of Aberystwyth.

Hutchings, Peter (2003), 'The Argento effect', in Jancovich, Mark, Lazario-Reboll, Antonio, Stringer, Julian and Willis, Andy, *Defining Cult Movies: The Cultural Politics of Oppositional Taste* (eds), Manchester: Manchester University Press, pp. 127–41.

Iannone, Pasquale (2016), 'Pietro Germi, Hybridity and the Roots of the Italo-Western', in Fisher, Austin (ed.), *Spaghetti Westerns at the Crossroads: Studies in Relocation, Transition and Appropriation*, Edinburgh: Edinburgh University Press, pp. 49–66.

Ignatieff, Michael (2000), *Isaiah Berlin: A Life*, London: Vintage.

Johnson, Malcolm L. (1975), 'Delon, Conte in "No Way Out"', *Hartford Courant*, 5 November, p. 26.

Judt, Tony (2010), *Postwar: A History of Europe Since 1945*, London: Vintage.

Kannas, Alexia (2017), 'All the colours of the dark: film genre and the Italian giallo', *Journal of Italian Cinema & Media Studies*, 5:2, pp. 173–90.

Kannas, Alexia (2013), 'No place like home: the late-modern world of the Italian giallo film', *Senses of Cinema*, 67. <http://sensesofcinema.com/2013/uncategorized/no-place-like-home-the-late-modern-world-of-the-italian-giallo-film/> (last accessed 5 December 2017).

Kelleter, Frank (2017), 'Five ways of looking at popular seriality', in Kelleter, Frank (ed.), *Media of Serial Narrative*, Columbus: The Ohio State University Press, pp. 7–36.

Kern, Ben (1970), 'Old fairy tale debased into modern movie', *Star Tribune*, 27 September, p. 53.

King, Claire Sisco (2010), 'The man inside: trauma, gender, and the nation in *The Brave One*', *Critical Studies in Media Communication*, 27:2, pp. 111–30.

Klein, Amanda Ann and Palmer, R. Barton (2016), 'Introduction', in Klein, Amanda Ann and Palmer, R. Barton (eds), *Cycles, Sequels, Spin-offs, Remakes, and Reboots: Multiplicities in Film and Television*, Austin: University of Texas Press.

Klinger, Barbara (1997), 'Film history terminable and interminable', *Screen*, 38:2, pp. 107–28.

Klinger, Barbara (1989), 'Digressions at the cinema: reception and mass culture', *Cinema Journal*, 28:4, pp. 3–19.

Koven, Mikel J. (2014), 'The giallo and the spaghetti nightmare film', in Bondanella, Peter (ed.), *The Italian Cinema Book*, London: British Film Institute, pp. 203–10.

Koven, Mikel J. (2006), *La Dolce Morte: Vernacular Cinema and the Italian* Giallo *Film*, Oxford: Scarecrow Press.

Laviosa, Flavia (2013), 'Editorial', *Journal of Italian Cinema & Media Studies*, 1:1, pp. 3–6.
Leake, Elizabeth (2011), 'Prototypes of the Mafia: Luchino Visconti's *The Leopard*', in Renga, Dana (ed.), *Mafia Movies: A Reader*, Toronto: University of Toronto Press, pp. 234–42.
Leitch, Thomas (2002), *Crime Films*, Cambridge: Cambridge University Press.
Leo (1975a), 'L'uomo della strada fa giustizia', *Il Messaggero*, 1 June, p. 14.
Leo (1975b), 'La città sconvolta: caccia spietata ai rapitori', *Il Messaggero*, 6 September, p. 10.
Leo (1975c), 'Il giustiziere sfida la città', *Il Messaggero*, 19 September, p. 14.
Leotta, Alfio (2013), 'Nostalgics, thugs and psycho-killers: neo-fascists in contemporary Italian cinema', *Journal of Italian Cinema and Media Studies*, 1:2, pp. 143–56.
Leyda, Julia (2002), 'Black-audience westerns and the politics of cultural identification in the 1930s', *Cinema Journal*, 42:1, pp. 46–70.
Lichtner, Giacomo (2013), *Fascism in Italian Cinema since 1945: The Politics and Aesthetics of Memory*, New York: Palgrave Macmillan.
Lumley, Robert (1990), *States of Emergency: Cultures of Revolt in Italy from 1968 to 1978*, London: Verso.
M.C. (1974), 'Il cittadino si ribella', *La Stampa*, 20 September, p. 7.
McDonagh, Maitland (2013), 'An exceptional vintage', *Film Comment*, July–August, pp. 44–7.
McElfresh, Tom (1973), '"Connection" is dreadful', *The Cincinnati Enquirer*, 20 October, p. 12.
Macherey, Pierre [1978] (2006), *A Theory of Literary Production*, London and New York: Routledge Classics.
MacNab, Geoffrey (2006), 'Italian B-movies: Tarantino's inspiration', *The Independent*, 2 February.
Markantonatos, Andreas (2002), *Tragic Narrative: A Narratological Study of Sophocles'* Oedipus at Colonus, Berlin: De Gruyter.
Marlow-Mann, Alex (2013), 'Strategies of tension: towards a re-interpretation of *The Big Racket* and the Italian crime film', in Rigoletto, Sergio and Bayman, Louis (eds), *Italian Popular Cinema*, Basingstoke: Palgrave Macmillan, pp. 133–46.
Mazower, Mark (1999), *Dark Continent: Europe's Twentieth Century*, London: Penguin.
Mendik, Xavier (2014), 'The return of the rural repressed: Italian horror and the *Mezzogiorno giallo*', in Benshoff, Harry M. (ed.), *A Companion to the Horror Film*, Chichester: Wiley-Blackwell, pp. 390–405.
Merlino, Rossella (2014), 'Sicilian mafia, patron saints, and religious processions: the consistent face of an ever-changing criminal organization', *California Italian Studies*, 5:1, pp. 109–29.
Mittlestadt, Chuck (1976), 'Crime movie is "pretty good"', *Albuquerque Journal*, 9 December, p. 28.

Moe, Nelson (2002), *The View from Vesuvius: Italian Culture and the Southern Question*, London: University of California Press.
Mootz, William (1971), 'Whodunit should have been whydoit', *The Courier-Journal*, 4 February, p. 32.
Moretti Franco (2005), *Graphs, Maps, Trees: Abstract Models for a Literary History*, London: Verso.
Moss, David (1989), *The Politics of Left-Wing Violence in Italy, 1969–85*, London: Macmillan.
N.A. (1970), '"The Bird" great for mystery fans', *The Post-Standard*, 12 October, p. 17.
Needham, Gary (2003), 'Playing with genre: defining the Italian *giallo*', in Schneider, Stephen Jay (ed.), *Fear without Frontiers: Horror Cinema across the Globe*, Godalming: FAB Press, pp. 135–44.
Nowell, Richard (2016), 'Cars and girls (and burgers and weed): branding, mainstreaming, and Crown International Pictures' SoCal drive-in movies', in Fisher, Austin and Walker, Johnny (eds), *Grindhouse: Cultural Exchange on 42nd Street, and Beyond*, New York: Bloomsbury Academic, pp. 107–28.
Nowell, Richard (2011), *Blood Money: A History of the First Teen Slasher Film Cycle*, New York: Continuum.
O'Leary, Alan (2014), 'Towards an ecology of cinema and history', *The Italianist*, 34:2, pp. 250–5.
O'Leary, Alan (2011), *Tragedia all'italiana: Italian Cinema and Italian Terrorisms, 1970–2010*, Oxford: Peter Lang.
O'Leary, Alan (2009), 'Moro, Brescia, conspiracy: the paranoid style in Italian cinema', in Antonello, Pierpaolo and O'Leary, Alan (eds), *Imagining Terrorism: The Rhetoric and Representation of Political Violence in Italy 1969–2009*, London: Maney, pp. 48–62.
O'Leary, Alan and O'Rawe, Catherine (2011), 'Against realism: on a "certain tendency" in Italian film criticism', *Journal of Modern Italian Studies*, 16:1, pp. 107–28.
O'Rawe, Catherine (2011), '"A past that will not pass": Italian cinema and the return to the 1970s', *New Cinemas: Journal of Contemporary Film*, 9:2–3, pp. 101–13.
Olesen, Giulio (2017), 'An interview with Sergio Martino: an American in Rome', *Journal of Italian Cinema & Media Studies*, 5:2, pp. 261–6.
Olney, Ian (2013), *Euro Horror: Classic European Horror Cinema in Contemporary American Culture*, Bloomington: Indiana University Press.
P.Per. (1978), 'Brividi a Venezia e catastrofe sulle rotaie', *La Stampa*, 17 August, p. 17.
P.Per. (1973), 'Sangue nella verde Umbria', *La Stampa*, 26 January, p. 7.
P.Per. (1972a), 'Sangue al pomodoro un giallo all'italiana', *La Stampa*, 22 December, p. 7.
P.Per. (1972b), 'Il tuo vizio è una stanza chiusa e solo io ne ho la chiave', *La Stampa*, 20 August, p. 7.

Palazzi, Renato (1977), 'Il giustiziere siciliano', *Corriere della Sera*, 13 November, p. 19.

Palmerini, Luca M. and Mistretta, Gaetano (1996), *Spaghetti Nightmares: Italian Fantasy-Horror as Seen Through the Eyes of their Protagonists*, Key West, Florida: Fantasma Books.

Pasolini, Pier Paolo (1974), 'Cos'è questo golpe? Io so', *Corriere della Sera*, 14 November, p. 3.

Pepoli, Massimo (1976), 'Poliziotti violenti', *Il Messaggero*, 12 June, p. 12.

Peretti, Luca (2018), 'Mafia, mobility, and capitalism in Italy circa 1960', in Larke-Walsh, George S. (ed.), *A Companion to the Gangster Film*, Hoboken: Wiley-Blackwell, pp. 244–61.

Pestelli, Leo (1976), 'Un thriller all'italiana tra magìa e sadismo', *La Stampa*, 21 August, p. 6.

Pestelli, Leo (1974), 'Due pugili da marciapiede', *La Stampa*, 1 March, p. 7.

Pestelli, Leo (1973), 'La mano nera', *La Stampa*, 13 April, p. 7.

Pestelli, Leo (1972a), 'La "Torino nera" dell'immigrato nel drammatico giallo di Lizzani', *La Stampa*, 6 October, p. 7.

Pestelli, Leo (1972b), 'Poliziotto rigoroso', *La Stampa*, 14 April, p. 7.

Pestelli, Leo (1970), 'Un "killer" non deve credere all'amore', *La Stampa*, 1 October, p. 7.

Pezzotti, Barbara (2016), *Investigating Italy's Past through Historical Crime Fiction, Films, and TV Series: Murder in the Age of Chaos*, New York: Palgrave Macmillan.

Porro, Maurizio (1975), 'Quasi tutti compromessi', *Corriere della Sera*, 15 April, p. 15.

Reggiani, Stefano (1972), 'Camorra', *La Stampa*, 15 September, p. 7.

Reich, Jacqueline (2001), 'The mother of all horror: witches, gender, and the films of Dario Argento', in Jewell, Keala (ed.), *Monsters in the Italian Literary Imagination*, Detroit: Wayne State University Press, pp. 89–105.

Renga, Dana (2013), *Unfinished Business: Screening the Mafia in the New Millennium*, Toronto: University of Toronto Press.

Renga, Dana (2011), 'The Corleones at home and abroad', in Renga, Dana (ed.), *Mafia Movies: A Reader*, Toronto: University of Toronto Press, pp. 3–31.

Rondi, Gian Luigi (1973), 'La polizia sta a guardare', *Il Tempo*, 24 November, p. 8.

Rosen, Philip (2001), *Change Mummified: Cinema, Historicity, Theory*, Minneapolis: University of Minnesota Press.

Rosenstone, Robert A. (2012), *History on Film / Film on History*, 2nd edn, London: Routledge.

Rosenstone, Robert A. (1995), 'Introduction', in Rosenstone, Robert A. (ed.), *Revisioning History: Film and the Construction of a New Past*, Princeton: Princeton University Press, pp. 3–14.

Rossi, Umberto (1997), 'Il pubblico del cinema', in Miccichè, Lino (ed.), *Il cinema del riflusso: film e cineasti italiani degli anni '70*, Venice: Marsilio, pp. 26–44.

Ryan, Desmond (1977a), 'Mister Scarface: incoherent and absurd', *The Salt Lake Tribune*, 3 October, p. 32.
Ryan, Desmond (1977b), '"Scarface a Roman squaliday', *The Philadelphia Inquirer*, 22 September, p. 30.
Ryan, Desmond (1975), '"No Way Out" puts a premium on exits', *The Philadelphia Inquirer*, 31 October, p. 26.
Ryan, Jack (1972), 'Good luck, Folmer Blangstead', *Detroit Free Press*, 9 April, p. 70.
S.V. (1978), 'Ultrà di sinistra dilaniato dalla sua bomba sul binario', *Corriere della sera*, 10 May, p. 13.
Santuari, Aurora (1975), 'Culta dell'odio invece della giustizia', *Paese Sera*, 22 August, p. 15.
Santuari, Aurora (1974), 'Revolver', *Paese Sera*, 26 May, p. 15.
Sarris, Andrew (1968), *The American Cinema: Directors and Directions, 1929–1968*, New York: Dutton.
Savioli, Aggeo (1973), 'La polizia sta a guardare', *L'Unità*, 24 November, p. 9.
Savioli, Aggeo (1970), 'L'uccello dalle piume di cristallo', *L'Unità*, 1 March, p. 9.
Scorer, James (2010), 'Once upon a time in Buenos Aires: vengeance, community and the urban western', *Journal of Latin American Cultural Studies*, 19:2, pp. 141–54.
Scott, Vernon (1972), 'Oscar entries number 334, bombs galore', *Fort Lauderdale News*, 5 February, p. 59.
Sisto, Antonella (2017), 'The practice of dubbing and the evolution of the soundtrack in Italian cinema: a schizophonic take', in Burke, Frank (ed.), *A Companion to Italian Cinema*, Oxford: Wiley-Blackwell, pp. 393–407.
Smelser, Neil J. (2004), 'Psychological trauma and cultural trauma', in Alexander, Jeffrey C., Eyerman, Ron, Giesen, Bernard, Smelser, Neil J. and Sztompka, Piotr, *Cultural Trauma and Collective Identity*, Berkeley: University of California Press, pp. 31–59.
Smiljanich, Dorothy (1974), 'Violence smothers pasta', *Tampa Bay Times*, 19 March, p. 58.
Sorlin, Pierre (1980), *The Film in History: Restaging the Past*, Oxford: Blackwell.
Sparks, Douglas (1970), 'Horror film has hold on mind', *The Daily News-Journal*, 9 August, p. 18.
Staiger, Janet (1992), *Interpreting Films: Studies in the Historical Reception of American Cinema*, Princeton: Princeton University Press.
Stanfield, Peter (2013), '"Pix biz spurts with war fever": film and the public sphere - cycles and topicality', *Film History*, 25:1–2, pp. 215–26.
Stearns, Robert (1973), 'Italian-style "Connection" loses something in translation', *The Pittsburgh Press*, 25 October, p. 23.
Sztompka, Piotr (2004), 'The trauma of social change: a case of postcommunist societies', in Alexander, Jeffrey C., Eyerman, Ron, Giesen, Bernard, Smelser, Neil J. and Sztompka, Piotr, *Cultural Trauma and Collective Identity*, Berkeley: University of California Press, pp. 155–95.

Tamburri, Anthony Julian (2011), 'Michael Corleone's tie: Francis Ford Coppola's *The Godfather*', in Renga, Dana (ed.), *Mafia Movies: A Reader*, Toronto: University of Toronto Press, pp. 94–101.

Tarrow, Sidney (1991), 'Violence and institutionalisation after the Italian protest cycle', in Catanzaro, Raimondo (ed.), *The Red Brigades and Left-Wing Terrorism in Italy*, London: Pinter Publishers, pp. 41–69.

Thomas, Kevin (1974), 'Boyle in role of Crazy Joe', *The Los Angeles Times*, 6 March, p. 78.

Thomas, Kevin (1973a), 'Crossing the mafia', *The Los Angeles Times*, 7 December, p. 111.

Thomas, Kevin (1973b), 'Bronson as a pro assassin', *The Los Angeles Times*, 16 March, p. 112.

Thomas, Kevin (1971), 'Dreams of murder come true in "Lizard"', *The Los Angeles Times*, 29 September, p. 88.

Thomas, Kevin (1970), 'Maniac sought in "Bird"', *The Los Angeles Times*, 27 August, p. 94.

Thomas, Kevin (1965), '"Young Dillinger" right on mark', *The Los Angeles Times*, 11 June, p. 84.

Thompson, Howard (1973), '"Italian Connection" opens at 3 theaters', *The New York Times*, 1 November, p. 48.

Thrower, Stephen (1999), *Beyond Terror: The Films of Lucio Fulci*. Godalming: FAB Press.

Tricomi, Antonio (2009), 'Killing the father: politics and intellectuals, utopia and disillusion', in Antonello, Pierpaolo and O'Leary, Alan (eds), *Imagining Terrorism: The Rhetoric and Representation of Political Violence in Italy 1969–2009*, London: Maney, pp. 16–29.

Urbano, Cosimo (2007), '*Don't Torture a Duckling*', in Steven Jay Schneider (ed.), *100 European Horror Films*, London: BFI, pp. 73–4.

Uva, Christian (ed.) (2007), *Schermi di Piombo: Il Terrorismo nel Cinema Italiano*, Soveria Mannelli: Rubettino.

Uva, Christian and Picchi, Michele (2006), *Destra e Sinistra nel Cinema Italiano: Film e Immaginario Politico dagli Anni '60 al Nuovo Millennio*, Rome: Edizioni Interculturali.

Valdata, Achille (1978), 'Un albergo poco ospitale', *La Stampa*, 11 March, p. 24.

Valdata, Achille (1976), 'Roma, l'altra faccia della violenza', *La Stampa*, 19 August, p. 12.

Valdata, Achille (1975), 'C'è già tutto nel titolo', *La Stampa*, 22 October, p. 7.

Valdata, Achille (1973a), 'Milano trema: la polizia vuole giustizia', *La Stampa*, 26 August, p. 7.

Valdata, Achille (1973b), 'L'amico del padrino', *La Stampa*, 25 February, p. 7.

Valdata, Achille (1972a), 'I familiari delle vittime non saranno avvertiti', *La Stampa*, 20 August, p. 8.

Valdata, Achille (1972b), 'L'ammazzadonne', *La Stampa*, 18 August, p. 7.

van den Oever, Annie (2010), 'Conversation with Laura Mulvey', in van den Oever, Annie (ed.), *Ostrannenie*, Amsterdam: Amsterdam University Press, pp. 185–203.
Vice (1973a), 'Milano trema: la polizia vuole giustizia', *Il Messaggero*, 1 September, p. 13.
Vice (1973b), 'L'onorata famiglia', *Il Messaggero*, 6 July, p. 12.
Vice (1973c), 'Milano rovente', *Il Messaggero*, 20 May, p. 21.
Vice (1973d), 'Gli amici degli amici hanno saputo', *L'Unità*, 14 April, p. 9.
Vice (1973e), 'La mano nera', *Il Messaggero*, 12 April, p. 13.
Vice (1972a), 'Afyon-oppio', *Il Messaggero*, 23 December, p. 15.
Vice (1972b), 'Non si sevizia un paperino', *L'Unità*, 30 September, p. 11.
Vice (1972c), 'La mano lunga del padrino', *L'Unità*, 20 August, p. 9.
Vice (1972d), 'Cosa avete fatto a Solange?', *L'Unità*, 26 April, p. 7.
Vice (1971a), 'I nuovi vampiri', *La Stampa*, 3 July, p. 6.
Vice (1971b), 'Gli occhi freddi della paura', *L'Unità*, 20 May, p. 7.
Vice (1971c), 'Un "giallo" per signora', *La Stampa*, 17 April, p. 8.
Vice (1971d), 'Una lucertola con la pelle di donna', *L'Unità*, 19 February, p. 9.
Vice (1971e), 'Lo strano vizio della signora Wardh', *L'Unità*, 12 February, p. 7.
Wagstaff, Christopher (2013), 'Italian cinema, popular?', in Rigoletto, Sergio and Bayman, Louis (eds), *Italian Popular Cinema*, Basingstoke: Palgrave MacMillan, pp. 29–51.
Wagstaff, Christopher (1998), 'Italian genre films in the world market', in Nowell-Smith, Geoffrey and Ricci, Stephen (eds), *Hollywood and Europe: Economics, Culture, National Identity 1945–95*, London: BFI, pp. 74–85.
Wagstaff, Christopher (1995), 'Italy in the post-war international cinema market', in Duggan, Christopher and Wagstaff, Christopher (eds), *Italy in the Cold War: Politics, Culture and Society 1948–1958*, Oxford: Berg, pp. 89–115.
Wagstaff, Christopher (1992), 'A forkful of Westerns: industry, audiences and the Italian Western', in Dyer, Richard and Vincendeau, Ginette (eds), *Popular European Cinema*, London: Routledge, pp. 245–61.
Warner, Nicholas O. and Riggio, Ronald E. (2012), 'Italian-American leadership in Hollywood films: images and realities', *Leadership*, 8:3, pp. 211–27.
Warshow, Robert (2001), *The Immediate Experience: Movies, Comics, Theatre and Other Aspects of Popular Culture*, London: Harvard University Press.
Weiler, A. H. (1965), 'Blood and Black Lace', *The New York Times*, 11 November, p. 58.
Weinberg, Leonard (1986), 'The violent life: an analysis of left- and right-wing terrorism in Italy', in Merkl, Peter H. (ed.), *Political Violence and Terror: Motifs and Motivations*, London: University of California Press, pp. 145–67.
White, Hayden (1988), 'Historiography and historiophoty', *American Historical Review*, 93:5, pp. 1193–9.
Wood, Mary P. (2012), 'Navigating the labyrinth: cinematic investigations of rightwing terrorism', in Glynn, Ruth, Lombardi, Giancarlo and O'Leary,

Alan (eds), *Terrorism Italian Style: The Representation of Terrorism and Political Violence in Contemporary Italian Cinema*, London: IGRS Books, pp. 29–44.

Wood, Mary P. (2005), *Italian Cinema*, Oxford: Berg.

Wood, Mary P. (2003), 'Revealing the hidden city: the cinematic conspiracy thriller of the '70s', *The Italianist*, 23, pp. 150–62.

DVDs

Gomarasca, Manlio (2011), 'Calibro 9', *Caliber 9*: Nocturno Cinema.

Gomarasca, Manlio and Pulici, Davide (2011a), 'Fernando Di Leo: la morale del genere', *Caliber 9*: Nocturno Cinema.

Gomarasca, Manlio and Pulici, Davide (2011b), 'Storie di mafia', *The Boss*: Nocturno Cinema.

Gregory, David (2013), 'Laying down the law: interviews with director Enzo G. Castellari and star Franco Nero', *Street Law*: Blue Underground.

Malloy, Mike (2012), *Eurocrime: The Italian Cop and Gangster Films That Ruled the '70s*: Nucleus Films.

Index

4 mosche di velluto grigio / Four Flies on Grey Velvet see Argento, Dario
9/11 *see* September 11 (2001) attack
1900 see Bertolucci, Bernardo

Action Party, 22
Afyon oppio / The Sicilian Connection see Baldi, Ferdinando
Agrama, Frank, 13, 99, 100, 155, 196
   L'amico del padrino / The Godfather's Friend, 13, 99, 100, 101, 113n, 155, 163, 185, 196, 200, 202
Angels with Dirty Faces see Curtiz, Michael
Anna, quel particolare piacere / Secrets of a Call Girl see Carnimeo, Giuliano
Anni di piombo, 3, 9, 10, 23, 37, 39, 41n, 44, 45, 46, 48, 49, 50, 62, 67, 77–8, 82, 83, 118–19
Aprà, Pierluigi, 98
Argento, Dario, 115, 118, 124, 125, 133, 152, 168, 169, 171, 195, 196
   4 mosche di velluto grigio / Four Flies on Grey Velvet, 124–5
   L'uccello dalle piume di cristallo / The Bird with the Crystal Plumage, 115, 124, 125, 127, 134, 138, 139, 146n, 168–70, 173, 175, 195, 201, 208, 209
   Profondo rosso / Deep Red, 115, 124, 132–3, 138, 139, 171–2, 196, 213
Aristotle, 56
Armstrong, Samuel, 170, 171
   Dumbo, 170–1
Ausino, Carlo, 11, 63, 197
   Torino violenta / Double Game, 11, 63, 64, 68–9, 186, 197
Avanguardia Nazionale, 3, 24
Avati, Pupi, 16, 116, 188, 197
   La casa dalle finestre che ridono / The House of the Laughing Windows, 16, 115–16, 125, 137–9, 142, 188, 197, 204

Baciamo le mani / Family Killer see Schiraldi, Vittorio
Baedeker guidebooks, 139
Balabanov, Aleksei, 64
   Brat / Brother, 64
   Brat 2 / Brother 2, 64
   Voyna / War, 64
Baldi, Ferdinando, 13, 100, 107, 196
   Afyon oppio / The Sicilian Connection, 13, 100, 101, 102, 105, 106–7, 108, 185, 196, 200, 202
Balsam, Martin, 97
Banda della Magliana, 112n
Banditi a Milano / The Violent Four see Lizzani, Carlo
Barilli, Francesco, 15, 18n, 123, 188, 197
   Pensione paura / Hotel Fear, 15, 18n, 123–4, 188, 197, 204
Barker, Reginald, 86
   The Italian, 86–7
Baudrillard, Jean, 114
Bava, Mario, 15, 114, 115, 117, 124, 130–1, 133, 135, 148, 149, 170, 171, 173, 187, 195
   Il rosso segno della follia / A Hatchet for the Honeymoon, 15, 124, 131, 132, 195
   La ragazza che sapeva troppo / The Evil Eye, 114, 115, 117, 127, 132
   Reazione a catena / A Bay of Blood, 15, 115, 117, 135–6, 148–9, 165, 170, 172–3, 174, 187–8, 195, 209, 210
   Sei donne per l'assassino / Blood and Black Lace, 15, 117, 130, 195, 208
Bazzoni, Luigi, 134, 162, 195
   Giornata nera per l'ariete / The Fifth Cord, 134, 162, 195
Bellocchio, Marco, 48, 49
   Sbatti il mostro in prima pagina / Slap the Monster on Page One, 49
Bells of San Juan see Dunlap, Scott
Ben Hur see Wyler, William
Benjamin, Walter, 18–19n

Bergonzelli, Sergio, 15, 119, 120, 188, 195
  Nelle pieghe della carne / In the Folds of the Flesh, 15, 119–22, 124, 188, 195, 201
Berlinguer, Enrico, 26
Bertolucci, Bernardo, 36
  1900, 36
Bianchi, Andrea, 14, 15, 100, 105, 131, 159, 160, 161, 196, 197
  Nude per l'assassino / Strip Nude for Your Killer, 15, 131–2, 133, 161–2, 197, 204
  Quelli che contano / Cry of a Prostitute, 14, 100, 102, 104–5, 106, 159–61, 165, 185, 196
Bianco di Saint Jorioz, Alessandro, 95
Bido, Antonio, 15, 16, 116, 121, 188, 197
  Il gatto dagli occhi di giada / Watch Me When I Kill, 15, 121, 122–3, 125, 188, 197, 204
  Solamente nero / Bloodstained Shadow, 16, 116, 125, 138–9, 142, 188, 197, 204
Bolkan, Florinda, 142, 165
Bologna bombing, 25
Bonnie and Clyde see Penn, Arthur
Bonomi, Nardo, 99, 100, 154, 195
  La mano lunga del padrino / The Long Arm of the Godfather, 99, 100, 101, 108–9, 113n, 154–5, 185, 191–2n, 195, 200, 202
Borghese, Junio Valerio, 24, 45, 53–4
Bouchet, Barbara, 141, 159
Brando, Marlon, 84, 89
Brat / Brother see Balabanov, Aleksei
Brat 2 / Brother 2 see Balabanov, Aleksei
Brescia, Alfonso, 15, 121m, 188, 195
  Ragazza tutta nuda assassinata nel parco / Naked Girl Killed in the Park, 15, 121–2, 123, 188, 195
Brescia bombing, 24, 46
Brigate Rosse, 3, 26, 51
Bronson, Charles, 67
Bullitt see Yates, Peter

Cabiria see Pastrone, Giovanni
Cadaveri eccellenti / Illustrious Corpses see Rosi, Francesco
Caetano, Israel Adrián, 64
  Un oso rojo / Red Bear, 64
Calabresi, Luigi, 34, 46, 68
Camorra, 108, 112n
Camorra / Gang War in Naples see Squitieri, Pasquale
Capolicchio, Lino, 138
Capone, Al, 87
Capponi, Pier Paolo, 80
Cardinale, Claudia, 92
Carnimeo, Giuliano, 14, 15, 100, 115, 129, 156, 161, 178n, 195, 196
  Anna, quel particolare piacere / Secrets of a Call Girl, 14, 100, 102, 110, 111, 161, 162, 185, 196
  Perché quelle strane gocce di sangue sul corpo di Jennifer? / The Case of the Bloody Iris, 15, 115, 129, 131, 132, 134, 146n, 156, 178n, 195, 201
Caserini, Mario, 34
  Gli ultimi giorni di Pompeii / The Last Days of Pompeii, 34
Castellari, Enzo G., 11, 20–1, 35–6, 45, 63, 69, 147n, 163, 184, 191n, 195, 196, 197
  Gli occhi freddi della paura / Cold Eyes of Fear, 147n, 195, 201
  Il cittadino si ribella / Street Law, 11, 20–1, 35–6, 39, 40n, 63, 64, 67, 68, 69, 75n, 76n, 119, 124, 184, 186, 187, 192n, 196, 198, 203
  Il grande racket / The Big Racket, 11, 45, 48, 52, 53, 59, 75n, 163, 197, 199, 204
  La polizia incrimina la legge assolve / High Crime, 76n
Catanzaro trials, 78
Catenacci, Luciano, 102
Christian Democrat Party (Italy) (DC), 22, 23, 25, 27, 29, 73
Christie, Agatha, 114
CIA (Central Intelligence Agency), 54
Cianciulli, Leonarda, 143
Cicero, 146–7n
Cimarosa, Tano, 63, 156, 197
  No alla violenza / Death Hunt, 63, 156, 186, 197, 199, 204
Cinecittà Studios, 27
Circeo massacre, 68, 72
Città violenta / The Family see Sollima, Sergio
CND (Campaign for Nuclear Disarmament), 58
Cobb, Lee J., 92
Cold War, 23, 27–8, 64
Collinson, Peter, 166
  Open Season, 166

Confessione di un commissario di polizia al procuratore della repubblica / Confessions of a Police Captain see Damiani, Damiano
Conte, Richard, 79, 84, 102, 161–3
Coppola, Francis Ford, 10, 13, 30, 78, 84, 85, 88, 89, 90, 102, 108, 109, 148, 154, 163, 184
  The Godfather, 10, 13, 30, 78, 84–5, 88–9, 90, 99, 102, 103, 105, 108, 109, 111–12, 113n, 148, 154–5, 163–5, 173, 184, 185, 192n, 200
  The Godfather: Part II, 89
Corbari see Orsini, Valentino
Corbucci, Sergio, 75n
  Django, 75n
Cosa avete fatto a Solange? / What Have You Done to Solange? see Dallamano, Massimo
Cosa Nostra, 77–8, 79–80, 89, 93, 104, 110, 112n
Cozzi, Luigi, 85
Craven, Wes, 173
  The Last House on the Left, 173
Crazy Joe see Lizzani, Carlo
Cristo si è fermato a Eboli / Christ Stopped at Eboli see Levi, Carlo
Curcio, Renato, 26
Curtiz, Michael, 30
  Angels with Dirty Faces, 30

Dallamano, Massimo, 1–2, 15, 125, 147n, 161, 170, 195
  Cosa avete fatto a Solange? / What Have You Done to Solange?, 15, 125, 131, 133–4, 147n, 170, 195, 201
  La polizia chiede aiuto / What Have They Done to Your Daughters?, 1–2, 161
Damiani, Damiano, 43, 60, 61, 90, 92, 97, 99, 109, 111
  Confessione di un commissario di polizia al procuratore della repubblica / Confessions of a Police Captain, 60, 97, 102, 109, 187
  Il giorno della civetta / Day of the Owl, 92–3, 97, 102, 103, 109, 185
  Io ho paura / I Am Afraid, 60–1
  Perché si uccide un magistrato / How to Kill a Judge, 97, 98–9, 102, 111
  Quién sabe? / A Bullet for the General, 92
De Lorenzo, Giovanni, 24, 53
De Maria, Renato, 49
  La prima linea / The Front Line, 49

De Martino, Alberto, 13–14, 100, 109, 155, 164, 195, 196
  I familiari delle vittime non saranno avvertiti / Crime Boss, 100, 101, 102, 110, 185, 191–2n, 195, 200, 202
  Il consigliori / Counselor at Crime, 13, 100, 101, 102, 103, 105, 108, 109, 155, 163–4, 185, 196, 200, 203, 213
de Sade, Marquis, 93
De Santis, Giuseppe, 29–30
  Riso amaro / Bitter Rice, 29–30
Death Wish see Winner, Michael
Delli Colli, Tonino, 92
Delon, Alain, 96, 111
Desert Love see Jaccard, Jacques
Di Leo, Fernando, 11, 12–13, 14, 60, 63, 68, 70, 78–84, 85, 89, 90, 91, 99, 100, 101, 104, 112n, 153, 154, 156, 162, 195, 196, 197
  I padroni della città / Rulers of the City, 12, 81, 91, 164, 174, 176, 197, 213
  Il boss / The Boss, 12, 79–81, 82, 83–4, 84, 89, 100, 102, 154, 155, 162, 185, 196, 200, 202
  Il poliziotto è marcio / Shoot First, Die Later, 99, 100, 102, 185, 196
  La città sconvolta: caccia spietata ai rapitori / Kidnap Syndicate, 11, 63, 64, 67, 68, 70–1, 153, 156, 163, 186, 197, 198, 204
  La mala ordina / The Italian Connection, 12, 82, 100, 104, 164, 173, 174, 175, 176, 185, 195, 211
  Milano calibro 9 / Caliber 9, 12, 70, 80–3, 85, 156, 185, 195, 200, 201
Dirty Harry see Siegel, Don
Django see Corbucci, Sergio
Dumbo see Armstrong, Samuel
Dunlap, Scott, 91
  Bells of San Juan, 91

Eastwood, Clint, 65
  Mystic River, 65
Ercole e la regina di Lidia / Hercules Unchained see Francisci, Pietro
Ercoli, Luciano, 11, 45, 131, 161–2, 196, 197
  La morte accarezza a mezzanotte / Death Walks at Midnight, 131, 132, 196, 202
  La polizia ha le mani legate / Killer Cop, 11, 45, 46, 49, 52, 58, 61, 75n, 76n, 161–2, 197, 198, 203

Fabian, Françoise, 97
Faccia a faccia / Face to Face see Sollima, Sergio
Falcone, Giovanni, 80
Fellini, Federico, 125–6
   La dolce vita, 125–6
Feltrinelli, Giangiacomo, 25, 49
Fenech, Edwige, 111, 128–9, 130, 131, 161–2
Ferrara (Massimo Felisatti), 72
   I violenti di Roma bene / Terror in Rome, 72
Fidani, Demofilo, 100, 196
   La legge della Camorra / The Godfather's Advisor, 100, 105, 185, 196
Fiddler on the Roof see Jewison, Norman
First World War, 83, 85
Fleischer, Richard, 116
   See No Evil, 116
Ford, John, 91
   My Darling Clementine, 91
Formazioni Comuniste Combattenti (FCC), 51
Fragasso, Claudio, 32
Franchetti, Leopoldo, 94
Francisci, Pietro, 33, 40n
   Ercole e la regina di Lidia / Hercules Unchained, 40n
   Le fatiche di Ercole / Hercules, 33, 34, 40n
Freud, Sigmund, 37, 38, 121, 124
Friedkin, William, 10, 30, 40n, 47, 102
   The Exorcist, 40n
   The French Connection, 10, 30, 47, 102, 173
Fritz, Roger, 166
   Mädchen mit Gewalt / Cry Rape, 166
Fronte dell'Uomo Qualunque, 178n
Fronte Italiano Liberazione Femminile, 133
Fronte Nazionale, 53
Fulci, Lucio, 15, 115, 128, 141, 165, 183, 188, 195
   Non si sevizia un paperino / Don't Torture a Duckling, 15, 16, 115, 139, 141–3, 146n, 188, 195, 202
   Una lucertola con la pelle di donna / A Lizard in a Woman's Skin, 128, 165, 176, 195, 201, 209

G-Men see Keighley, William
Gable, Clark, 89
Gaddi, Carlo, 102
Gaipa, Corrado, 84, 102
Garibaldi, Giuseppe, 95, 96
Garko, Gianni, 79
Gatti rossi in un labirinto di vetro / Eyeball see Lenzi, Umberto
Germi, Pietro, 29, 90, 91, 92
   Gioventù perduta / Lost Youth, 29
   In nome della legge / In the Name of the Law, 29, 91–2, 93, 102
Giannettini, Guido, 45–6
Ginger see Schain, Don
Gioia, Giovanni, 80
Giordana, Marco Tullio, 49
   Pasolini: un delitto italiano / Who Killed Pasolini?, 49
Giornata nera per l'ariete / The Fifth Cord see Bazzoni, Luigi
Gioventù perduta / Lost Youth see Germi, Pietro
Girolami, Marino, 11, 63, 151–2, 156, 197
   Roma, l'altra faccia della violenza / Rome: The Other Side of Violence, 11, 63, 64, 68, 71, 72–3, 76n, 156, 186, 197, 199, 204
   Roma violenta / Violent City, 11, 63, 73, 151–2, 153, 186, 197, 198, 204
Gli amici degli amici hanno saputo see Marcolin, Fulvio
Gli occhi freddi della paura / Cold Eyes of Fear see Castellari, Enzo G.
Gli ultimi giorni di Pompeii / The Last Days of Pompeii see Caserini, Mario
Grau, Jorge, 170
   Non si deve profanare il sonno dei morti / Don't Open the Window, 170
Great Depression, 87
Gruppi d'Azione Partigiana, 25
Guazzoni, Enrico, 34
   Quo Vadis?, 34
Guglielmi, Marco, 98

Harrison, Richard, 31–2
Harvey, Laurence, 170
   Tender Flesh, 170
Hawks, Howard, 87
   Scarface, 87–8
Hayworth, Rita, 89
Heffron, Thomas N., 86
   Tony America, 86–7
Helen of Troy see Wise, Robert
Hemmings, David, 132
High Noon see Zinnemann, Fred
Hill, George Roy, 164
   The Sting, 164

Hindley, Myra, 118
Historic Compromise, 26–7, 73
Hitchcock, Alfred, 115, 168, 173
Hitler, Adolf, 23
Holocaust, 37, 119, 120, 121
Hooper, Tobe, 166
   The Texas Chain Saw Massacre, 166
Huston, John, 30, 112n
   The Asphalt Jungle, 30

I corpi presentano tracce di violenza carnale / *Torso see* Martino, Sergio
I familiari delle vittime non saranno avvertiti / *Crime Boss see* De Martino, Alberto
I guappi / *Blood Brothers see* Squitieri, Pasquale
I padroni della città / *Rulers of the City see* Di Leo, Fernando
I ragazzi della Roma violenta see Savino, Renato
I violenti di Roma bene / *Terror in Rome see* Segri *and* Ferrara
Il bandito / *The Bandit see* Lattuada, Alberto
Il boss / *The Boss see* Di Leo, Fernando
Il cittadino si ribella / *Street Law see* Castellari, Enzo G.
Il consigliori / *Counselor at Crime see* De Martino, Alberto
Il contesto see Sciascia, Leonardo
Il gatto dagli occhi di giada / *Watch Me When I Kill see* Bido, Antonio
Il gattopardo / *The Leopard* (book) *see* Tomasi di Lampedusa, Giuseppe
Il gattopardo / *The Leopard* (film) *see* Visconti, Luchino
Il giorno della civetta / *Day of the Owl* (book) *see* Sciascia, Leonardo
Il giorno della civetta / *Day of the Owl* (film) *see* Damiani, Damiano
Il giustiziere sfida la città / *Syndicate Sadists see* Lenzi, Umberto
Il grande racket / *The Big Racket see* Castellari, Enzo G.
Il poliziotto è marcio / *Shoot First, Die Later see* Di Leo, Fernando
Il postino / *The Postman see* Radford, Michael
Il rosso segno della follia / *A Hatchet for the Honeymoon see* Bava, Mario
Il tuo vizio è una stanza chiusa e solo io ne ho la chiave / *Your Vice Is a Locked Room and Only I Have the Key see* Martino, Sergio
Illustrazione Italiana (magazine), 139, 147n
Impastato, Giovanni, 77
In nome della legge / *In the Name of the Law see* Germi, Pietro
Indagine su un cittadino al di sopra di ogni sospetto / *Investigation of a Citizen Above Suspicion see* Petri, Elio
Infascelli, Roberto, 11, 45, 161, 178n, 196
   La polizia sta a guardare / *The Great Kidnapping*, 10–11, 45, 48, 52, 59, 161, 178–9n, 187, 196, 198, 203
Io ho paura / *I Am Afraid see* Damiani, Damiano
Isasi, Antonio, 11, 63, 197
   Ricatto alla mala / *Summertime Killer*, 11, 63, 64, 67, 70, 197
Italian Communist Party (PCI), 23, 24, 25, 26, 27
Italian Social Movement (MSI), 24
Italian Socialist Party (PSI), 23, 24, 25, 27
Italicus Express bombing *see* San Benedetto Val di Sambro bombing

Jaccard, Jacques, 91
   Desert Love, 91
Jack the Ripper, 118
Jewison, Norman, 148
   Fiddler on the Roof, 148
Jordan, Neil, 65
   The Brave One, 65
José, Edward, 86
   My Cousin, 86–7

Keaton, Diane, 89
Kefauver Committee hearings, 88
Keighley, William, 46
   G–Men, 46
Kubrick, Stanley, 30
   The Killing, 30

L'altra faccia del padrino / *The Funny Face of the Godfather see* Prosperi, Franco
L'amico del padrino / *The Godfather's Friend see* Agrama, Frank
L'onorata famiglia – Uccidere è cosa nostra / *The Big Family see* Ricci, Tonino
L'uccello dalle piume di cristallo / *The Bird with the Crystal Plumage see* Argento, Dario
L'uomo della strada fa giustizia / *Manhunt in the City see* Lenzi, Umberto

La caduta di Troia / *The Fall of Troy see* Pastrone, Giovanni
La casa dalle finestre che ridono / *The House of the Laughing Windows see* Avati, Pupi
La città sconvolta: caccia spietata ai rapitori / *Kidnap Syndicate see* Di Leo, Fernando
La dama rossa uccide sette volte / *The Red Queen Kills Seven Times see* Miraglia, Emilio
La dolce vita see Fellini, Federico
La legge della Camorra / *The Godfather's Advisor see* Fidani, Demofilo
La mala ordina / *The Italian Connection see* Di Leo, Fernando
La mano lunga del padrino / *The Long Arm of the Godfather see* Bonomi, Nardo
La mano nera / *The Black Hand see* Racioppi, Antonio
La morte accarezza a mezzanotte / *Death Walks at Midnight see* Ercoli, Luciano
La padrina / *Lady Dynamite see* Vari, Giuseppe
La polizia accusa: il servizio segreto uccide / *Silent Action see* Martino, Sergio
La polizia chiede aiuto / *What Have They Done to Your Daughters? see* Dallamano, Massimo
La polizia ha le mani legate / *Killer Cop see* Ercole, Luciano
La polizia incrimina la legge assolve / *High Crime see* Castellari, Enzo G.
La polizia ringrazia / *Execution Squad see* Vanzina, Stefano
La polizia sta a guardare / *The Great Kidnapping see* Infascelli, Roberto
La prima linea / *The Front Line see* De Maria, Renato
La ragazza che sapeva troppo / *The Evil Eye see* Bava, Mario
La resa dei conti / *The Big Gundown see* Sollima, Sergio
La violenza: quinto potere / *The Sicilian Checkmate see* Vancini, Florestano
Lacenaire, Pierre-François, 118
Lancaster, Burt, 95
Lattuada, Alberto, 29, 113n
  Il bandito / *The Bandit*, 29
  Mafioso, 113n
  Senza pietà / *Without Pity*, 29
Le fatiche di Ercole / *Hercules see* Francisci, Pietro

Lenzi, Umberto, 11, 13, 15, 31, 60, 63 100, 126, 127, 155, 156, 191n, 195, 196, 197
  Gatti rossi in un labirinto di vetro / *Eyeball*, 126–7, 196, 203
  Il giustiziere sfida la città / *Syndicate Sadists*, 11, 63, 71, 73, 76n, 155–6, 186, 197, 199, 204
  L'uomo della strada fa giustizia / *Manhunt in the City*, 11, 63, 64, 67, 69, 73, 156, 186, 197, 198, 204
  Milano rovente / *Gang War in Milan*, 13, 100, 101, 104, 106–7, 110, 156, 185, 196, 200, 203
  Paranoia / *A Quiet Place to Kill*, 15, 126, 128, 131, 132, 195
  Un posto ideale per uccidere / *A Quiet Place to Kill*, 15, 127–8, 132, 195
Leone, Sergio, 78, 92, 112n
  Per un pugno di dollari / *A Fistful of Dollars*, 112n
LeRoy, Mervyn, 34, 87
  Little Caesar, 87–8
  Quo Vadis, 34
Levi, Carlo, 143
  Cristo si è fermato a Eboli / *Christ Stopped at Eboli*, 143
Liberation of Italy, 22, 25, 27
Little Caesar see LeRoy, Mervyn
Lizzani, Carlo, 10, 30, 72, 100, 172, 196
  Banditi a Milano / *The Violent Four*, 10, 30–1
  Crazy Joe, 100, 101, 105–6, 109, 172, 175, 185, 196, 200, 203, 211, 212
  San Babila ore 20: un delitto inutile / *San Babila 8 pm*, 72
  Torino nera, 100, 101, 109–10, 185, 196, 200, 202
Lo strano vizio della signora Wardh / *Blade of the Ripper see* Martino, Sergio
Lotta Continua (journal), 50–1, 53
Lounsbery, John, 170, 171
  Winnie the Pooh and Tigger Too, 170–1
Lucky Luciano see Rosi, Francesco

Macherey, Pierre, 39, 74
Mädchen mit Gewalt / *Cry Rape see* Fritz, Roger
Mafioso see Lattuada, Alberto
Magnani, Anna, 28
Malden, Karl, 67
Mangano, Silvana, 30
Mano Nera (extortion rackets), 88

Marcolin, Fulvio, 100, 196
  Gli amici degli amici hanno saputo, 100, 109–10, 185, 196, 200, 203
Mark colpisce ancora / Mark Strikes Again see Massi, Stelvio
Mark il poliziotto / Blood, Sweat and Fear see Massi, Stelvio
Mark il poliziotto spara per primo / Mark Shoots First see Massi, Stelvio
Martinelli, Renzo, 62
  Piazza delle cinque lune / Five Moons Plaza, 62
Martino, Sergio, 10, 11, 15, 16, 34, 45, 55, 115, 116, 124, 128–9, 134, 146n, 153, 165, 167, 170, 171, 188, 191n, 195, 196, 197
  I corpi presentano tracce di violenza carnale / Torso, 15–16, 115, 116, 125, 139, 143–4, 145, 165–7, 170–1, 188, 196, 202, 210, 212, 213
  Il tuo vizio è una stanza chiusa e solo io ne ho la chiave / Your Vice Is a Locked Room and Only I Have the Key, 129, 132, 134–5, 195, 202
  La polizia accusa: il servizio segreto uccide / Silent Action, 11, 45, 48, 52, 54–6, 57, 59, 67–8, 75n, 153, 197, 198, 203
  Lo strano vizio della signora Wardh / Blade of the Ripper, 15, 124, 128–9, 134, 195, 201
  Milano trema – la polizia vuole giustizia / The Violent Professionals, 10, 34–5, 45, 46, 48, 52, 58, 59, 75n, 76n, 146n, 187, 196, 198, 203
  Tutti i colori del buio / All the Colors of the Dark, 129
Massi, Stelvio, 31, 75n
  Mark colpisce ancora / Mark Strikes Again, 75n
  Mark il poliziotto / Blood, Sweat and Fear, 75n
  Mark il poliziotto spara per primo / Mark Shoots First, 75n
Maury, Alfred, 93–4
McCutcheon, Wallace, 88
  The Black Hand, 88
Mediterraneo see Salvatores, Gabriele
Melford, George, 86
  The Organ Grinder, 86–7
Melville, Jean-Pierre, 112n
Merenda, Luc, 46, 67
Miceli, Vito, 54

Milano calibro 9 / Caliber 9 see Di Leo, Fernando
Milano rovente / Gang War in Milan see Lenzi, Umberto
Milano trema – la polizia vuole giustizia / Violent Professionals see Martino, Sergio
Milian, Tomas, 71, 103, 142
Miraglia, Emilio, 131
  La dama rossa uccide sette volte / The Red Queen Kills Seven Times, 131
Monicelli, Mario, 76n
  Un borghese piccolo piccolo / An Average Little Man, 76n
Montesquieu, Charles-Louis de Secondat, 96
Morath, Max, 148
Moro, Aldo, 3, 4, 24, 46, 62, 77
Movimento Liberazione delle Donne, 133
Murder She Wrote (television show), 116
Musante, Tony, 124
Mussolini, Benito, 22, 23, 24, 27, 40n, 87
My Cousin see José, Edward
My Darling Clementine see Ford, John
Mystic River see Eastwood, Clint

NATO (North Atlantic Treaty Organization), 28, 54
'Ndrangheta, 112n
Negri, Gaetano, 95
Nelle pieghe della carne / In the Folds of the Flesh see Bergonzelli, Sergio
Nero, Franco, 20, 92, 93, 97, 98, 107, 162
Niceforo, Alfredo, 94
Nichols, Mike, 159
  The Graduate, 159
Nixon, Richard, 26, 47
No alla violenza / Death Hunt see Cimarosa, Tano
Non si deve profanare il sonno dei morti / Don't Open the Window see Grau, Jorge
Non si sevizia un paperino / Don't Torture a Duckling see Fulci, Lucio
Nude per l'assassino / Strip Nude for Your Killer see Bianchi, Andrea
Nuovo Cinema Paradiso / Cinema Paradiso see Tornatore, Giuseppe

Oedipus at Colonus see Sophocles
Oklahoma bomb, 39
On Dangerous Ground see Ray, Nicholas
Open Season see Collinson, Peter
Ordine Nuovo, 3, 24

Orsini, Valentino, 36
   Corbari, 36

P2 (Masonic lodge), 54
Pacino, Al, 84
Palance, Jack, 176
Pani, Corrado, 161
Paranoia / A Quiet Place to Kill see Lenzi,
   Umberto
Pasolini, Pier Paolo, 51, 58
*Pasolini: un delitto italiano / Who Killed
   Pasolini? see* Giordana, Marco Tullio
Pastrone, Giovanni, 34
   Cabiria, 34
   La caduta di Troia / The Fall of Troy, 34
Pellegrin, Raymond, 102
Penn, Arthur, 128
   Bonnie and Clyde, 128, 164
Pensione paura / Hotel Fear see Barilli,
   Francesco
Peplum, 34, 177, 182
*Per un pugno di dollari / A Fistful of Dollars
   see* Leone, Sergio
*Perché quelle strane gocce di sangue sul corpo
   di Jennifer? / The Case of the Bloody
   Iris see* Carnimeo, Giuliano
*Perché si uccide un magistrato / How to Kill
   a Judge see* Damiani, Damiano
Peteano bombing, 24, 54
Petri, Elio, 43, 48, 60, 61, 90
   *Indagine su un cittadino al di sopra di ogni
   sospetto / Investigation of a Citizen
   Above Suspicion*, 60, 61, 187
Piano di Rascino (training camp), 46, 68
*Piazza delle cinque lune / Five Moons
   Plaza see* Martinelli, Renzo
Piazza Fontana bombing, 3, 4, 24, 26, 40n,
   46, 49, 50–1, 53, 68, 78, 118
Pinelli, Giuseppe, 4, 50, 71
Pistilli, Luigi, 81, 134
Poliziotti violenti / Crimebusters see
   Tarantini, Michele Massimo
Pontecorvo, Gillo, 48
Preminger, Otto, 47
   Where the Sidewalk Ends, 46–7
Prima Linea, 51
Profondo rosso / Deep Red see Argento,
   Dario
Prohibition era, 87
Prosperi, Franco, 99
   *L'altra faccia del padrino / The Funny
   Face of the Godfather*, 99
Puzo, Mario, 103

Quelli che contano / Cry of a Prostitute see
   Bianchi, Andrea
Quién sabe? / A Bullet for the General see
   Damiani, Damiano
Quo Vadis see LeRoy, Mervyn
Quo Vadis? see Guazzoni, Enrico

Racioppi, Antonio, 18n, 100, 196
   La mano nera / The Black Hand, 18n,
   100, 101, 102, 105, 107, 108, 185,
   196, 200, 202, 203
Radford, Michael, 139
   Il postino / The Postman, 139
*Ragazza tutta nuda assassinata nel parco /
   Naked Girl Killed in the Park see*
   Brescia, Alfonso
Ray, Nicholas, 47
   On Dangerous Ground, 47
Reazione a catena / A Bay of Blood see
   Bava, Mario
Red Brigades *see Brigate Rosse*
Reed, Oliver, 66
Republic of Salò, 24
Resa dei conti ('settling of accounts'),
   15, 22–3, 38, 69, 119, 123, 124
Resistance (Italian), 4, 20, 21, 22–3,
   25–6, 36, 38, 69, 120, 122–3,
   124
Revolver / Blood in the Streets see Sollima,
   Sergio
Ricatto alla mala / Summertime Killer see
   Isasi, Antonio
Ricci, Tonino, 13, 100, 153, 162, 196
   *L'onorata famiglia – Uccidere è cosa
   nostra / The Big Family*, 13, 100,
   102–3, 106, 107, 108, 153, 162, 185,
   196, 200, 203
Richardson, John, 161
Riso amaro / Bitter Rice see De Santis,
   Giuseppe
Risorgimento (unification of Italy), 13, 83,
   94–5, 108, 141
Ritt, Martin, 88
   The Brotherhood, 88
Rivolta Femminile, 133
Roma città aperta / Rome, Open City see
   Rossellini, Roberto
*Roma, l'altra faccia della violenza /
   Rome: The Other Side of Violence see*
   Girolami, Marino
Roma violenta / Violent City see Girolami,
   Marino
Rosa dei Venti, 45, 54, 68

Rosi, Francesco, 43, 48, 60, 61, 73, 90, 91, 96–7, 153–4
   Cadaveri eccellenti / *Illustrious Corpses*, 60, 61, 73–4
   Lucky Luciano, 91
   Salvatore Giuliano, 96–7
Rossellini, Roberto, 120, 121
   Roma città aperta / *Rome, Open City*, 120–1
Ruffini, Cardinal Ernesto, 80

Sabato, Antonio, 110
Sacra Corona Unita, 112n
Salvatore Giuliano see Rosi, Francesco
Salvatores, Gabriele, 139
   Mediterraneo, 139
San Babila ore 20: un delitto inutile / *San Babila 8 pm see* Lizzani, Carlo
San Benedetto Val di Sambro bombing, 24–5
Sarris, Andrew, 112n
Savalas, Telly, 67
Savino, Renato, 72
   I ragazzi della Roma violenta, 72
Sbatti il mostro in prima pagina / *Slap the Monster on Page One see* Bellocchio, Marco
Scarface see Hawks, Howard
Scavolini, Romano, 100, 196
   Servo suo / *Your Honor*, 100, 185, 196
Schain, Don, 166
   Ginger, 166
   The Abductors, 166
Schiraldi, Vittorio, 13, 100, 196
   Baciamo le mani / *Family Killer*, 13, 100, 101, 102, 103, 105, 108, 109, 185, 196, 200, 202
Sciascia, Leonardo, 73, 103, 114
   Il contesto, 73
   Il giorno della civetta / *Day of the Owl*, 103
Second World War, 3, 4, 7, 10, 14–15, 18n, 19n, 20, 21–3, 25–6, 27, 36, 38, 40, 69, 74, 76n, 83, 104, 110, 119–25, 137, 144
See No Evil see Fleischer, Richard
Segni, Antonio, 24
Segri (Sergio Grieco), 72
   I violenti di Roma bene / *Terror in Rome*, 72
Sei donne per l'assassino / *Blood and Black Lace see* Bava, Mario
Senza pietà / *Without Pity see* Lattuada, Alberto

September 11 (2001) attacks, 39, 65
Servizio Informazione Difesa (SID), 46
Servo suo / *Your Honor see* Scavolini, Romano
Shavelson, Melville, 148
   The War Between Men and Women, 148
Siegel, Don, 10, 30, 35, 47, 85, 187
   Dirty Harry, 10, 30, 34–5, 47–8, 85, 163, 187
Silva, Henry, 67, 104, 105, 159, 162
Solamente nero / *Bloodstained Shadow see* Bido, Antonio
Sollima, Sergio, 11, 63, 66, 76n, 153, 164, 165, 195, 196
   Città violenta / *The Family*, 11, 63, 64, 66–7, 70, 71–2, 99, 153, 164–5, 172, 173, 176, 186, 195, 198, 201, 210, 211
   Faccia a faccia / *Face to Face*, 66
   La resa dei conti / *The Big Gundown*, 66
   Revolver / *Blood in the Streets*, 11, 63, 66, 67, 68, 71, 72, 186, 196, 198, 203
Sophocles, 56
   Oedipus at Colonus, 56
Spaghetti Westerns, 30, 34, 35, 66, 75n, 156, 175–6, 177, 182, 188
Spanish Civil War, 127
Sperli, Alessandro, 104
Spillane, Mickey, 114
Squitieri, Pasquale, 18n, 100, 153, 195, 196
   Camorra / *Gang War in Naples*, 100, 101, 102, 107, 109, 153, 155, 185, 191–2n, 195, 200, 202
   I guappi / *Blood Brothers*, 18n, 100, 101, 102, 107–8, 185, 196, 200, 203
Steffen, Anthony, 103
Stevenson, Robert, 170, 171
   The Island at the Top of the World, 170–1
Stragismo, 3, 24–5, 40n
Strategia della tensione ('strategy of tension'), 7, 19n, 24, 26, 34, 45, 48, 52, 57, 58, 67, 73, 118

Tarantini, Michele Massimo, 11, 45, 197
   Poliziotti violenti / *Crimebusters*, 11, 45, 48, 52, 59, 75n, 197, 199, 204
Tender Flesh see Harvey, Laurence
Tessari, Duccio, 14, 91, 100, 196
   Tony Arzenta / *No Way Out*, 14, 91, 100, 102, 108, 110–11, 185, 196, 200, 203, 212, 213
Testi Fabio, 66, 107
Teti, Vincenzo, 116

The Abductors see Schain, Don
The Asphalt Jungle see Huston, John
The Black Hand (1906) *see* McCutcheon, Wallace
The Black Hand (1950) *see* Thorpe, Richard
The Brave One see Jordan, Neil
The Brotherhood see Ritt, Martin
The Exorcist see Friedkin, William
The French Connection see Friedkin, William
The Godfather see Coppola, Francis Ford
The Godfather: Part II see Coppola, Francis Ford
The Graduate see Nichols, Mike
The Island at the Top of the World see Stevenson, Robert
The Italian see Barker, Reginald
The Killing see Kubrick, Stanley
The Last House on the Left see Craven, Wes
The Organ Grinder see Melford, George
The Sting see Hill, George Roy
The Texas Chain Saw Massacre see Hooper, Tobe
The Valachi Papers see Young, Terence
The War Between Men and Women see Shavelson, Melville
Thorpe, Richard, 88
  The Black Hand, 88
Togliatti, Palmiro, 25
Tomasi di Lampedusa, Giuseppe, 95, 98
  Il gattopardo / The Leopard, 95, 96
Tony America see Heffron, Thomas N.
Tony Arzenta / No Way Out see Tessari, Duccio
Torino nera see Lizzani, Carlo
Torino violenta / Double Game see Ausino, Carlo
Tornatore, Giuseppe, 139
  Nuovo Cinema Paradiso / Cinema Paradiso, 139
Totò, 28
Tozzi, Fausto, 102
Tutti i colori del buio / All the Colors of the Dark see Martino, Sergio

Un borghese piccolo piccolo / An Average Little Man see Monicelli, Mario
Un oso rojo / Red Bear see Caetano, Israel Adrián
Un posto ideale per uccidere / A Quiet Place to Kill see Lenzi, Umberto
Una lucertola con la pelle di donna / A Lizard in a Woman's Skin see Fulci, Lucio

Vai gorilla / The Hired Gun see Valerii, Tonino
Valerii, Tonino, 11, 63, 68
  Vai gorilla / The Hired Gun, 11, 63, 68, 186
Vancini, Florestano, 106
  La violenza: quinto potere / The Sicilian Checkmate, 106, 107
Vanzina, Stefano, 10, 42, 43, 73, 146n, 161–2, 187, 195
  La polizia ringrazia / Execution Squad, 10, 42, 43, 44, 45, 47–8, 52, 54, 57, 58, 59, 67–8, 73–4, 75n, 76n, 146n, 161–2, 178–9n, 187, 195, 198, 201
Vari, Giuseppe, 99, 100, 196
  La padrina / Lady Dynamite, 99, 100, 102–3, 105, 107, 185, 196
Viale Lazio massacre, 78
Vichy (regime), 23
Vietnam War, 65
Villari, Pasquale, 94
Visconti, Luchino, 95, 96, 98
  Il gattopardo / The Leopard, 95–6, 97–8, 102, 107, 108, 109
Volontè, Gian Maria, 61
Voyna / War see Balabanov, Aleksei

Wallace, Edgar, 114
Where the Sidewalk Ends see Preminger, Otto
Winner, Michael, 10, 30, 36, 65, 85, 154, 184
  Death Wish, 10, 30, 36, 40n, 65, 85, 154, 163, 184, 186, 187
Winnie the Pooh and Tigger Too see Lounsbery, John
Wise, Robert, 34
  Helen of Troy, 34
Wolff, Frank, 81
Wyler, William, 34
  Ben Hur, 34

Yates, Peter, 30, 47
  Bullitt, 30, 47
Years of Lead see Anni di piombo
Young, Terence, 102
  The Valachi Papers, 102

Zinnemann, Fred, 34–5, 91
  High Noon, 35, 91

EU representative:
Easy Access System Europe
Mustamäe tee 50, 10621 Tallinn, Estonia
Gpsr.requests@easproject.com

www.ingramcontent.com/pod-product-compliance
Lightning Source LLC
Chambersburg PA
CBHW071836230426
43671CB00012B/1979